From War to Peace

From War to Peace

JANINE CHANTEUR

translated by
SHIRLEY ANN WEISZ

Westview Press

BOULDER ■ SAN FRANCISCO ■ OXFORD

English edition copyright © 1992 by Presses Universitaires de France

English edition published in 1992 in the United States of America by Westview Press, Inc., 5500 Central Avenue, Boulder, Colorado 80301-2847, and in the United Kingdom by Westview Press, 36 Lonsdale Road, Summertown, Oxford OX2 7EW

French edition copyright © 1989 by Presses Universitaires de France

Published in French in 1989 by Presses Universitaires de France as *De la guerre à la paix* by Janine Chanteur

Library of Congress Cataloging-in-Publication Data
Chanteur, Janine.
[De la guerre à la paix. English]
From war to peace / Janine Chanteur ; translated by Shirley Ann Weisz.
    p. cm.
  Translation of: De la guerre à la paix.
  Includes bibliographical references and index.
  ISBN 0-8133-1257-4. — ISBN 0-8133-1258-2 (paperback).
  1. Peace (Philosophy) 2. War (Philosophy) I. Title.
B105.P4C43 1992
327.1′72—dc20   92-7818
                                                                                 CIP

Printed and bound in the United States of America

 The paper used in this publication meets the requirements
of the American National Standard for Permanence of Paper
for Printed Library Materials Z39.48-1984.

10   9   8   7   6   5   4   3   2   1

To Ilias Lalaounis, my Athens friend
To Yirmiahu Yovel, my Jerusalem friend

CONTENTS

PREFACE

This project has a double ancestry. The message I received from the Greeks combined within me, a child of the Christian, rationalist West, with the discovery I made of the wealth of meanings latent in the Old Testament. This was a true discovery, made in spite of conventions that rarely inquire about what they fail to know. Like many who "have faith" and who do not "have faith," I was familiar with the tragicomic story of the apple that our primal parents bequeathed us as a questionable gift. I also knew a few other stories. But the metaphysical significance of a text, its living word, does not yield itself to a half-hearted listener.

One day, partly by chance, the Middle Eastern roots of my own civilization no longer seemed to me a dead past but began to fill me with an inexhaustible nourishment for which I had had a long-standing thirst without knowing it. Yet the rootstock of Hellenism did not wither. To become who we are, we must, I believe, consecrate within ourselves the union of our father and mother. I therefore try to celebrate the marriage of my Jewish and Hellenic "parents." This is the path I follow. It is hard to do, for I must avoid the pitfalls of excluding one voice, suppressing the other, or falsely assimilating them to each other. To hear without distortion—and then integrate—two voices that on first analysis seem to have no natural vocation for union is a task not without conflict. For that matter, war and peace, whatever you take them to be, are my life experience—are indeed my life. Each of us, I think, could say the same. The question of their relationship confronts me; I can neither escape it nor answer it.

But my personal history aside, my concern here is to clarify elements of the political domain. Why write yet another book on war and peace, unless in an attempt to ask questions without prejudging the answer? Certainly, we must not invent an answer particular to the historical juncture at which we find ourselves. But can we discover an answer that will lead to helpful innovations? Or have we perhaps always known the answer without recognizing it as such? This, then, is my task—to tease out answers, to make them explicit and timely, yet to avoid the inflexibility of dogma, that marriage of bias and poor memory; to dare nonetheless to "tear open the silent portals / Past which all creatures slink in silent dread";[1] for to seek understanding of war and peace is to encounter, whether we wish to or not, the mystery of life and death. Our resources are few: as much good faith as we can muster and the effort to avoid self-deception so that we may hear clearly even the most discordant voices.

The reader will understand that to initiate the union I intended, I had to renounce an old loyalty. From the age when I began to try to make sense of things, one philosophy had been my bulwark against the multiplicity, contradiction, and dizzying tacks of conclusions endlessly asserted and refuted. In Plato I found "the upward way," to use Socrates' words from the end of the *Republic*.[2] Now I had to tear myself away from Plato and to accept seeing things by the light of other lamps than his. We must separate ourselves from serene childhood and even from a source of happiness if it also holds us prisoner.

I know it is not customary to speak of oneself in philosophical works, let alone of one's loves and crises. Still, let me explain myself a little. The religious education I received in a somewhat puritanical Christian family filled me with the truth of the equivalence of *soma* and *sema* [body and grave]. My soul, which I believed to be the whole of my real self, expected bliss beyond imagining after death—which would, however, assign this wretched, this shameful body to a perfectly real grave. The dissociation of matter and spirit and the worth assigned their separation caused me to be a harsh judge of the delights of "my five senses and some others," as Guillaume Apollinaire puts it. Though I could not believe I would have to die, I harbored an ineffable confidence that pure happiness would be found in the afterlife. When Plato captivated my mind, my heart, and my senses (to reverse the order of the *Symposium*), he helped me endure the burden of the Fall: a body of clay, female on top of that, disgrace. It was a use for the myth of Er and the myth of the *Phaedrus* that Plato could hardly have foreseen. Ignorant of my own ignorance, I could exclaim with Saint Paul, "Who shall deliver me from the body of this death?"[3] I aspired to a peace that could be *perpetual* for the soul alone, and I considered the contraries of war and peace to be the necessary and irrevocable worldly condition of those suffering the awkward pairing of body and soul, whom only that other pairing, thought and understanding, came to comfort.

I would probably have been satisfied with a dualistic, impoverishing interpretation of Plato had I not discovered, in the course of a long journey, that in the here and now the body and soul are not dual. The cost was onerous, for departure from early allegiances and the furrows of habit remains unthinkable for a long time. Yet hope regarding this earthly life has risen within me; it rests on the adventure that began for those of us who have succeeded in leaving father and mother, as Scripture prescribes, and in contemplating ourselves as that indissolubly earthly and spiritual reality that constitutes a human being. Then peace will not be a utopian dream, though the battle for peace will surely be more surprising and more difficult than what we usually call war; for we must become aware that war is less an external assailant than it seems. War will perhaps destroy the world by being, paradoxically, the last alibi our fears and blindness hide behind.

On my journey I of course turned to several great philosophical systems—those of Machiavelli, Hobbes, Rousseau, Kant, and others—to steady my footsteps. I did not choose them at random. Some I had already found helpful, and others, on the contrary, threatened my passage. There was something to be learned from these, too, because disagreement and even distrust, if kept from becoming rejection, are also ways of questioning. I might have chosen other or more "interlocutors"; I have certainly not exhausted the possibilities. Therefore this book is by no means a history of the philosophy of peace and war. Other philosophers allow us, by understanding the difficulties they have met, to ask our own questions in better ways. In this spirit, I eschewed a survey and instead asked myself if peace, though it seems to be a basic human goal, *is* actually so central an interest and, if it should prove to be so, why we continue to wage war.

I have taken my bearings from only some of the relevant philosophical analyses and even then without fully presenting them. Yet I have tried to take each on its own terms and to formulate questions that each seemed to call for. I started with no preconceived ideas. Certain of the themes of the war philosophers have caught my interest and helped organize my thinking. Because my plan is not to recount the history of research into peace (or its impossibility), I bring with me only an itinerary. It determines my life; its paths are what I know I must rediscover each day, because they are lost so quickly through haste and forgetfulness. Where will I end? I have no idea. Like everyone else, I know that we live in a world at war and that war seduces us and terrifies us by turns. I know, too, that hope and freedom can replace fascination and fear. But we must also know what brings us joy or sorrow, anguish or serenity. And we must also dare to examine our own inner rift and so avoid erring through complacency as well as through despair.

Janine Chanteur

NOTES

1. Johann Wolfgang von Goethe, *Faust*, trans. Walter Kaufmann (Garden City, N.J.: Anchor Books, 1962), p. 117.

2. Plato, *Republic* 621c, trans. Paul Shorey, in Bollingen Series 71, *The Collected Dialogues of Plato*, ed. Edith Hamilton and Huntington Cairns (Princeton, N.J.: Princeton University Press, 1987).

3. Rom. 8:24 (Revised Standard Version).

INTRODUCTION

On first consideration, we agree that our well-being depends upon peace, following Saint Augustine, for whom "there is no one who does not love peace. . . . It is for the sake of peace that men wage wars . . . and even brigands strive to keep the peace with their comrades."[1] True, but wars exist, and so do brigands who wage the wars we are supposed to refrain from and to whom we do not often give the chance to attack first. Furthermore, it is not always easy to tell who is a brigand. History is left to make the designation, which it generally does according to who has won or lost.

Apparently, therefore, we cannot think about peace without inquiring at the same time, or perhaps even first, into war. Each term summons the other, but their relation has this peculiarity, that a study focused solely on peace would see its object become blurred if detached from its opposite. What is peace per se, peace without reference to its opposite, the very thing it is supposed to put an end to? What is peace without war?

It goes without saying that we have experienced much more war than peace. We see that stories of a golden age are mere myths when we compare them to the oldest writings and monument inscriptions, which are usually concerned with war. War seems inseparable from the reality of human life under whatever conditions it is lived, at whatever time, in whatever place. Descriptions of peace without reference to war are most often only imaginary visions designed to sustain us in our real lives. They speak of a "paradise lost," the memory of which early generations supposedly passed on but that no generation has actually known. There are myths and legends about war, too, but war is above all a reality that impinges on our immediate experience, either by its presence, by fresh memories of its past occurrence, or by the fear of its approach.

Today the whole world knows that war is potentially synonymous with unimaginable destruction. The nature of our industries and the profound anxiety characterizing our era keep us aware of this truth. The arsenal that we have invented to destroy one another is incommensurate with anything produced before. Although the existence of war is a historical constant, we may persuade ourselves that these quantitative differences will alter the nature of our analysis. Certainly, some phenomena are so overwhelming, in part because of new technology, that they defy judgment according to usual criteria. We take it for objective truth that the Third Reich lost World War II. On 8 May 1945, an armistice was signed that put an end to hostilities. Germany had surrendered; the Nazi state was collapsing amid the ruins of its people, country, and political regime; the Allies had won. Yet it may be more accurate to say that despite these facts, Hitler triumphed, for after 1945 torture came into frequent, even commonplace use in numerous conflicts. Is it not also one of Nazism's greatest, though unintended, victories that we were slow to discern the profound similarity of its methods to those of the Soviets, precisely because we could not believe such brutality could occur again? Yet the Soviets, starting from a different ideology, arrived at identical methods and used them far longer.

We are *immersed* in war and its consequences; they poison even the time when arms are officially silent. It is not the least surprise of the twentieth century's end that we are utterly unable to define peace, incomprehensible wars ceaselessly taking place before our very eyes. When terrorism occurs daily, is there such a thing as a country at peace? What is peace? What is war? It is not, moreover, the least paradox of our age that a vision of peace can serve the ends of war, as the phenomenon of pacifism clearly demonstrates.

We traditionally mean by *war* the armed confrontation of two armies from two separate countries, endangering the lives of at least some of their soldiers and civilians. This kind of war is generally preceded by a declaration of war, depending on the customs of the parties involved and on their intentions. War implies movement, which over time has become increasingly restricted to the movement of projectiles hurled from greater and greater distances. Today, without recourse even to the movement of planes and their skilled crews, we can with great precision dispatch missiles that destroy the enemy's troops.

Whatever technology it employs, war as so defined obviously is a matter of life and death to the involved individuals and peoples. Hence behind every war there are philosophical convictions, explicit or implicit, that underlie the political convictions. Though not always asked openly, a question always exists as to the legitimacy of the decision to engage in war. Is it a legitimate act of government to risk the lives of citizens whose country it is responsible for (and of course also the lives of those it defines as enemies)? Remember that one of the reasons for political power is to assure the safety of citizens. Whether a war of offense undertaken to make national safety less dependent on luck, or a war of defense intended to ward off an imminent threat, war obviously requires the sacrifice of a certain number of lives. A war may be caused by a single person's ambition or the ambitions of a state, by some ideology or the need to defend territory; whatever the hecatomb's cause, we can always find a philosophy of human nature underlying that cause and explaining it. Hence we can begin to see the form that the problem of pacifism, for example, will take: What definition of a person accounts for the behavior of one who, faced with the loss of a national identity, a way of life, and all that he or she values, renounces in advance all usual means of defense against foreign aggression and prefers to take refuge in some such formula as "Better red than dead"?

The existence of war forces us to inquire into a widely accepted assumption of political science.[2] Is it true that those in political life cannot avoid separating into friends and enemies? Does this separation force us to accept what we might call an ontological gap, a break in the unity of the human race, so that it becomes impossible to speak of humankind without mention of the fissure dividing it? War highlights an inevitable opposition at the heart of human nature, that of "same" and "other"; the combination is in no way dialectical at the beginning, even though it may become so. We see this opposition persist, moreover, in the treaties that put a provisional end to wars. A so-called peace treaty does not oblige us to redefine the status of otherness; the other, the vanquished, incapable of being the victor, must bow before the decisions of the victor. Partial destruction or assimilation of the other, the diminution of the other's territory, tribute that must be paid—whatever the clauses of a peace treaty, they always imply to a greater or lesser extent the absorption of the "other" into the "same."

To make war is to measure myself against another in such unawareness of the other's nature that I accept that the other must die so that I may live. Paradoxically, I must also be willing to risk my own life to try to prevent the other from killing *me*. In this situation, the otherness of the enemy is absolute. A poet might call it "black otherness," but no alchemy can transmute such blackness, because war without death is impossible. We die, either in war or by the consequences of war, and we cause death. Think of troops wallowing in the mud of fields ripped by shells, of corpses decomposed beyond recognition, of babies decapitated in the collapse of houses built to shelter them. . . . Why go on listing scenes too horrible to forget?

The clash between "same" and "other" is so brutal that despite other conclusions we might draw from its frequency, people find it intolerable. This is why they have relied on "rules of war" to restrict death's field of operation. International agreements, international laws, all manner of conventions exist to preserve certain values even in the heat of battle. Is the attempt at legal control at odds with a purpose that works through war? Are human beings obliged to kill one another to be truly human? It is too early in our quest to say.

Another characteristic of war is that it gives human beings a broken image of time. Although time flows regularly into the future, and the steady rhythms of evening and morning, season and year never fail, the quality of time changes inevitably, if unpredictably. A time of war, which is the same for all as they risk death and fight for their lives, is followed by a time of peace, which has a different quality for the vanquished than it does for the victors. And as for peace, we are well acquainted with its brevity. So war and peace break history into bits, explode it into fragments without apparent reason or meaning. In the most seemingly intense war, there is always something beyond our comprehension that allows success at peacemaking, just as in the most seemingly stable peace, something may trigger a war when least expected.

Far from exhausting the nature of international war, these comments touch on only its surface aspects, those most commonly recognized by individuals and nations. Does war have a meaning that—for better or worse—makes it inevitable? It is a question we cannot avoid asking.

War has a second form, usually called civil war—armed struggle within a single country between two or more segments of the population. In this case the goal of combat is typically to overthrow an existing regime in order to replace it with either new rulers or a different form of government. Whether civil war occurs as mere rebellion against authorities or in the more extreme form of revolution, its point is always to seize power—regardless of illusions held by certain anarchical elements. In this kind of war, a nation's solidarity is lost. The enemy, whom we usually think of as outside the country, is inside it. Otherness, now deep in the "same" of the body politic, will force it into irreconcilable factions. In this kind of war, what rules of war could be possible? All legal protection disappears. When the seditious speak of justice, their words are contradictory because they have no legitimate judiciary power. The threatened government, meanwhile, is forced to rely on that dangerous weapon, *raison d'état*. More than any other type of war, civil war brings about the reign of arbitrary power. Virtually unanimously, philosophers have taken civil war to be the worst calamity a country can undergo. Even when it has some satisfactory outcomes, armed conflict between citizens results in the crimes of one generation weighing on the following generations, who unconsciously shoulder the burden and lose their innocence, so to speak.

Although we recognize as war in the strictest sense only the two types just discussed, we cannot ignore conflicts between private individuals, which can also become intense enough to lead to death. They may arise from an accidental wrong; from bitter arguments that end in violence, premeditated or otherwise; or from private enmities that, passed on for generations, break out in fighting on seemingly mysterious pretexts, as happens in the vendetta.[3]

Disputes between individuals reveal the hostility that is inseparable from war. Despite the sangfroid of a soldier thousands of miles from the target he is bent on destroying, he is not an automaton tapping computer keys as if to control some harmless procedure; he is a human being. In every act of war we must uncover what has enabled human beings—and still enables them—to kill others; what causes otherness to become so mysterious, so unknowable, and finally so intolerable that it must be destroyed. Although individual fights and wars are hardly the same thing, there is a sort of blind spot, a kernel of obduracy common to both in the belief that the relationship of "same" and "other" can be mediated only by the unthinkable—death. Does humanity harbor an indestructible root of hostility from which grows every form of conflict? If it withered, would humanity still exist?

Everyday speech is far more often contaminated by the terminology of war than enriched by the language of peace. We *cross swords* in an argument; we try to *outmaneuver* our rivals. We *slaughter* an opposing team; our projects are *shot down*. At dinner we fight like *men-of-war*; in the boardroom we plan market *strategies*. In our love lives we *overcome resistance* and *conquer* affection. We *attack* a steak with gusto. The battle metaphors mount up and make us wonder.

We must concede that every living thing is embattled—people, animals, and, in a sense, even plants. Life's propensity to aggression is universal. It is interesting to reread Dino Buzzati's novella *Douce nuit*. "Everything reposed in that surprising and marvelous way that nature has of sleeping in the moonlight, which no one has ever been able to explain." While the novelist contemplates the garden, however,

> terror, anguish, dismemberment, agony, death for thousands upon thousands of God's creatures—that is the nocturnal slumber of a garden thirty meters by twenty. And it is the same thing everywhere when the night is barely begun: extermination, annihilation, and carnage. And when night dissipates and the sun appears, another carnage begins, with new assassins, but the same ferocity. It has been so since the beginning of time, and it will be the same for centuries to come, till the end of the world.[4]

Must we then conclude that we are condemned to individual and collective combat? Are we like animals whose battles have the ultimate purpose of assuring the species' survival or satisfying the need for food, even when the apparent stake is territory or control of the herd? In spite of the alternation of wartime and peacetime, must it be true that whatever we do, we only encounter this dilemma: That war is now and forever our inescapable reality? Would respite from war serve only to make us drop our guard? Historical writings are not, of course, nursery tales. They do not show us war and peace as genuine alternatives so much as they reveal the unacknowledged nature of peace. Peace is the moment when history catches its breath in order to hurl itself once more into war. Our era is far from an exception in this respect. It is endowed with weapons that though not changing the intrinsic nature of war and peace, have made us more hesitant to make war. They have also made us, however, even less sure of peace because of the threat of virtually total annihilation that a global nuclear war would entail. One of the combatants, trying to surprise the other in the belief that the first to use nuclear weapons would be the only one to use them, would find that a response had been readied. In every corner of the planet a bomb waits to be activated. The vitrification of immense regions would not wipe out all enemy supplies—humanity has always filled its arms depots before its granaries. It would be a naive government that thought it could attack without provoking a counterattack in kind from any country with the capability to do so.

In this day and age we can no longer live in ignorance of the least disturbances among distant peoples or of their danger to others. Newspapers, films, television, novels, science fiction keep us informed even against our will. Their alarmist predictions have reasonable grounds. In the oppressive atmosphere of the twentieth century's final years, diverse and sometimes contradictory attitudes have arisen, based on the most passive pessimism and the most exalted optimism.

We may find it logical and even comforting that humanity should suffer for its improvidence and wickedness; we may believe in the balance of power that prevents cataclysms by tolerating limited disasters;[5] we may take peace to be the late-ripening but inevitable fruit of freedom's growth through history or the result of moving beyond contradictions on the economic plane. Whatever our belief, at this moment none of us knows what peace is, how to attain it, or perhaps even whether it is desirable. It seemed to me that some plain questions had to be asked once again and that it was important to try to answer them. Why do humans fight? Are they "programmed" to do so? Of what worth are various historical approaches in controlling their penchant for destruction? Must we simply accept humanity's obvious leaning toward war without asking what might lie behind it?

Despite the end of the cold war, and in view of the mounting dangers of nationalism, it is better to acknowledge the truth than to be trapped in illusions. The history of humanity is far less the history of peace than the history of war. This truth is not particularly consoling, I admit, but to ignore it is to invite longer wars and shorter periods of truce. Most philosophers, moreover, maintain that humans are "made for fighting." War is both their natural state *and* the condition of their emergence from nature into culture. Initially tied to the basic creaturely tendency to try to stay alive, war is humanity's way of surviving through attack and defense. But war is more than instinct, more even than instinct brandishing all the weapons that human intelligence can invent. Philosophers have claimed it to be the necessary and perhaps sufficient condition of human life as such. In their view, human beings cannot be characterized within the limits of any kind of basic nature because they create their own nature, and therefore, out of a compulsion specific to humankind, they are driven to surpass that nature in endless spiral, destroying for the sake of rebuilding. When an animal loses aggressiveness, its life is in danger. If humans ceased fighting, they would risk losing not only biological life but a genuinely human life—in other words, the meaning that humans alone can give their lives. For human life is more than procreation and length of days.

Though facing the facts of history and their implications, we must note that the aspiration to peace is also a reality. We are not always eager to begin fighting, nor will we agree to keep fighting indefinitely. Are we speaking of the mere need for a truce? Then peace would be like a sleep that revives our strength. It would be the pause needed to train a new generation for combat, to tap a reservoir of fresh aggressivity. In this case, peace would not be valued as an end in itself but as a means. Unless otherwise enlightened, analysis takes the alternation of war and peace for a tiresome, repetitious rhythm in which the cannon's silence simply gives time for blood to dry, scars to replace wounds, supplies to be built up, new techniques to perfect better weapons, and, of course, humans to reproduce in order that new lives might encounter their distinctive humanity in war.

Might not a continual yearning for peace then be the sign of the exhaustion of ancient civilizations no longer capable of self-defense? The life force once swept them into battle to extend their boundaries and prolong their fame, to civilize others as they went, and to impose their own norms and ideals. Now it has ebbed. They have lost confidence because they dominated the world too brilliantly; exhaustion follows every exertion. Now they want only a comfortable existence. They are like wealthy old ladies warming themselves in the sun: Their rich adornments conceal decrepit bodies; their idle conversation does not rouse their drowsy souls. They will vanish; they are doomed. The peace that our civilizations extol after centuries of victory in war is merely their final defeat. Nothing, especially not peace, could slow the wave of youthful strength that will take over and dictate, in its turn, its own law.

So must we be either near death or simply in need of catching our breath in order to want peace? Has peace no other meaning than truce or exhaustion? Does the longing for peace arise merely because victor and vanquished alike need occasional rest? Or does it so little represent humanity's true nature that it is characteristic only of the weak, those who are either temporarily or permanently powerless? Beyond these apparent truths, I believe, we can make out a different reality—that peace may belong to the essence of men and women, may be built into their nature. (If this is the case, however, we still must know which peace we mean and which human reality.) Though everything seems to require war, to live at peace, here and now, would then be to live as human beings and to discover the truth of humankind. It may be that our misunderstanding and perversion of human nature have allowed war to offer itself, however paradoxically, as the sole path to the affirmation of life, preferable to the peace we usually depict as the time in which we await the next war or as the first symptom of degeneration and death.

The Reality of War

For we have compelled every land and sea to open a path to our daring and have everywhere planted eternal memorials of our triumphs and misfortunes.

—Thucydides, *Peloponnesian War* 2.41

CHAPTER 1

─────────────────────────────────

War, the World Order, and God's Order

The questions we ask today about war and peace are relatively new. That war is the source of evils has apparently never been disputed, but this has not always sufficed to class war itself as an evil. Particular wars have elicited varying opinions. The Median wars, which gave the Greeks victory over the Persians, were, for example, a source of pride to the league of Hellenic city-states. Yet the Peloponnesian War gave them cause to castigate their disastrous rivalries but inspired much less criticism of war as such. "We are not yet to speak . . . of any evil or good effect of war," says Socrates in discussing the education of soldiers, the guardians of the City.[1] Each time the theme of war recurs, in fact, Plato neglects this question.[2]

In contrast, what is taken to be an indisputable evil—absolute evil, as we say today—is war within the City, war pitting citizen against citizen, civil war, *stasis* [standing] in contrast to *polemos* [war]. "Do we know of any greater evil for a state than the thing that distracts it and makes it many instead of one, or a greater good than that which binds it together and makes it one?" asks Socrates.[3]

Condemnation of civil war is so far from being condemnation of all war that war against those who would rob the City of its independence, its freedom, or its self-respect and pride is a duty a citizen cannot and must not evade. In the face of war, the important thing is to know how the political community should act. How can it effectively defend itself? When should it attack and upon what conditions? Here, it appears, are the problems posed by war that give the *Republic* the most obvious outlines of its structure. It is foreign to ancient thought to inquire into the legitimacy of war where the City's best interest is concerned and, a fortiori, to inquire into the duty or the possibility of suppressing war.

This is not to imply that peace both without and within the City is not good and desirable, especially if honorably, even gloriously, won. Peace permits the harmonious development of a flourishing City and thereby improves its chances of winning any future wars. The Greeks, like the

Romans, were well aware of the benefits of peace. But even the Pax Romana relied on the might and victory of armies kept in a state of perpetual readiness.

We need hardly recall that education in ancient Greece was based on epic poems and that the nature of virtues was learned from the bloodiest episodes, in which these virtues are forged and made manifest. *Areté*, "excellence," soon to be widely identified with virtue, is above all the accomplishment of the warrior who wins glory in combat both for himself and for his family. We find Agamemnon "driving eagerly toward the fighting where men win glory."[4] Diomedes is amazed that he has never before met Glaucos "in the fighting where men win glory,"[5] though now he comes "striding far out in front of all others" to boldly face his threatening spear.[6] At the mere thought of being "like a coward . . . to shrink aside from the fighting," Hector feels himself blush with shame. Though moved by Andromache's suffering, he yet replies to her fears, "I have learned to be valiant / and to fight always among the foremost ranks of the Trojans, / winning for my own self great glory, and for my father."[7] When his son takes fright at the bronze of his helmet, Hector dandles him, smiling, yet leaves with him, as his farewell, a prayer to Zeus that is both a wish and a rule of conduct:

> Zeus, and you other immortals, grant that this boy, who is
> my son,
> may be as I am, pre-eminent among the Trojans,
> great in strength, as I am, and rule strongly over Ilion;
> and some day let them say of him: 'He is better by far than
> his father',
> as he comes in from the fighting; and let him kill his enemy
> and bring home the blooded spoils, and delight the heart of
> his mother.[8]

Such is the original and sole *areté* from which the classic moral virtues will be elaborated. One among them, courage, will inherit the attributes that once constituted the complete definition of excellence. Homer, moreover, will always be cited by the Greek philosophers, whether or not the poet was considered a member of the City. Plato thus says of courage that it is the virtue "of a citizen,"[9] that it is proper to the group of citizens that "defends [the City] and wages war on its behalf."[10] It is not in respect to all citizens but solely the warriors[11] that we can define courage as "this power in the soul, this unfailing conservation of right and lawful belief about things to be and not to be feared."[12] This is why we must accord warriors the greatest honors. Homer's lesson was not lost. Although the poet was banished from the City, the virtue that he praised and that is acquired only in war received philosophy's rigorous definition. This characteristic of war is clear—it is the condition that makes it possible to acquire a civic and moral virtue.

Though war and peace are defined by each other, they are nonetheless tied to the reality of the world, that is, to its immutable and intangible order, which humankind has not made and cannot unmake. The order of the world does not depend upon man. In this sense it is transcendent. Humanity and the City have their place in this eternal order, but insofar as war and peace also belong to the order of the world, no human could abolish either one; they are both necessary, each in its way, to the life and perfection of the whole. Thus are war and peace necessarily linked. In their opposition they imply each other, as the pre-Socratic philosophers had already noted. Whether successive or simultaneous, opposites are at the origin of things. This explains, according to Heraclitus, why the world is intelligible, subject as it is to the divine law, the Logos. Aristotle relates that the philosopher of Ephesus criticized Homer for wishing "'that Conflict might vanish from among gods and men!' For there would be no attunement without high and low notes nor any animals without male and female, both of which are opposites."[13] To pay for his lack of logic, the poet "deserves to be expelled from the competition and beaten with a staff."[14] He had not understood, in effect, that "the counter-thrust brings together, and from tones at variance come perfect attunement, and all things come to pass through conflict."[15]

In fact, in the passage Heraclitus censures, Homer is not attacking war at all but quite the opposite. After Patroclus' death, Achilles is grieving in the presence of his mother, Thetis. "I must die soon, then," he cries, "since I was not to stand by my companion / when he was killed."[16] He despises his own inactivity, which he considers the cause of Patroclus' death, and he curses its cause, the quarrel with Agamemnon that led him to lay down his arms:

Why, I wish that strife would vanish away from among gods
    and mortals,
and gall, which makes a man grow angry for all his great
    mind,
that gall of anger that swarms like smoke inside of a man's
    heart
and becomes a thing sweeter to him by far than the dripping
    of honey.
So it was here that the lord of men Agamemnon angered
    me.[17]

It is discord among the Greeks that is being denounced, not war against the Trojans. On the contrary, it is war that one must return to, even knowing that one goes to death.

> So I likewise . . .
> shall lie still, when I am dead. Now I must win excellent
>   glory,
> and drive some one of the women of Troy, or some deep-girdled
> Dardanian woman, lifting up to her soft cheeks both hands,
> to wipe away the close burst of tears in her lamentation,
> and learn that I stayed too long out of the fighting.[18]

Achilles is hardly making an apologia for peace, nor had he stopped fighting out of love of peace.

War and peace, in their eternal opposition, cannot exist—nor even be thought of—without each other, for together they are the source of all future events. "Graspings: wholes and not wholes, convergent divergent, consonant dissonant," says Heraclitus, "from all things one and from one thing all."[19]

As paradoxical as this aphorism seems, it exactly represents the fecundity of contradiction; to abolish contradiction by expunging either term would annihilate the world. "One must realize that war is shared and Conflict is Justice, and that all things come to pass . . . in accordance with conflict."[20] How can we oppose war if war, reciprocally and successively with peace, is "the father of all and the king of all,"[21] founder of the political community in which people are ranked according to their worth and of the order of moral values that manifest the order of the world?[22] For this reason "gods and men honor those who fall in battle."[23] Behind the opposition of life and death, as of war and peace, value and life triumph, but only if we do not abandon the movement that creates and conserves, the struggle that prevents dissolution. For "even the potion separates unless it is stirred."[24]

It is interesting to observe a similar intuition expressed by Empedocles, even though when Aristotle is trying to understand friendship in the *Nichomachean Ethics*, before arriving at his own definition of it,[25] he contrasts the two pre-Socratic philosophers. According to Heraclitus' ideas, Aristotle recalls, what is opposed is useful, and "from tones at variance come perfect attunement, and all things come to pass through conflict."[26] But the opposite opinion, he adds, is maintained by Empedocles, according to whom "like attracts like."[27]

Empedocles makes this attraction one of the principles of his philosophy. It is nonetheless true that the four elements that make up "all that was or is or evermore shall be"[28] must submit to the action of two forces, love and strife, that "were strong of yore . . . shall have their hereafter; nor . . . shall endless Age be emptied of these Twain."[29] Strife's role is far from negligible. Empedocles calls it "deadly,"[30] but without it love would gather everything into a mass, peaceful, indeed, but one from which nothing would emerge, neither object nor individual existence. It is strife that puts the four elements into equilibrium,[31] then by scattering them permits their recombination, although no longer into an indistinguishable mixture, as Aristotle reminds us.[32] For "the Many . . . / Spring from primeval scattering of the One, / So far have they a birth and mortal date."[33] Strife is the individuation principle. Our lives are thus in the grip of this twofold dynamic, for life is destroyed when the elements that make up reality are dispersed and destroyed again when love reassembles the original unity. Men and women are born, live, and die in the alternation of these tensions and through their double action—through this "world-wide warfare of the eternal Two."[34] Each is as necessary as the other, even though—as Aetius tells us, citing Empedocles[35]—the reign of strife, obedient to the world's order, cannot help but be painful.[36] In "The Purifications," Empedocles exclaims: "O mortal kind! O ye poor sons of grief! / From such contentions and such sighings sprung!"[37] But lamentation cannot change reality:

Twofold the birth, twofold the death of things:
For, now, the meeting of the Many brings
To birth and death; and, now, whatever grew
From out their sundering, flies apart and dies.
And this long interchange shall never end.[38]

I have referred to most of the fragments that speak of this opposition because though its meaning is not strictly the same in Heraclitus and Empedocles, it is nonetheless a concept that illuminates our understanding of conflict. Whether we deplore it or rejoice in it, conflict is necessary; there could be no life without it, even what we call human life, our life. Plato partly shares this perspective, it seems, when he reminds us, in the myth of Cronus, that the world we live in is the product of a movement that has reversed itself since the days when that god held sway.[39] If this movement attained its maximum momentum, the world would be "wracked by storms and confusion, and be dissolved again in the bottomless abyss of unlikeness,"[40] but if there were no movement at all, the world we know and our very lives would not exist.

Conflict, then, cannot be separated from life, even when it may destroy life. Though Greek philosophy was not entirely comfortable in doing so, it nonetheless developed without breaking free from the idea of this necessity that appeared to be the condition of human life. Human beings are not to blame for war, which in its opposite and indestructible relationship to peace makes them what they are. When war stifles its contrary, it is a scourge; but if peace banished war forever, peace, too, would be a catastrophe. To find the balance between these necessary tensions, to prevent either from dominating, was the goal toward which the political philosophers of antiquity strove.

It may seem obvious to contrast the Judeo-Christian tradition with the Greek view of war and peace. The former bases its stand on divine precept as found in the absolute rigor of the formula "Thou shalt not kill." Alone among the nations, the Hebrews received the commandment forbidding the slaying of one human being by another. Whereas the Greeks never generalized a prohibition against killing to all humanity, do we not find in scriptural texts a clear and definitive condemnation of war—any form of war—delivered to a people *chosen* to make it known to the world by first of all respecting it themselves?

The prohibition is uttered by God himself, in the twentieth chapter of Exodus.[41] Its place in the text precedes the commandment in Leviticus that enjoins love of one's neighbor.[42] In its spareness, clarity, absence of commentary, it is sufficient in itself. It follows four precepts concerning God—to worship him, to make no images of him, not to take his name in vain, to honor the day that he chose as his own day of rest. It also follows the charge to honor one's parents. Because we have been created by God and produced after the flesh by parents, we have duties of gratitude implied by such an ontological status; and after these obligations comes the duty to refrain from killing. The universal and primary precept of human conduct concerns the life of relationships and, in sum, makes such a life possible. This commandment will be developed in practical detail in Leviticus 19:17–18. "You shall not hate your brother in your heart, you must reprove and correct your neighbor, and you will incur no guilt because of him. You shall not seek revenge, you shall not bear a grudge against the children of your people, but you shall love your neighbor as yourself." Leviticus elaborates into commands and prohibitions what Exodus proclaims in simplest terms, brevity giving the commandment its power.

It goes without saying that in the New Testament we again encounter both the prohibition against killing and the commandment to love our neighbor. Taken as a whole, the scriptural writings emphasize the idea of peace, the very opposite of the idea of war. Christ did not come "to abolish the law and the prophets . . . but to fulfill them."[43] He himself also teaches: "Blessed are the peacemakers, for they shall be called sons of God";[44] "You have heard that it was said to the men of old, 'You shall not kill; and whoever kills shall be liable to judgment.' But I say to you that every one who is angry with his brother shall be liable to judgment."[45] Citations abound, from the first words of Christmas night, "On earth peace among men with whom he is pleased,"[46] through the words uttered before the Passion, "Peace I leave with you, my peace I give to you,"[47] to the clear-cut threat, "For all who take the sword will perish by the sword."[48] All point to what the Holy Spirit brings—peace as the true way.

Should we see in these formulations that have helped shape the Western soul a pure and simple condemnation of war—which Western nations have nonetheless waged so often in their histories and for which they continually and actively prepare when not actually fighting? If we restore the biblical words to their contexts we understand that, in spite of recent interpretations, their intent is not to forbid war. They definitely prohibit us from killing our fellow, but the prohibition concerns death by a private act, what we would call homicide or assassination. The passages in question do not apply to political acts. The Catholic catechism interprets the fifth commandment of the Decalogue in a way that leaves no room for doubt and is perfectly faithful to the text: "Homicide point ne seras, sans droit ni volontairement" [You shall not deliberately kill another human without legal right].[49] It is precisely as a moral precept that we should take the interdict "Thou shalt not kill." It is a precept bearing on private, individual-to-individual relationships, not a prohibition regarding war. In the Bible we read, moreover, that the Israelites were often led to wage war because God required it of them and that God himself takes sides for or against his people, according to whether they deserve help or punishment. Turning to the writings of the New Testament, we find even less concern with the political realm. In addition, it would be impossible to resolve their apparent contradictions if we took these texts as applying to war in the sense that we understand it when we speak of foreign war and perhaps even of civil war. Though Jesus gives peace, he says just as clearly that he has not "come to bring peace, but a sword. For I have come," he says, "to set a man against his father, and a daughter against her mother, and a daughter-in-law against her mother-in-law; and a man's foes will be those of his own household."[50] Theological exegetes must explain the meaning of these family conflicts and show how they are consistent with the gift of peace, but there is no possible way that they can attribute a political significance to either passage.

Having said this, I still cannot avoid asking what relation the prohibition against killing has to warfare. Does "thy neighbor" mean a member of the same nation? Are we obligated to conduct ourselves morally in private relations, whereas we may kill in good conscience those who live on the other side of the river from our country if we are at war with them?

Reflection on the texts in question, I suspect, will lead to a less summary conclusion.

I must first of all state that the notion of neighbor as it appears in scriptural texts is not synonymous with people in general or with humanity. *Neighbor* refers to one of a group selected from all of humankind, a definite set, neither the whole nor some imprecise part. It is the group of human beings with whom we are in a relationship of proximity (as the French and Latin terms indicate).* It is those toward whom we have real, concrete feelings because we know them, we have common concerns, we share a common history. But they are also those with whom we fall into conflict and disharmony, precisely because the "neighbor" is the one who is "nigh," who is close by; for the nearer and more concrete their object, the stronger our emotions.

In addition, the notion of neighbor does not have a clearly defined limit. The nearest "neighbor" is a family member, a father, a brother, a son. The term, then, extends to cover more distant relatives, then friends, colleagues, acquaintances, and finally fellow citizens. It also includes strangers whom circumstance puts in our way and with whom we may more or less temporarily develop a common cause, for in this case the "neighbor" is still a real person, not an anonymous member of the human species. It is clear that the more the group expands, the more the sense of being in the presence of a "neighbor" weakens, just as a long separation can turn those who were once close into strangers. Finally, it seems indeed that to love people in the very vague sense of humankind in general is only a convenient way of loving no one in particular and of giving ourselves a conscience so clear that we feel exempt from loving our neighbor.

If love of those near us is natural, then the commandment not to kill is universal and takes us back to the original question: When causing death is the issue, are we defining this action as appropriate in our relations with some persons but not others? Or, on the contrary, must a human being, as addressed by Judaism or Christianity, cease from waging war under any circumstances at all? No matter how complex the interpretations we give them, we have seen that the texts do not answer this question. Indeed, they do not ask it. The Church Fathers, in compensation, took it upon themselves to find answers, both acknowledging the commandment and facing the problems it presented. Some of the Church Fathers are categorical: A Christian is essentially defined by an expectation of eternal life, preparing in the here and now for the kind of life that totally excludes

---

*Fr. *prochain* and *proximité*, Lat. *propinquus* and *proximitas* (neighbor and nearness). Both pairs derive from *prope* and *proximus* (near and nearest).

warfare. War is incompatible with the evangelical ideal, and because existence here below has no goal but salvation and the life eternal, it is better to let oneself and one's household be massacred than to resist assault and endanger the life of an assailant. Arguments of this sort can be found in Tertullian, Origen, and Lactantius.

For Saint Augustine, however, war is lawful under carefully defined conditions that are mentioned in various places in his copious writings. War, he argues, is a consequence of original sin, a sign of the finite and fallen nature of humankind.[51] Is the Christian, the redeemed man or woman who must try to live according to the precepts of the gospel, nevertheless allowed to wage war in certain circumstances and sometimes even obligated to do so? Although the answer is given in full by Saint Augustine, it was Thomas Aquinas who gathered his predecessor's scattered arguments and organized them under the heading, the *quaesitio*, of "War."[52]

Bringing together, according to his method, speakers of different and indeed opposed opinions, Saint Thomas catalogs the possible replies to the question, Is there such a thing as a lawful war, or is it, in other words, always a sin to wage war? The debaters in the first group answer that it is indeed a sin, appealing to the authority of Scripture. The teachings of Christ and the church give grounds for condemning war. These are the teachings Saint Thomas is referring to when, without mentioning them by name, he recalls those Church Fathers who had formerly denied all possibility of war in the name of the gospel and cites the same passages as they. It is true that they had limited themselves to a simple condemnation of war, taking the texts that were the subject of their commentary as decisive. Christ's words as reported by Matthew, "All who take the sword will perish by the sword,"[53] become in Saint Thomas a sort of law of retaliation implying that the punishment for disobedience to the commandment "Thou shall not kill" will be identical to the act. Saint Thomas reminds us that Christ adjures us not to resist evil,[54] which amounts to not enforcing justice ourselves, but to wait on God's justice.[55] Even when we are the victim of another, we may not judge that other. Consequently, we cannot punish the other, for we must not usurp a purely divine prerogative. From this point of view, living in peace is synonymous with living righteously, whereas waging war is the same as living sinfully, and acts of preparation for war are included in the full condemnation.

The structure of the *disputatio*, however, requires the exposition of opposing arguments according to the dialectic method, in the Aristotelian sense of the term.[56] War is not a topic suited to investigation through mathematical reasoning. The premises established are uncertain, as the variety of discordant opinions witnesses. Though rigorously deduced, conclusions remain merely probable due to their dubious starting points.

They fail to reach the truth, although they approach it, thanks to the juxtaposition of differing points of view.[57] The second series of arguments derives from those of Saint Augustine: Because Christ did not condemn the army when he accepted the centurion's plea to restore his child to life, we can conclude that he did not condemn war.[58] The demonstration would be rather slight if it relied on no more than this statement from an Augustinian letter (no. 138), so Saint Thomas repeats all of Augustine's theses relating to war in order to classify them and to determine from them when and on what condition war is lawful and whether it is or is not a sin to wage war. Here we find the well-known doctrine of the "just war," which, as transmitted by Saint Augustine and Saint Thomas, became the church's own doctrine on the subject. I will briefly summarize its essential points.

For a war to be lawful, it must first of all be initiated by a legitimate authority. An individual without rank or a group, even a political one, is by definition never a public authority. The purpose of political power is to assure the common welfare; it hence becomes the ruler's responsibility to guarantee and answer for it. Those who govern must preserve the well-being of the community internally and defend its frontiers against external threats. It is the prince's duty to prevent enemies, either within or without, from harming the community that is under his care. The prince's obligation to use force, if he has no other recourse, to carry out the function that is his raison d'être arises from the natural order of things. "The natural order," writes Saint Augustine regarding worldly peace, "ordains that the monarch should have the power of undertaking war."[59] (We should understand the word *monarch* to mean one who governs legitimately.)

In the second place, the reason for waging war must be a "just cause." The only just war is a war of defense against an unjust and unavenged attack. The state is "natural," as Aristotle taught, because outside it no man or woman could live other than as an animal. We are each, in our own place in the community, part of the equilibrium of the whole. This is why no one may decide that his or her life is not worth defending against an unjust attack. A human being may not choose whether to live or die; it would be contrary to divine authority, whose *minister* [agent] in civic society is the prince.

Finally, a defensive war must only be undertaken for the direct purpose of reestablishing peace. Although it is sometimes a necessary means, war is never an end. It should be waged dispassionately and with peace as its aim, even though—we must not deceive ourselves—it provides the opportunity for the passions to rage uncensured. Albeit attempting to control war, the theory of the just war does not suppress it nor expect its disappearance. On the contrary, it would actually increase the necessity of war, lest humans forget that they are only creatures, which would be completely satanic.

From neither classical nor Christian tradition could the idea be born that, in this world, war will one day yield to peace. Whether taken as inherent in the order of the universe or in the God-given and fallen nature of humanity, the relationship of opposition indeed appears to be inescapable. Just or not, war demands analysis before we can investigate the hypothesis of the reality of peace. The doctrine of the just war makes apparent that some *sinful* party must be rejecting peace. There are also those who, in good faith, believe their war is just, at the same time their adversaries are equally convinced that it is they who are in the right. The ethical requirement that the Church Fathers insist on does not decide what is moral. And supposing it were always possible to point to the wrongdoer, still it is only force, we are obliged to admit, that can quell that malfactor. *Dieu et mon droit* [God and my right] proclaims the British crown; but the escutcheon is framed by the lion and unicorn, who also know how to sail to the Falkland Islands. *Honi soit qui mal y pense* [Shamed be he who thinks evil of it]. . . . Justice without force is ineffective. The doctrine of the just war is a sort of recognition of the ineluctable reality of war. In the kingdom of this world, war is analyzed in a way that makes the divine commandment unfathomable—though it does not apply solely to private relations, neither can it unqualifiedly govern public life. Pious hopes and good intentions can do no better than delude the imagination or conceal hypocritical plots.

CHAPTER 2

Desire and War

That human beings fight is a fact. Is fighting part of the human condition, is it so much a part of our nature that to expect the final elimination of war, whether soon or in the distant future, is only utopian fantasy? Observation of human nature has led many a philosopher to find it so intertwined with the existence of war that peace has never been seen as other than contrary to that nature and hence impossible to establish in all places and for all time. If war arises from human nature itself, we must conclude that only the permanent threat of the evils an outbreak of war might bring allows truces to be made and respected. How precarious is peace, when danger lurks on every hand; yet how necessary is peace for humankind's survival and productivity.

Where does war come from? Is it in the makeup of human beings? Can we say that it is a defining attribute of human nature, whereas peace is only one of its accidental properties? All living species are engaged in struggle. A priori, there is no reason that humankind should be otherwise. We can begin from the biological point of view: War appears necessary to the survival of the species. We are familiar with the conclusions Konrad Lorenz drew from his observations. Species without defenses against aggression are nearing extinction, but even the better-armed species do not survive unless their members attack before being attacked. What is true for species is true for individuals, and, contrary to what we might suppose from superficial observation, not only are animals of different species pitted in battle but so, too, in accord with instinctual patterns, are those of the same species.[1] An animal is, moreover, constantly on guard. It is never completely absorbed, for example, in feeding. It remains alert to its surroundings, from which unpredictable danger may arise. It seems natural, as Spinoza writes in the *Tractatus Theologico-Politicus*, that "the greater [fish] devour the less,"[2] yet fish of the same size and appearance also behave like enemies when it comes to defending their feeding territory.

Humans' war against humans is embedded in their nature in a much more complex way than as mere expression of instinct. It is not linked solely to opportunities to satisfy a biological need, as is true of other animals. The latter are strictly products of nature, every moment from their birth to their death. The cycle of need and satisfaction is the process by which an animal—and from this perspective, a human being—maintains its existence. The shrewd Stoics demonstrated the spontaneous interest a living creature has in self-preservation and in preferring what contributes to self-preservation.[3] A person, however, is other than this. He or she is of course an animal and, as such, compelled to satisfy natural needs and pay the necessary price for doing so, even to the risk of life in war; yet at the same time we can say that a person is in no way comparable to an animal. Do human beings even have biological needs in a pure state, except in limiting cases such as that of the newborn or the individual facing death by starvation? Even though the same members and organs of the body are engaged, in a human being we do not see the action of need but of desire.

Desire is neither a complex need nor an inessential need but the specifically human way of experiencing, and of trying to satisfy, the wants of the flesh and the mind we all feel. Desire profoundly affects the cycle of self-preservation. It participates in the cycle but may also withdraw from it to such an extent that individuals following their desire are capable of renouncing the satisfaction of essential natural needs for satisfactions irrelevant to mere survival. Desire brings into play a synergy of powers: Intelligence, memory, imagination, strength, and courage place themselves at its service and combine in a dynamic that strives toward an infinity of ends—with which it will never be satisfied. This is the mainspring of human life. To continue living is, for men and women, to continue desiring, to continue seeking what they lack, in order to become, paradoxically, always other than they are.

This is why desire contributes to establishing a sense of time, though not as time is measured by biological rhythm. Humans are obviously aware of this kind of repetitive time, but because of desire, they are in time and create time, are in history and possess a history. The history of humankind is the history of its desires.

It must be stressed that the desiring person is always in relationship with other persons, yet in contradictory ways. Although desire is of course the expression of a social existence, to desire is also to separate oneself from others. Desire, in effect, makes use of others, starts rivalries, starts hostilities. We cannot affirm our own desires except in relation to, and in conflict with, another's desire; we cannot desire in a vacuum. Hence, the root of war is coiled inside desire like a snake; and because there is no human being (in the full sense of the term) who is without desire, there is no human community without war.

In the confrontation between desires, it is not so much their desires that humans affirm as their right to impose them. What could possibly make us betray life's driving force? If another is the means of fulfilling my desire, why would I yield to the other any more than that other would to me? Desire seeks the single form of domination that is of fundamental value to humanity, that which gives human life its meaning and uniqueness—one human being's domination of another. We must have the courage to acknowledge this and also to measure all the implications of a truth we pretend not to know—that it is always the others we accuse of wanting to impose their desire. Yet in each of us, hidden with more skill or less, the protean taste for power grows more restless, whether it be for the little power that those disadvantaged by limited talent or adverse circumstances still insist on seeking, or for the many forms of power, and especially political power, reserved for those whose zeal and perspicacity have cleared their way to success.

Moral outrage is beside the point. Desire cannot bend to laws. It is anarchic, in the original sense of the word. Without a principle, with no origin but itself, it need not justify itself. Besides, are not those who have won power and taken command always anarchic? If a person creates the law and pronounces the law, is he or she not therefore above the law? But even though the desires of others have proved weaker, when they continue to exist, war is always at least possible, as much within a particular political community as between different communities. History is the tale of desires imposed and resisted, and politics is always and necessarily a confrontation, a struggle, a clash of strengths of which civil and foreign war are the extreme manifestations. Consequently, any political power, in asserting itself, is characterized not only by anarchy but by at least a minimum of tyranny. In a political joust, the winner's desire, subject to no law, is imposed on all others. The vanquished hold to the hope of overturning the victory in order to dominate in their turn. What is true of relations within the boundaries of a single nation is true of relations between nation and nation. If desire renounces this dialectic of anarchy and tyranny, it disappears as desire. The only person without desire, they say, is a dead one; we can apply the same adage to states.

This is what Callicles shows he understands when, in the *Gorgias*, he argues that desire is the fundamental human reality, defining humanity better than do other concepts, such as "animal" and "reason." Nevertheless, though all men and women desire, they do not all desire in the same way; the strength of their desire and the means they have for satisfying it are not identical: Human beings are not equal. When their desires conflict, they go to war; some conquer, some are conquered. But Plato shows us, through the words of Callicles, that desire's irrational violence leads to the actualization of reason and courage, specifically human traits that would not develop without it; for in order to be realized, desire must be served by these traits. "Anyone who is to live aright should suffer his appetites to grow to the greatest extent and not check them, and through courage and intelligence should be competent to minister to them at their greatest and to satisfy every appetite with what it craves."[4] Most are incensed when they read these words; they should rather let introspection show them the truth of the lesson. The power of a desire, no matter which, has always been the basis for human action, has always justified policies, perhaps even morality, and has always succeeded in dictating the law. Without desire, actions might possibly be imagined but could not be carried out, for they would sink in the quicksand of indifference. Because it springs from the whole personality and impels it toward courage and intelligence, desire thrusts a human being ahead in time, pointing the way to what he or she must do to become what he or she must be. To desire is to escape living unconsciously, moved by the mechanical determinism of instinct. The stronger and more abundant one's desires, the more one achieves. Desire is a double infinity: Combined with the infinite strength of some of our desires is the infinite number of all our desires.[5]

In *The Republic*, Plato has Glaucon say that to follow one's desire is to be "among mankind as the equal of a god."[6] Desire is *epiphany*, revealing the human being. At the same time, however, it reveals that the order reigning within a City or among Cities comes about through the universal imposition of a single person's desire. For this reason, order is always unstable and swings from armed peace to open war as soon as more powerful desires seek to overthrow it for their own advantage. The only limit on desire is its own weakness.

Rather than be discomfited by these ideas, we do better to ask whether their inspiration is not a truth that we refuse to accept, a truth that would account for the origin of all power that, from its humblest to its most intricate form, is inseparable from human life. It is a truth that is painful to acknowledge when expressed so plainly, for it brutally confronts us with the knowledge that each desire to be satisfied brings with it not peace but conflict. Perhaps we can move past analysis only if we plunge into it and accept its outcomes. It is not the least evidence of Plato's greatness that he decisively shows that no *ethical* code is persuasive enough to prevail by itself against the claims of desire, in the broadest meaning of the term. The style of the *Gorgias* is skeptical. Socrates' arguments fail to convince Callicles, who easily shows them to be masks behind which ill-equipped desires strive to have their turn at domination. Plato repeatedly points out the connection between desire and war that makes hopes for peace vain. He devotes a great deal of effort to the question of how to control that particular species of the genus *Desire*, political ambition; he hopes to guarantee the unity of the City through civil peace, the City providing for its own safety by arming effectively and appropriately against a possible war beyond its borders.

———————

Although Machiavelli does not systematically work out a theory of the relation between desire and war, he makes a remarkable analysis of its complexity. This analysis is worth examining at some length, for though we cannot strictly say that Machiavelli initiates a change in thought that overturns old concepts of war, he is nonetheless among those who have depicted with precision and realism the unbreakable bond linking the existence of war to human nature. After Machiavelli, the character of peace will be clear—desirable under certain conditions, but not an expression of the ultimate truth about humanity. Human beings live at peace when war is not a better means of self-preservation or, more especially, when peace better contributes to the actualization of a nature that finds its greatest fulfillment in self-assertion through political power. In the here and now, individuals identify their own worth with works that they intend should endure and that inevitably require warlike means for their accomplishment. If we first acknowledge the role of desire, we can then understand the true nature of humankind, most often associated with war even though political communities have sometimes, in certain periods, happened to live in peace. In the final analysis, humanity is defined by its works, and Machiavellian anthropology makes clear the indissoluble bond between human works and war.

To the most basic desire within each of us, the desire of all creatures to avoid death, there corresponds primarily one type of war. Machiavelli does not hide its terrifying yet ineluctable character. When outward circumstances—hunger, epidemics, war—are bringing certain death, people are driven to do what they must to stay alive. What they do is not dependent on governmental decision nor on deliberate agreement among the members of a group, and yet what we could call a mass movement occurs. To resist a threat that can only end in disaster, the potential victims, in the hope of escaping their fate, will turn what began as a war of *defense* (a struggle against an external scourge) into a war of *offense* against peaceful populations whose destruction has become the aggressors' only means of survival.

Machiavelli shows that this war is natural, primitive, and inescapable and that no precautions could have restrained it, as it is the deadly result of a human being's all-powerful will to live in the face of calamities beyond human control. It occurs "when an entire people, constrained by famine or war, leave their country with their families for the purpose of seeking a new home in a new country, not for the purpose of subjecting it to their dominion . . . but with the intent of taking absolute possession of it themselves and driving out or killing its original inhabitants. This kind of war is most frightful and cruel."[7] Machiavelli takes special note of the inevitability of this kind of war; it is as natural as life. "These tribes migrated from their own countries . . . driven by hunger, or war, or some other scourge, which they had experienced at home and which obliges them to seek new dwelling-places elsewhere."[8] "Great migrations," as historians demurely name this sort of chronic calamity, are the consequence, then, of "the extremest necessity,"[9] a necessity that condemns men and women to leave a "cold and sterile country, whence they were compelled to migrate, the population being very great and the country too poor to support it."[10] It condemns them to turn migration into the savage warfare of those who would save their own skin at the cost of the skin of a more fortunate populace from a more congenial countryside. War, not peace, is what gives them their chance to stay alive, just as the populations they invade will, in turn, only have their chance for survival if they can raise "formidable armies" against the waves of invaders breaking upon them.[11] War can thus be likened to an impulse, to every living creature's drive to continue living, a drive that propels one, invaded and invader alike, to defend one's individual life, even at the risk of that life and the lives of others. There is no original *philia* [affection] among humans—none between attackers and those attacked, needless to say, but neither is there any among members of the same group. There is an atrocious free-for-all, for "when an entire people aims to possess itself of a country and to live upon that which gives support to its original inhabitants, it must necessarily destroy them all," while the latter, "each fighting for [his or her] very existence," try to drive back the assault.[12]

War, we see here, is based first on individual animal need, without involving what we would strictly define as desire. On the level of mere subsistence, humans engage in what could be called aggressive herd movements.[13] They intend in this way to meet vital needs. War caused by need does not resemble classic warfare nor does it know anything of group tactics. It is a survival reflex. Nevertheless, whatever the instinctive force that triggers each invader's behavior, it relies on cleverness and the use of arms, and thus on things unknown to mere beasts. In this regard, war for survival is a sign of humanness, but it does not constitute a sufficient definition of war as a specifically human activity. Because of its relation to need, this kind of war resembles a natural means at the service of a basic drive that must be satisfied at any cost. Economic behavior—that is, behavior essential for survival—reaches, in human populations, a familiar complexity (another mark of the difference between humans and animals). Yet actions taken on solely economic grounds, grounds of primitive need, do not in themselves separate humankind from the beasts. Without stating it explicitly, Machiavelli makes this perfectly apparent.

In this kind of war, men and women defend only their own lives, whether they are members of the horde—the swarm, to use Machiavelli's image—or members of a normal citizenry trying to drive back the horde's assault. But even the Roman people lost its coherence in resisting such invasions, each person fighting solely for herself or himself when immersed in the wave of invaders. It is only after one side or the other finally triumphs that human institutions come into being or reappear. While the battle rages, the character of the individual reveals itself, as the individual rediscovers the instincts of the beast fighting for its life. At any rate, to continue to live peaceably on either side, invader's or defender's, would be to sign one's own death warrant.

But this kind of war, however natural and inevitable, is not the kind that principally interests Machiavelli. In fact he considers it a minor type; he mentions it only after another to which he devotes far more attention. Whereas war for survival, either offensive or defensive, depends on humans' biological similarity to other animals, the first form of war Machiavelli analyzes originates in the specifically human trait—desire. It originates particularly in the desire one human being has to displace another, to dominate another—that is, in ambition. "The one [kind of war] springs from the ambition of princes or republics that seek to extend their empire. . . . These wars are dangerous, but never go so far as to drive all its inhabitants out of a province, because the conqueror is satisfied with the submission of the people, and generally leaves them their dwellings and possessions, and even the enjoyment of their own institutions."[14]

The type of war previously discussed was the war of natural and vital need, whereas this war is specifically the war of desire. Although in this passage Machiavelli associates it with the ambition of princes and republics, he sees it no less as the war that each of us dreams of waging; for it is desire that defines human beings, with our boundless impulse to appropriate what is *valued* by others, an impulse endlessly repeated, as possession quickly pales and one person's desire takes aim forever at the equally limitless desire of another.

"Meditate a little deeper on mortal craving," Machiavelli writes to Francesco Guicciardini's brother, "from the sun of Scythia to that of Egypt, from Gibraltar to the opposite shore . . . what province or what city escapes it? What village, what hovel? Everywhere Ambition and Avarice penetrate." To which he adds this very significant sentence, "O human spirit . . . through your longing so ambitious, the first violent death was seen in the world, and the first grass red with blood!" Desire, whether expressed in pride, ambition, avarice, or some other vice, is born with humankind. "From this it results that one goes down and another goes up; on this depends, without law or agreement, the shifting of every mortal condition." And because "so always the world has been, modern and ancient," it follows that "every man hopes to climb higher by crushing now one, now another, rather than through his own wisdom and *virtù* [excellence]. To each of us another's success is always vexatious; and therefore always, with effort and trouble, for another's ill we are watchful and alert. To this our natural instinct draws us."[15] When it was a question of mere survival, we could not speak of innate *philia* between humans. Neither do we find it in the definition of what is unique to the human species. Lightened by a breath of poetry, this little work on the subject of ambition presages the teachings of *The Prince* and the *Discourses*.

"As human desires are insatiable," Machiavelli writes in the *Discourses on the First Ten Years of Titus Livius*, "(because their nature is to have and to do everything whilst fortune limits their possessions and capacity of enjoyment), this gives rise to a constant discontent in the human mind and a weariness of the things they possess; and it is this which makes them decry the present, praise the past, and yearn for the future, and all this without any reasonable motive."[16] Machiavelli recognizes, then, that all are desire's creatures and that desire has no limits inasmuch as its peaceable fulfillment inspires not calm enjoyment but boredom that can be relieved only through war.[17] To be is to desire to have, that is, to turn toward the future, toward what one is not because one has not. To be is also to recall the past with nostalgia or bitterness, as what no longer exists and cannot be possessed again is for that very reason desirable. Desire feeds on imagination. The imagined object, past or future, is rich with all possibilities, whereas the possessed object is proved limited by reality. We will value it only if we can imagine it snatched away at some future time by another's conquering will. Political ambition would surely be less fiery, less enterprising (for better or worse) if it were not nourished by the image of humanity it has itself created. This image is so much more brilliant than the reality, always necessarily constrained by the immediate situation, that it motivates an attempt to make the real and the imaginary coincide. *Quo non ascendam?* [To what heights shall I not rise?] Here is the unconcealed hope of the ambitious, the driving force, the boundless purpose. Here also is the source of humanity's greed and inconstancy. If what we mean by human reason is the ability to form well-defined and stable relationships that allow us to peacefully enjoy what we have, without wistful glances at imagined visions of what we might have, then we must recognize that it is not reason that defines humanity. Reason only mediates desire, furnishing it the best means for its fulfillment. We must conclude, however, that what we value cannot be *owned*. No possession, indeed, is definitively owned when it is coveted by others whose desire renders it both precious and precarious. Because the *cupiditas habendi* [passion for possessing] is infinite in each of us, in the struggle between contending desires, every desire's strategy must be to clear a path, without illusions, to its unconstrained gratification. This path inevitably leads through war: The ambitious person's most self-affirming dream is to force the disavowal of others' desires. In disavowing desire, a human being ceases to live as a human being.

Machiavelli wonders "which was the more ambitious, he who wanted to preserve power or he who wanted to acquire it; as both the one and the other of these motives may be the cause of great troubles. It seems, however," he continues, "that they are most frequently occasioned by those who possess; for the fear to lose stirs the same passions in men as the desire to gain, as men do not believe themselves sure of what they already possess except by acquiring still more; and, moreover, these new acquisitions are so many means of strength and power for abuses."[18] The strategy of the winners gives them such a great sense of their superiority that the weak, spurred by envy, dream only of dispossessing the powerful. Some satisfy desire through the struggle for ever more possessions; others follow it in search of a way to ruin and humiliate the first group. Recognizing this, how can we not identify war as the particular activity that most accords with human nature?

To acquire power, to keep it by ceaselessly increasing its vigor, these are the aims desire chooses. In other words, an individual who has the capacity for waging war is concerned with waging the kind of war that destabilizes the state the individual wishes to take over, playing on its weaknesses, contradictions, and latent conflicts until civil war breaks out, the aggressor using even foreign war to further this end. For people impelled by ambition to distinguish themselves, and capable of doing so, acquisition means braving confrontation with others until they are forced to acknowledge the instigators' power over them. This implies an action that necessarily puts in question the order that, willingly or otherwise, a community has lived under fairly successfully. Desire rejects the prevailing state of affairs, negates it, without troubling itself with questions of legitimacy. When what exists is devalued, there is no restraint on the planning and execution of actions that deliberately deviate from the prevailing order. The resulting chaos eventually demands the rise of a new order. It will be imposed by the triumphant desire of the victor. Machiavelli does not analyze the connection between the determinism of desire and its realization in deeds that constitute freedom. He does not even use the word *freedom* with the meaning it will later have; he does, however, describe the clash of untamed freedoms, each trying to impose its own law. The *next* order will always be the law of the victor. The defining behavior of humankind is to confront others in the disorder of the war of desires, all battling for the sake of their own contradictory—or even similar—orders. An order that conquers, compels, and is obeyed will prove beyond doubt the vitality of an *individual* who has triumphed over other individuals.

Around those raised by the strength of their will to power above the mass of others who would also conquer but cannot, there forms a coalescence of individuals with less robust desires. And so groups of "partisans" appear. Their rivalry furthers the ambitions of the winners but also, secretly, the designs of each of their members. The war to accede to power is always apt to spread. Machiavelli finds examples in Roman history and especially in Italian history of his time. Changing configurations of foreign alliances may mix war abroad with civil war. It is rare that the former does not precipitate the latter. Sometimes a serious reversal in a war between states draws the ambitious to take advantage of the defeat to instigate a civil war they hope to turn to their benefit.

In a political community at peace inside its borders, the success of an individual's desire or of the desire of a stable government is also, almost automatically, the inspiration for foreign wars. "When through her own nature a country lives unbridled, and then, by accident, is organized and established under good laws, Ambition uses against foreign peoples that violence which neither the law nor the king permits her to use at home."[19]

"To this," Machiavelli says, "our natural instinct draws us, by our own motion and our own feeling"[20]—that is to say, to the intolerable evils a civil war would give rise to but that a war against strangers luckily deflects. What could this mean except that a person is by nature, and because goaded by desire, given to fight another for a place, even within the same political community—where peace is never assured? Border wars are fortunate and necessary opportunities for giving an outlet to desires eager to battle for dominance. Passages abound in which Machiavelli develops this theme. In *The Art of War* he writes: "[A citizen army] makes the people bolder against foreigners but does not make them in any way more disunited. . . . In this way you remove cause for dissensions, and furnish cause for union. . . . The disunited and quarrelsome ones unite and turn to the public benefit that energy which they are in the habit of using contrary to law."[21]

If the world has an order, we do not know it. We know only the violent passions shared by all and how to use their inevitable consequences, making them serve us by lending our own desire more strength and coherence than our adversaries' at the moment we measure ourselves against them. In our zeal to dominate others, and because others resist our domination, we cannot help considering others *bad*. But badness is not a vice, nor is it the opposite of virtue. It is not in the domain of ethics. The bad person is the one who affirms his or her desire over mine—and who judges me in the same way. It is not the one whose conduct is a refusal to actualize the essence of the human being. When it is our desire that defines us, our essence cannot be pinned down in a definition. Badness lies in the real barriers that one side's desire raises before the other's, in order to block its way to fulfillment. Machiavelli says very clearly: "Whoever desires to found a state and give it laws, must start with assuming that all men are bad and ever ready to display their vicious nature, whenever they may find the occasion for it. If their evil disposition remains concealed for a time, it must be attributed to some unknown reason; and we must assume that it lacked occasion to show itself; but time, which has been said to be the father of all truth, does not fail to bring it to light."[22]

Social relations, then, are based on conflict. Because emotions that are identical in all do not have identical chances of gratification, they are the source of the constantly challenged inequalities among humans. Every historical situation is an unstable one that may be replaced by a different, even opposite, situation. The law of politics, between countries as much as within them, is success. "It is a very natural and ordinary thing to desire to acquire, and always, when men do it who can, they will be praised or not blamed; but when they cannot, and want to do it anyway, here lie the error and the blame."[23] Desire is guiltless. Its worth depends on the trumps it holds. Judgments we make about it have nothing to do with morality. The ability to get and keep is the basis of rank for the human race. The essential thing is not to distinguish the good from the bad but leaders from all others. Though war alone does not make the distinction, it is indispensable to it.

As long as a person's strength and accomplishments last, a certain stability can resist the basic inconstancy of the human heart. But accomplishments are inevitably temporary; at the least sign of weakness, they will be attacked and replaced by others, even though the old may have been in no need of improvement. "For government," says Machiavelli, "consists mainly in so keeping your subjects that they shall neither be able nor disposed to injure you."[24] This is attainable for longer or shorter periods, depending on whether a state's founder has given it laws that enhance or detract from its chances of enduring. Because stability is never permanently attained, far from eliminating foreign wars, it actually requires them. In addition, the greater the internal cohesiveness of a state, the more chance it has, and can retain, of overcoming its neighbors, whether attacking them or defending against them. Hence, the broader and more coherent a ruler's political vision, the more sure the ruler can be of both military and civic success.

By itself, of course, desire cannot build the political edifice; for it is in everyone's nature to feel desire, and the enemy will also try to further its own. What is more, the prince, like any of us, must deal with *luck*, "arbiter of half of our actions."[25] But if an action undertaken on his own behalf does more than he intends, if his taste for power works, even without his knowledge, for the benefit and safety of the community, then a man becomes what Machiavelli calls a *virtùose*. He possesses *virtù*, the quality of the *vir*, the man who is both warrior and statesman. This does not imply that he is virtuous in the ethical sense. Politics is not morality, even if certain facets of moral virtue, such as temperance and courage, are components of *virtù*.

The *virtùose* is the man whose desire for dominance is so strong that he forces it to transform luck into necessity. Most often we can escape neither the limitations of our origin, the circumstances of our death, nor the countless incidents that batter us throughout our lives. A few can transform a given situation and bend it to their purposes—as all would, if only they knew how and had the power. "As one examines their actions and lives," writes Machiavelli, "one does not see that they had anything else from fortune than the opportunity, which gave them the matter enabling them to introduce any form they pleased. Without that opportunity their virtue of spirit would have been eliminated, without that virtue the opportunity would have come in vain."[26] Cesare Borgia, born on the steps of the pontifical throne, might have been nothing but an idiotic sybarite. Severus, of lowly birth, should never have been emperor, but his *virtù* left "astonished and stupefied" the populace he "overburdened," left the soldiers he commanded "reverent and satisfied."[27] Machiavelli's opinion of Severus implies not only that war, part and parcel with the thrust of desire, is the most typical condition under which desire reaches its goal, but also that to wage war and win requires strength and cunning, even shrewdly used cruelty. There is no altruism in desire. On the contrary, desire affirms the personality that succeeds in enforcing its own desire against that of others by correctly calculating the cost that unpredictable and risky circumstances may impose. "Thus whoever examines minutely the actions of [Severus] will find him a very fierce lion and a very astute fox, will see that he was feared and revered by everyone, and not hated by the army, and will not marvel that he, a new man, could have held so much power. For his very great reputation always defended him from the hatred that the people could have conceived for him because of his robberies."[28]

It is important to correctly situate the relation of desire and war within the whole of political activity. History unfolds against, and is contained within, a background of hostility that is frequently expressed and always latent. The transcendence of desire through accomplishments owed to war inaugurates for civil society an order guaranteed by legislation, yet this is not the permanent peace that Machiavelli shows so well to be unrealistic, as it would be tantamount to the disappearance of all the desires harbored by all individuals. "There are two kinds of combat," Machiavelli writes, "one with laws, the other with force. The first is proper to man, the second to beasts."[29] Laws are a sort of combat to the extent that they hamper the desires of those who have not made the laws and compel them to relinquish their hope of satisfaction. Nevertheless, laws as such, though imposed by the desire of the victor, are not what we understand to be *war*. On the contrary, so long as they are obeyed, they allow a community to live in peace.

Machiavelli considers legislation of primary importance. It is the scaffold of community life. Military success does not build states. It conquers them, participates in preserving them, but does not organize them. Though we cannot say that legislation is the purpose of war, in the final analysis, it is what makes sense of the relationship between force on the one hand and the establishment of and respect for law on the other. Law is not the imposition of an order independent of humanity, as Plato believed. It is, on the contrary, laid down by those who prove capable of imposing their own ideas on others. Once law is formulated, it initiates and guarantees a stable order that force defends. "A well-ordered city," Machiavelli writes in *The Art of War*, "will then decree that this practice of warfare shall be used in times of peace for exercise and in times of war for necessity and for glory, and will allow the public alone to practice it as a profession, as did Rome. Any citizen who in such an activity has another purpose is not a good citizen, and any city that conducts itself otherwise is not well governed."[30] Moreover, laws must be obeyed. "Men who are well trained fear the laws whether armed or unarmed,"[31] provided that breaking the law seems riskier than rebellion. Laws are good if they are both generally accepted and well enough enforced to discourage acts of contempt.

Machiavelli speaks of the rare good luck of Cities that escape civil war thanks to sound legislation. "When," he says, "a good, wise, and powerful citizen appears (which is but seldom), who establishes ordinances capable of appeasing or restraining these contending dispositions, so as to prevent them from doing mischief, then the government may be called free, and its institutions firm and secure; for having good laws for its basis, and good regulations for carrying them into effect, it needs not, like others, the virtue of one man for its maintenance."[32] Notice the terms that describe the genuine founder of a state, the person who helps Cities endure by giving them good laws. It is the unusual merit of this passage that it joins political virtues—wisdom and integrity—that are undeniably kin to moral virtues to a purely political quality, might. Clearly we do not often encounter someone of this stamp. Although antiquity had known their like, most states need "the *virtù* and the good fortune of some individual."[33] Such an individual will make the most of circumstances.

Although the *virtùose* knows how to do combat in the first way, which Machiavelli calls "proper to man," he cannot stop there. Laws alone are seldom able to curb desires. "Because the first (laws) is often not enough, one must have recourse to the second (force). Therefore it is necessary for a prince to know well how to use the beast and the man."[34] The same idea reappears in *The Art of War:* "All the arts that are provided for in a state for the sake of the common good of men, all the statutes made in it so that men will live in fear of the laws and of God, would be in vain if for them there were not provided defenses, which when well ordered, preserve them, even though they themselves are not well ordered."[35]

What should we conclude from this? First, that in the best-constituted, most vigorous states with the most likelihood of a long history (such as those established by Moses, Cyrus, Romulus, Theseus,[36] or, closer to our own time, by the kings of France contemporary with Machiavelli), law is the most basic need yet is inadequate to its own preservation. Without the constant possibility of using force, internally as well as externally—without, in a word, war—law would be impotent.

The lifework of the *virtùose*, however, does not consist wholly of war, even though it is, of course, partly the fruit of war. *Virtù* brings order to a world that has none, brings it and preserves it. In the headlong rush of desire as it wages wars of conquest or protection, there is more than what lures the prince. Even when fighting for himself alone or decreeing and enforcing laws for the sake of his own power, the prince, in Machiavelli's phrase, "introduces a form that would bring honor to him and good to the community of men."[37] The same theme appears in the *Discourses:* "A sagacious legislator of a republic, therefore, whose object is to promote the public good, and not his private interests, and who prefers his country to his own successors, should concentrate all authority in himself."[38] Someone reaching for power cannot be said to exhibit self-denial; it may be more correct to assert that such a person serves the common good without strictly intending to. Machiavelli adds, in fact, "Wise minds will never censure any one for having employed any extraordinary means for the purpose of establishing a kingdom or constituting a republic. It is well that, when the act accuses him, the result should excuse him; and when the result is good . . . it will always absolve him from blame."[39] He goes on to cite the example of Romulus. The desire that takes aim at its *skopos* [target], that is, its own satisfaction, unintentionally attains its *telos* [purpose]—the common good.

In this way is war justified as the means to a particular end, the satisfaction of the desire for power. But unlike Callicles, the prince (that is, the Machiavellian legislator) is great because, halting the course of events, he makes history, produces his masterwork by violent means, and preserves it without fear of "enter[ing] into evil, when faced by necessity."[40] By these acts, even though only pursuing his taste for power—for he has accepted fortune's challenge out of self-interest—he becomes the bulwark of order and stability for his people. We see, then, that it is foolish to self-righteously criticize Machiavelli for justifying the means by the end. It was indisputably immoral for Cesare Borgia to have Remirro de Orco commit crimes in his stead, even worse to execute him for cruelty once his work was done.[41] Would it have been better for Borgia to have abandoned Romagna to civil war and anarchy? Should he then have refused, because of the anger against his interference, to endow it with laws to ensure its future? Cesare Borgia obviously wished to establish his own power by conquering provinces and forcing their submission; yet he was far from forgetting that he could not govern, no matter how great his military power, without favorable public opinion. He knew that he must *seem* just, even though he was not, and that he must respect the beliefs of peoples he had subdued.[42] On such policies, claims Machiavelli, depended the peace and public order that the laws made possible. Considering what is risked by the politician who recognizes no middle ground between victory and defeat, Machiavelli does not begrudge him, as a *virtùose*, the means to succeed in achieving his end.

Virtù can do more—it can even resist the tide of events. Machiavelli goes so far as to say that "a truly great man is ever the same under all circumstances. . . . The fickleness of fortune has no power over him."[43] Yet he must not hesitate to use appropriate means. In order that "the fatherlands [be] ennobled and [become] very prosperous"[44] through the presence of a man capable of seizing control, this man must not retreat before any situation possibly advantageous to the common good. One must not "rely on prayers" to lead desire to success: "Things will always turn out badly and nothing be accomplished." On the contrary, if one relies solely on one's own powers, one will rarely fail. "From this it arises," Machiavelli comments, "that all armed prophets conquered and the unarmed were ruined."[45] He therefore is not satisfied with advising the prince who wants a long life to practice "to be able not to be good, and to use this and not use it according to necessity";[46] nor is he satisfied with having written the seven books of *The Art of War*. He must further proclaim as one of the rare truths that will never be called into question because based on human nature, that "a prince should have no other object, nor any other thought, nor take anything else as his art but the art of war . . . for that is the only art which is of concern to one who commands. And it is of such virtue that not only does it maintain those who have been born princes but many times it enables men of private fortune to rise to that rank."[47]

A prince with scruples would not be loved any better for all that; he would simply jeopardize the security of his person and his states. "One should note that hatred is acquired through good deeds as well as bad ones."[48] A means has no intrinsic worth, it is judged by its utility.

Machiavelli insists time and again, "In the actions of all men, and especially of princes . . . one looks to the end."[49] For a civil society, the end consists in good laws—and at some times peace, at others victory in battle. The Pax Romana is a real peace because subdued tribes leave off quarrelling and obey the laws, but for Rome it is a nearly perpetual war that inspires courage and rouses intelligence to productivity.

But though it is true that the most brilliant civilizations are born of war and sustained by victories, it is no less true that "time sweeps everything before it and can bring with it good as well as evil and evil as well as good."[50] The works of a great leader make history and are meant to be irreversible. Here desire deludes itself. The works of all men and women are ephemeral; they can only hope to outlast their author by a little. The earthly god of whatever *virtù* and whatever luck cannot preserve a creation for eternity. Every institution, however sturdy, is mortal. For Machiavelli, history never brings significant progress as it unfolds over time. Even the most admirable *virtùose* generates a sequence of events that have meaning only so long as they last. Other events will follow, as others preceded, with no essential connection to them. Brilliant civilizations may crumble and stagnate in conflict among desires without grandeur, as the history of Florence demonstrates.

> The nature of mundane affairs not allowing [provinces] to continue in an even course, when they have arrived at their greatest perfection, they soon begin to decline. In the same manner, having been reduced by disorder, and sunk to their utmost state of depression, unable to descend lower, they, of necessity, reascend; and thus from good they gradually decline to evil, and from evil again return to good. The reason is, that valor produces peace; peace, repose; repose, disorder; disorder, ruin; so from disorder order springs; from order virtue, and from this, glory and good fortune.[51]

No sure ways have been found to halt the unceasing flow of human events. At best, we can slow it—first, by knowledge of its workings. "Wise men have observed, that the age of literary excellence is subsequent to that of distinction in arms; and that in cities and provinces, great warriors are produced before philosophers," writes Machiavelli.[52] Are we to believe that when desire has been fulfilled by victory, it can be corrupted by culture? Machiavelli adds, in fact, "Arms having secured victory, and victory peace, the buoyant vigor of the martial mind cannot be enfeebled by a more excusable indulgence than that of letters; nor can indolence with any greater or more dangerous deceit," he stresses, "enter a well regulated community."[53]

A state may be ruined for a second, very similar reason. Once the charms of peace inspire the postponement of war, an opportunity arises for the person who is always there to grasp it.[54] Pacifists have been shortsighted since the beginning of time. Machiavelli reminds us of this with abundant examples. But pacifists, probably from fear of dying, have lost that desire to live that asserts itself only through risk and combat. "A man with no more desires is a dead man," says the proverb. It is paradoxical that, in order to live, we must risk our lives, make war, and consider peace to be no more than the truce that gives us a chance to catch our breath and regain strength. Yet war is surely our fate, for it is the sign of our inner selves being actualized on the stage of history and defined by the power of our desire. A warrior determined to win does not believe in death, for he thinks only of victory. It is the same for the one who creates a state. Both will finally be overtaken by death, but they will have lived their lives with that enormous vigor without which life is worth no more than death.

Such is Machiavelli's lesson when for Lorenzo de' Medici he recalls Livy's words, "War is just to whom it is necessary, and arms are pious when there is no hope but in arms."[55] Then, in the final analysis, is war not just for the person who finds it necessary to be truly human?

CHAPTER 3

■ ═══════════════════════════════════ ■

Nature, Destiny, and War

If ambition is the essence of the human being, we must conclude that a sort of aggressive energy constitutes human nature and that war, not peace, is humanity's primary goal. Still, should we not ask whether there is not another passion within the drive to remain alive that is quite as real and that makes a human being fear death as the worst of all evils? That humanity is inherently inclined to fight would then be false. War would not be an act of self-assertion but an act of defense forced on a being fundamentally content to live in peace. It would be, to use an Aristotelian term, the *essential accident* of peace, which would have a positive character, ill defined by such inadequate words as *truce* or *exhaustion*.

The will to live would be linked with a drive more basic than the desire to triumph over others—the fear of dying. If it happened that human beings no longer feared one another, they would live at peace, lovingly seeking, as the Stoics observed, what keeps them alive, retreating from what might do them harm. It is insecurity that gives us arms and causes wars; *safety* is confident and lives in peace.

If this is true, then war is no longer the sign of a life force expressing itself through aggression; it is only a means of defense invented by one who fears losing his life. And consequently, a human being is no longer defined by an enterprise that is continually stimulated by the limitless unfolding of desire. Machiavelli speaks of the "rage of men for novelty, a rage felt by the fortunate no less than the unfortunate," so that "men lament poverty and loathe well-being. Such a rage," he adds, "opens the portals of nations to the innovator."[1] We can take this to be a secondary aspect of human psychology, albeit making one of the causes of wars remarkably clear, but we find Machiavelli truer to reality (though he is referring only to the attitude of soldiers before a masterful military leader) when he says, "There are two great motives for men's deeds, love and fear."[2]

Rather than rushing after what is always lacking—which desire endlessly claims to be increased possessions and greater power—human beings, as they truly are, would be creatures seeking to remain *what* they are, attacking only for self-protection and so that they may withdraw into individual selves they only wish to preserve, without further ambitions or goals. At its origin, combat would always be combat for security alone; it would be necessitated by fear of death, dark corollary of the love of life.

However correct these observations may be, they still raise a question: If in their concern for self-preservation men and women have a nature that is peace-loving, why do humans fear each other? Why would they have to fight to defend themselves if they were not attacked? If there were no reason for fear, fear would not exist. In principle, we are not afraid without cause. And as cause precedes effect, it is not fear that comes first but its source. No one has analyzed the dynamic of fear better than Thomas Hobbes, who thought it as basic as love of life but at the same time due to yet another fundamental passion—glory—that also leads one human to harm and dominate another. We know that in the course of a trip to Florence, Hobbes and Galileo became friends. We do not know if Hobbes was influenced by the works of Machiavelli. Though he owned few books himself, Hobbes was an indefatigable bookworm in the libraries of his teachers and friends. In all likelihood, Hobbes had read, though he does not mention them, *The Prince* and probably the *Discourses*. His study of essentially the same emotions we find analyzed by Machiavelli is the more rigorous for being developed in the framework of a mechanistic philosophy. Although Hobbes does not explicitly acknowledge Machiavelli, he does systematize certain of Machiavelli's intuitive conclusions. He explains the relation of human nature to war and peace with such exactitude that we are hard put to find fault. When a century later even Rousseau gives up his belief in the human's total independence—a state, he says, "which no longer exists, which perhaps never existed, which probably never will exist"[3]—and when John Locke, writing before Hobbes, describes humanity's second state of nature,[4] neither delineates the relation among persons differently than does Hobbes.

According to Hobbes, peace is the first natural law; but we would be greatly mistaken to believe, as Saint Thomas taught, that this law abides in the human heart as a *lumen naturale*. "Natural law," he wrote, "is nothing but the presence of divine law in a rational creature."[5] The world order, willed by God, is peace. By submitting to eternal law (which we know because it is part of our being), by obeying divine law (which is revealed in Scripture) and human law (which is derived directly from natural law), we will live naturally in peace.

Hobbes believes, probably sincerely, in the existence of God and divine law, but his philosophy cannot admit of the *lumen naturale*. Natural law is "a precept or general rule, found out by reason,"[6] but it is by no means God's trace in man, enabling him to tell good from evil and to obey divine rule. "For REASON," he says in the *Leviathan*, "is nothing but *reckoning*— that is, adding and subtracting—of the consequences of general names agreed upon for the *marking* and *signifying* of our thoughts."[7] Reason is *ratiocinatio*, which meant to the Romans the act of counting. Entries in account books were *nomina*, "names." *Ratio*, "reason," is the ability to calculate in all domains, starting from the conventionally accepted names of objects.[8] There can be no confusion about the meaning of *reason* in Hobbes's nominalism.

A human is a system of movements in which sensations (which are themselves movements) provoke another movement, the conception of a perceived object, whereupon the human is "apt to inquire the consequences of [this object] and what effects he might do with it. . . . He can by words reduce the consequences he finds to general rules, called *theorems* . . . that is, he can reason or reckon not only in numbers but in all the other things whereof one may be added unto or subtracted from another."[9] We discover the theorems of geometry by carefully drawing, in a series of syllogisms properly arranged into a proof, conclusions that follow from the conventional definitions of objects. In the same way, but much more simply and directly, we are each able—though there are few geometricians—to calculate that it is to our advantage to live in peace, that our survival and safety depend on peace; and each of us is equally capable of calculating the necessary means to this end. Hence natural law is, as Hobbes puts it, the conclusion of a calculation within the capacity of the dullest, without study and without recourse to anything except personal experience. "These dictates of reason men used to call by the name of laws," says Hobbes, "but improperly, for they are but conclusions or theorems concerning what conduces to the conservation and defense of themselves, whereas law, properly, is the word of him that by right has command over others." He adds, "But yet if we consider the same theorems as delivered in the word of God, that by right commands all things, then are they properly called laws."[10] Indeed, and perhaps Hobbes considered them laws himself; but in the framework of his system, there is no need to appeal to God, as reason—understood as the ability to calculate what is in one's best interest—can by itself deduce natural law from everyday observation.

Before analyzing the implications of this proposition, let us note that in its most general sense "a law of nature (*lex naturalis*) is a precept or general rule, found out by reason, by which a man is forbidden to do that which is destructive of his life or takes away the means of preserving the same and to omit that by which he thinks it may best be preserved."[11]

Who forbids? What is forbidden? Why is it forbidden? This is certainly not an attempt to smuggle God back in. What forbids a person to let himself or herself be destroyed is that very self as a vital movement and an animal movement. Though the vital movement drives our vegetative functions to continue without our awareness, the animal movement, product of the movement we call intelligence, is the effort that tends to "bring us toward something that causes it . . . or fromward something."[12] It has two forms, desire and aversion. The course of a person's life is not affected by the same desires and aversions at every moment. It is therefore characterized by variability. And all the desires of the whole human race diverge so much that people cannot agree about the worth of a single object.[13] Each will consider a desired object good, a repellant object bad, but there is "nothing simply and absolutely so, nor any common rule of good and bad to be taken from the nature of the objects themselves."[14] Nevertheless, in spite of the radical subjectivity of our judgment of objects, each of us is still composed of the same movements, "one of approaching, the other of retiring,"[15] which are the source of all our actions. Hobbes is speaking of willed movements, for what we usually call will, more or less consciously meaning freedom to make reasoned choices, is only—in Hobbes's mechanistic theory of all human reality—"in *deliberation*, the last appetite immediately adhering to the action."[16] Deliberation is itself only the sum of our desires, aversions, hopes, and fears, tumbling one after the other, but all directed toward a single object;[17] and the last act of this drama is the movement of the winning appetite, or "will."

We are forbidden, then, by none other than ourselves defined as movement toward what preserves or attracts us and movement of retreat from what displeases or might destroy us. The law of nature is thus the simple conclusion of a calculation in which the terms are our desires and their objects in relations that are as complex as they appear to be until we have detected the underlying simplicity of this twofold movement that enables us to understand every person's behavior.

The first law of nature, however, the one Hobbes calls fundamental because it leads to the second law, from which the third is deduced—and so on, to the nineteenth—is stated thus: "It is a precept or general rule of reason *that every man ought to endeavor peace, as far as he has hope of attaining it; and when he cannot obtain it, that he may seek and use all helps and advantages of war.* The first branch of which rule contains the first and fundamental law of nature, which is *to seek peace and follow it.*"[18] Does this not appear to be the law of nature of beings who want to live, though the world they live in condemns them to death, and who possess no power likely to assure their own survival except the ability to calculate first this law and then how to act in light of this first calculation? Though peace may be a natural law, it does not define human nature as it develops in accord with the logic of its reality. And as for reality, Hobbes considers it so unimportant that he does not hesitate to write, "These are the laws of nature dictating peace for a means of the conservation of men in multitudes."[19] Peace is the *means* of preserving one whose nature is war, whether impulsive or calculated to satisfy a passion. To be propelled into war by their nature is so widespread and daily an occurrence for human beings that they indeed need to calculate the means of avoiding a violent death. Peace is this means. It is neither an innate ambition nor an original state of being; but Hobbes can still speak of a "first law of nature," for this law is the first, the primordial conclusion arrived at by a being whose nature it is to want to live and whose condition is yet the constant, hated threat of death. Because individuals are by nature capable of calculating what is in their best interest, appalled at their actual, natural situation, they contrive a plan for survival. That plan is peace, along with the measures for bringing it about and for preserving it as well as possible. But the essence of their plan is neither peaceful nor peaceable; on the contrary, it is characterized by war to a much greater degree than by peace.

Although typical of its time in its concept of an apolitical state of nature and of a contract as the foundation of communities, Hobbes's analysis is no less applicable today. His descriptions display deep understanding of people, and he shows us the kind of relations their passions impose on them. He himself realizes, moreover, that he has exposed traits that do not change with circumstances, the measures we can take against them, and the art with which we hide them from ourselves.

Hobbes believes that people are not naturally inclined to associate with each other. Aristotle thought that he had proved the human being to be a "political animal," but Hobbes shows in his powerful description of the *multitude* that the human is not. In a state of nature, a human being is set beside another human being as one grain of sand next to another. Who would dream of making a society from a mound of sand? Whatever momentary form a transient set of forces gives, juxtaposition is not the same as mutual attraction. An individual is merely in close spatial relationship with other individuals. We come into the world surrounded by those whose last thought is to prepare us a tender cradle or conditions for happy growth. Caught in a force field determined by both others' movements and our own, we are each subject to its mechanical laws of association and confrontation. Only rarely does anyone benefit from this situation. Forces may be added or subtracted; they may be favorable or unfavorable. In this way all learn the easy calculation of what is to their advantage and disadvantage. The multitude that constitutes each person's natural milieu has no unity. It has no principle and can have no organization. Only the philosopher, viewing it from without, can describe it as a set of forces, acting concurrently but never conjointly, that confront each other in chance meetings beyond human understanding. The multitude is not a being. Our usual way of speaking does not apply to it: We can speak of *the* people or *a* people, but we cannot meaningfully combine the same terms with "multitude," for it can be neither definite nor indefinite, neither singular nor plural. It does not act. Every action implies an actor, a unified intention. But Hobbes correctly observes that because of ignorance of the meaning of words,

> men cannot distinguish, without study and great understanding, between one action of multiple men and many actions of one multitude; as for example between one action of all the senators of Rome in killing Cataline, and the many actions of a number of senators in killing Caesar; and therefore are disposed to take for the action of the people that which is a multitude of actions done by a multitude of men, led perhaps by the persuasion of one.[20]

In condemning Cataline to death, an official body acts as such through its decision. In murdering Caesar, even though one might persuade others, the senators do not act as a single unit but as private individuals, each striking on his own account; for their momentary collusion has no organic unity and therefore cannot effect a common, single action. Corresponding in its basic structure to the nonbeing we call "multitude" is the anarchy of individual actions by individual actors in pursuit of their individual goals.

We can easily understand that such an essential condition would predispose the human being to war rather than to peace. It would be a miracle—and Hobbes's mechanism admits of none, unless it be self-sacrifice—were each person to so act that the product of all individual forces would be a harmonious symphony. The opposite is of course the case, because it is precisely the passions that determine actions.

Now the chief of all passions, in Hobbes's view, is fear. In an anecdote recounted by John Aubrey, according to which the philosopher's mother was brought to childbed by "a fright induced by the Spanish invasion," we learn of Hobbes's fear, confided to Aubrey, of being murdered in the night "for five or six pounds that some scoundrels might think he kept in his room" and of his "sanguineo-melancholicus" temperament.[21] We leave to Hobbes's biographer and to the psychologists the problem of elucidating the relationship between his mother's frights and the importance her son gave to the emotion of fear. It is more worthwhile to return to our initial line of inquiry and ask why people fear, what they fear, and why the basic emotion of fear is related to war rather than to peace; for after all, rather than killing each other when they are afraid, people could remain perfectly still and have so little contact with each other that their stupor would resemble peace.

Fear, says Hobbes, is "*aversion* with opinion of HURT from the object."[22] What do people hate, then, and from what do they expect mostly ill? The answer is clear: People fear people. And we must now consider, as they relate to war, the many reasons Hobbes gives for this disastrous state of affairs.

According to Hobbes—and here we meet an element of human nature already familiar to us—"A man [cannot] any more live whose desires are at an end than he whose senses and imagination are at a stand."[23] To live is to desire. There is no human life without desire. Hobbes shows how desire spawns more desire, to the point that a human's happiness depends less on enjoying the satisfaction of desire than on the opportunity to continue desiring. A human's need is to desire; a human's desire is to desire; a human *is* the desire to desire.[24] "Felicity," says Hobbes, "is a continued progress of desire from one object to another, the attaining of the former being still but the way to the latter. The cause whereof is that the object of man's desire is not to enjoy once only and for one instant of time, but to assure forever the way of his future desire."[25] What are the objects of desire in its ceaseless quest for itself and the world? "In the first place," says Hobbes, "I put for a general inclination of all mankind a perpetual and restless desire of power after power that ceases only in death."[26] How could we better depict the insatiability of this inclination that defines us all? How could we fail to recognize the never sated greed, the demands that, in endless renewal, are synonymous with life itself?

If we recognize the truth of our nature in the infinitude of desire that only our death can limit and if we are also aware of a separateness from others so complete that there is no inclination naturally able to bring about coherent relations among us, then we must conclude that desires are necessarily rivalrous and that in defending our desire—equivalent to defending our life—none of us will be greatly concerned for another's life, or even for the risk of our own. The command that would stop the anarchic ravages of desire, at least within a given geographic area, could only issue from the accepted and acknowledged authority of one person over all others living there. But such a person does not exist, for by nature all persons are equal.

Because humans are desire and all humans are equal, each fears every other indiscriminately. No one is ever confident that he or she can assert desire without meeting another's conflicting claim, nor can anyone hope for lasting superiority over those who are always in opposition. Because of human equality, no one is by nature able to organize the world for her or his own good in a way that might lead in the end to the good of all. As early as 1640, Hobbes wrote in the *Elements of Law*, "Men considered in mere nature, ought to admit among themselves equality."[27] *De Cive* gives the reason for this equality—not by reference to a divine creation that makes all of us children of God in original fraternity, for we must not forget that Hobbes describes human beings in the language of physics and that he is intent on knowing the strength of forces that meet in desire. "They are equals," he writes, "who can do equal things one against the other; but they who can do the greatest things (namely, kill) can do equal things. All men therefore among themselves are by nature equal; the inequality we now discern, hath its spring from the civil law."[28]

Is Hobbes unaware that there are weak and strong, bright and dull, and that aptitudes can vary so much from one person to another that we question whether we are dealing with members of the same species? Obviously not. What does strength matter if wit can arm the weak, or intelligence, if it can be overcome in turn by physical strength? The difference in aptitudes is compensated for in the result: Anyone can kill anyone. In 1651 (as in 1640 and also in 1642 and 1647, in the two editions of *De Cive*) Hobbes claims in the *Leviathan* that "Nature has made men so equal in the faculties of the body and mind as that, though there be found one man sometimes manifestly stronger in body or of quicker mind than another, yet, when all is reckoned together, the difference between man and man is not so considerable as that one man can thereupon claim to himself any benefit to which another may not pretend as well as he."[29]

The equality of human beings is the first source of fear. When Hobbes affirmed this equality in *The Elements of Law*, he had already described its character. "If we consider," he wrote, "with how great facility he that is the weaker in strength or in wit, or in both, may utterly destroy the power of the stronger, since there needeth but little force to the taking away of a man's life; we may conclude that men considered in mere nature, ought to admit amongst themselves equality."[30] He is speaking, then, of an equality of condition among human beings that results in the equal potential of each to die a violent death at the hands of another. Each person knows this, and this primitive knowledge produces in each a constant fear of losing his or her life. In *De Cive* Hobbes had written in the same vein, "The cause of mutual fear consists partly in the natural equality of man."[31]

There are two principle causes for one human being's always representing a potential threat of death to another. These causes in turn are the source of fear, continually providing it with reasons to arise, grow, and mutate. Despite the multiplicity and variability of the desires of every human heart, it usually happens that individuals simultaneously desire an object that all, or even two of them, cannot have jointly: "The most frequent reason why men desire to hurt each other, arises hence, that many men at the same time have an appetite to the same thing; which yet very often they can neither enjoy in common, nor yet divide it."[32] We know how little desire is prepared to renounce what it craves, how much it would be against its nature (that is, against life) if it yielded of its own free will. Hobbes therefore concludes, "It follows that the strongest must have it."[33] In other words, when two individuals or several or all desire the same thing, a war of each against each ensues; its outcome is the victory of the strongest, lasting only as long as the victor's strength. Now as we have learned, *all* human beings desire power, and whatever the reason for the victory, superior strength or keener judgment, the one who triumphs is always at the mercy of a strength that will one day be greater or a craft more subtle than the former victor's own. We come to the conclusion that, surrounded as we are by the hostility of other desires, to desire is to fear not winning, to win is to fear losing our gains.

In the *Leviathan* Hobbes clarifies the mechanism of war as an expression of desire, of life moving forward. "From this equality of ability," he says, "arises equality of hope in the attaining of our ends. And therefore if any two men desire the same thing, which nevertheless they cannot both enjoy, they become enemies; and in the way to their end, which is principally their own conservation, and sometimes their delectation only, endeavor to destroy or subdue one another."[34] (He does not use the term *ability* as we usually understand it but simply as the potential of animal strength to overwhelm intelligence or of the latter to invent stratagems that will defeat the former.) Whether it is a question of preserving one's life or merely of pleasure, it makes no difference. Insofar as desire of any kind is the manifestation of life, it must succeed. The uncertainty of dominance inspires fear in everyone; the result is recourse to preventive war, with each striving for gratification at the expense of others before they have so much as given an indication of their own desires or of any animosity. "Among so many dangers therefore," says Hobbes,

as the natural lusts of men do daily threaten each other withal, to have a care of one's self is not a matter so scornfully to be looked upon, as if so be there had not been a power and will left in one to have done otherwise. For every man is desirous of what is good for him, and shuns what is evil, but chiefly the chiefest of natural evils, which is death; and this he doth, by a certain impulsion of nature, no less than that whereby a stone moves downward.[35]

The mechanism of desire and its consequences could not be better described.

To desire, we would say in following Hobbes, is to live. It follows that we must overcome whatever opposes our desire, even what *might* oppose it. Avoidance of death justifies all means—of which the most effective is to kill before one who would do the same to us has the time to act. This is what is meant by this passage from the *Leviathan:* "From this diffidence of one another there is no way for any man to secure himself so reasonable as anticipation—that is, by force or wiles to master the persons of all men he can, so long till he see no other power great enough to endanger him; and this is no more than his own conservation requires, and is generally allowed."[36]

The logic of desire, then, accounts for fear and for both preventive and aggressive war. They are products of a calculation that seeks the most effective way of protecting life, liberty, the fruits of labor, and one's own desire against the existence and efficacy of another's desire.[37] Because fear is a consequence of aversion, we would expect it first to inspire withdrawal or flight; yet the opposite occurs—in order to protect desire, it chooses aggression against the desire of others. As this movement is part of human nature and will occur unless prevented by a more powerful movement, we conclude that the natural state of humankind is war and not peace.

Hobbes defines fear as "a certain foresight of future evil."[38] It is an emotion felt in the present, based on past experience, affecting the future. Like every emotion, it is a sensation combined with memory and imagination. And therefore it already constitutes a natural calculation of the measures most likely to afford protection against a future evil. By means of fear, we learn that we are destined to a violent death and that we are made to wage war, the only guarantee of our desire. The whole human mechanism is thus directed toward war, destined for war. It is its direct means of maintaining its life—which is desire.

Hobbes does not end his analysis here, however. A second cause of fear, and hence indirectly of war, can be also and by itself an immediate cause of war. This is glory, another basic yearning that outwardly seems to typify only some individuals but that in its broadest sense exists in all.

Glory is first of all an impulse that some use to good advantage and that drives them both to outdo others and to insist on acknowledgment of their own superiority. Although desire has many objects, its principal object, in the case of glory, is to enthrall the desire of others and force that desire to renounce its own claims. After Machiavelli, but before Rousseau and Hegel, Hobbes clearly saw the behavior that defines humankind as a species: an individual's demand that others bow before his superiority and withdraw in his favor, acts that no one is inclined to by nature and so must be forced to perform.

The target glory has in its sights is fame:

Considering the great difference there is in men from the diversity of their passions, how some of them are vainglorious, and hope for precedency and superiority above their fellows, not only when they are equal in power, but also when they are inferior; we must needs acknowledge that it must necessarily follow, that those men who are moderate, and look for no more but equality of nature, shall be obnoxious to the force of others, that will attempt to subdue them. And from hence shall proceed a general diffidence in mankind, and mutual fear one of another.[39]

We may wonder who these men are "who are moderate, and look for no more but equality of nature," as Hobbes himself seems to forget their existence when he writes in *De Cive* that "all the mind's pleasure is either glory (or to have a good opinion of one's self) or refers to glory in the end."[40] Does he not mean only those who are weary or who, from a natural defect, lack the strength to dominate?

The best way to compel others to humble themselves is to conquer them. Hobbes very discerningly notes that though people are equal by nature, they detest equality. If another is awarded the same decoration as I, the very honor I risked everything for has lost all value for me. Submissiveness and adulation keep their charm only so long as no one else receives them. "Glory," says Hobbes, "is like honour, if all men have it, no man hath it, for they consist in comparison and precellence; neither doth the society of others advance any whit the cause of my glorying in myself; for every man must account himself, such as he can make himself, without the help of others."[41] In these few lines we already find the whole of Rousseau's analysis of pride. Hobbes also traces the consequences of glory that emphasize the logic linking glory to war. For Hobbes, glory is one of the passions that define human nature; according to Rousseau, pride is a degraded form of self-love, which is the only original and innocent emotion, though once its degeneration has begun Rousseau will agree with Hobbes on its disastrous results. "Since all the pleasure and jollity of the mind consists in this," the latter writes, "even to get some, with whom comparing, it may find somewhat wherein to triumph and vaunt itself; it is impossible but men must declare sometimes some mutual scorn and contempt, either by laughter, or by words or by gesture, or some sign or other; than which there is no greater vexation of mind, and than from which there cannot possibly arise a greater desire to do hurt."[42]

Mutual vengeance, in other words the war of each against all—such is the natural state brought about by glory. For the *vainglorious*, to stay alive means to satisfy their desire to be above comparison by the natural and necessary act of fighting with any who would challenge them. It also means attacking preventively, from fear of losing preeminence, any who might someday dare a challenge. For the vainglorious are fearful, too. They fear for their desire, and they fear losing their lives as much as they fear losing their glory.

Glory is a basic passion in that it sharply separates the human species from the other animals and does so better than the will, which even beasts are capable of experiencing.[43] "But among men," says Hobbes, "there is a contestation of honour and preferment; among beasts there is none:

whence hatred and envy, out of which arise sedition and war, is among men. . . . But man scarce esteems anything good which hath not somewhat of eminence in the enjoyment, more than that which others do possess."[44]

We might expect that, driven by the desire for glory, a person would succeed—thanks to that natural, necessary, direct form of combat, an offensive war for the sake of glory—in gaining enough control over others to create order—that individual's order—at least for a period of time that would properly be called peaceful. War would be the necessary prelude to the founding of states. This is how Machiavelli analyzed centuries of historical events related only through the chance rise of a *virtùose* able to grasp opportunities.

Hobbes, however, also carefully distinguishes republics "by institution" from what he calls "despotic dominations" or republics "by acquisition," in which sovereign power is seized by force. But he shows clearly that force alone does not suffice to establish a state; it is also necessary that "the future subjects recognize and authorize once and for all, out of fear for their lives, all the acts of him who holds their lives and liberty in his power."[45] According to the logic of glory's evolution, the force that it uses is directed only toward war, the single means appropriate to a limitless desire for power.

Still, glory as such is nothing but the will to harm, and the response of whoever fears glory must also be the will to harm. Hobbes stresses, particularly in *De Cive*, the traits of this passion. Several paragraphs insist, like hammer blows, on humans' will to do each other harm. Together with equality, "their mutual will of hurting"[46] is a source of mutual fear. "All men in the state of nature have a desire and will to hurt."[47] We have seen that seeking an object that can neither be possessed by more than one at a time nor shared between them is "the most frequent reason why men desire to hurt each other."[48] The desire to do harm is in each human heart; it is "this natural proclivity of men, to hurt each other, which they derive . . . chiefly from a vain esteem of themselves."[49] So the war spawned by this tendency is begun over and over forever.

Hobbes shows also that the mechanism of the complex interactions of the desire for self-preservation, the desire to be superior to another, and the fear of death justifies war, and that there is nothing in it to blame. It is our "natural right" to do anything in our power to further the expansion of our desires and the satisfaction of our passions. Because it is our nature to define ourselves as desire, hence as affirmation of power over people and things, and because we are not aided by others, but quite the opposite, then we can rely only on ourselves to discover whatever means we possess for asserting ourselves and assuring the success of our undertakings. Hobbes has made a remarkable distinction between natural *right* and natural *law*, demonstrating how the former cannot exist without warfare, whereas the latter, in contrast, is a precept about peace. We must follow his analysis in order to clearly understand what the chances of peace are for humanity.

In a world where all are in contact but none naturally inclined to relationship, where each is more alone in the midst of the crowd than Rousseau's "perfect and solitary whole"[50] in his woods where berries slake his hunger and springs his thirst, the contact between human beings is the opposite of a penchant for sociability. The passions that move men and women—the desire to best others and the fear of destruction at another's hands—flourish whenever they encounter no obstacle. This power within each one can only be checked by the same power within every other, but there is no *law* that can hinder us, neither from a transcendent source nor arising from the organizing powers of one more gifted than others. For if there is a transcendent law, it is ineffective; and though a person is fortunate enough to dominate others temporarily, he is at the mercy of whoever will of course try to harm him. When war—ever a possibility—pits one person against another, we each have by nature the right to do what we want, that is, what we can, to win or at least to protect ourselves. "The right of nature," says Hobbes, "is the liberty each man has to use his own power, as he will himself, for the preservation of his own nature—that is to say of his own life—and consequently of doing anything which, in his own judgment and reason, he shall conceive to be the aptest means thereunto."[51] Hobbes's lesson does not vary. He earlier taught in *The Elements of Law*: "Every man by nature hath right to all things, that is to say, to do whatsoever he listeth to whom he listeth, to possess, use, and enjoy all things. . . . Nature hath given all things to all men."[52] He repeats in *De Cive* that

> nature hath given to everyone a right to all; that is it was lawful for every man in the bare state of nature . . . to do what he would, and against whom he thought fit, and to possess, use, and enjoy all what he would, or could get. Now because whatsoever a man would, it therefore seems to him to contribute towards his preservation, . . . it follows, that in the state of nature, to have all, and do all, is lawful for all. And this is that which is meant by that common saying, nature hath given all to all.[53]

Such, then, is our nature. And when Hobbes speaks of "natural" right or of "nature" giving us a right, he uses the word *nature* as physicists do. He is referring neither to a providence that existed before creation nor to any entity but to inevitable relations among natural movements linked in accord with the determinism of cause and effect. Natural right is thus not susceptible of any moral judgment. It is the expression of the power that, according to our individual makeup, we each have for sustaining our being—a being that is desire, that is passion, both fear and glory. This power seeks our being's preservation and preeminence, using any means possible. The most direct and obvious means, though also the most baneful, is war.

Because everyone has a natural right to everything, in practice no one has a right to anything. Natural right is "invalid," says Hobbes, for "one man invadeth with right, and another with right resisteth."[54] Hence "the estate of hostility and war [are] such, as thereby nature itself is destroyed, and men kill one another."[55] This is echoed in *De Cive*: "The natural state of men, before they entered into society, was a mere war, and that not simply, but a war of all men against all men."[56] Without illusions, Hobbes states in the *Leviathan* the ultimate consequence of this right that is, by nature, the right of each of us: "Every man," he says, "has a right to everything, even to another's body."[57]

From whatever point of view we define human beings—whether we focus on their will to live, their passions, their natural right, or even their reason that calculates ways to satisfy itself and use its power effectively— all converge on war, part and parcel with human nature, like a fate residing in the mechanism of their existence and history. Peace receives only *negative* definitions. It is that which is *not* war. War is the primary reality. "The time which is not war is peace," Hobbes writes in *The Elements of Law*.[58] In almost the same words in *De Cive* he states, "The time remaining, is termed peace."[59] And in the *Leviathan*, after having shown that the natural condition of humanity "is called war, and such a war as is of every man against every man," Hobbes concludes, "all other time is peace."[60]

Nevertheless, if nature is war, it is also and above all desire for life, and because war cannot guarantee life, even to those who attack out of desire for glory, it is natural to calculate how to survive through means not provided by nature. Natural though it may be, war in fact produces only disasters. In referring to "savage nations" that live in accord with nature and can therefore illustrate what we all know to be true of ourselves, Hobbes says, "We find the people few and short lived, and without the ornaments and comforts of life, which by peace and society are usually invented and procured."[61] In *De Cive* he considers humanity in general: "Yet cannot men expect any lasting preservation continuing thus in the state of nature, that is, of war."[62] And in the *Leviathan* he arrives at the same conclusion, but with a strong emphasis on the negative character of humanity's natural state, both as it is in its basic form, which civilized society is in fact obliged to prohibit, and as it becomes in times of crisis, when it is precisely civilization's products that it allows to be swept away. "Whatsoever, therefore, is consequent to a time of war," Hobbes writes, where every man is enemy to every man, the same is consequent to the time wherein men live without other security than what their own strength and their own invention shall furnish them withal. In such condition there is no place for industry because the fruit thereof is uncertain: and consequently no culture of the earth; no navigation nor use of the commodities that may be imported by sea; no commodious buildings; no instruments of moving and removing such things as require much force; no knowledge of the face of the earth; no accounts of time; no arts; no letters; no society; and, which is worst of all, continual fear and danger of violent death; and the life of man solitary, poor, nasty, brutish, and short.[63]

Notice the gradation of assets that are stripped away by the war of each against all. From the means of satisfying the most urgent needs and assuring survival, through technology and commerce to the sciences and the arts, all the gifts of civilization are forgotten or destroyed, replaced by fear of death as the dominating feature of an existence governed only by its passions.

We must stress how easily Hobbes assimilates the state of nature to the state of war and consequently notice his insistence on defining human nature by war. Human nature is never eliminated by the contrivances of civilization, although some must take responsibility for restraining it because human beings cannot survive in their natural state. Because living in their natural state brings death, people calculate a sort of theorem: To live, we must live in peace. Then they calculate the means of carrying out this *natural law*—to give up, along with all others, their *natural right*, which is worthless, because it does not guarantee their security.

According to the modalities of Hobbesian philosophy, the agreement among all to renounce their personal right to anything and to place this right in the hands of an individual or a governing group creates a community that is immediately a political community, responsible for enforcing peaceful relations among its members. Hobbes's solution is to eliminate natural equality and replace it with the greatest possible political inequality, the subordination of the governed to a sovereign, be it an individual or an assembly. Although in nature no one is born to command or obey and although we all strive to command whereas none consents to obey, still we are each capable of comprehending that others' right to kill us jeopardizes our life and that our own right to kill others is inadequate to protect us. If a power enormously superior to the power of a single person—in fact, superior to the sum of all individual powers—guaranteed that everyone would renounce his or her personal power, then there could be peace. Peace would even be the ultimate purpose of the "contract" that we must accept in order to stay alive. And so although peace is a natural law, because all can calculate it as the best means of escaping death, it is nonetheless the product of an artifice—the mutual agreement by which we abjure our natural right.

For this reason, even a safeguarded peace remains fragile. Indeed, what sort of peace is meant? By nature a person is either a means of satisfaction for another or an obstacle to the other's successful movement. This implies that one person's value to another is basically utilitarian as soon as the first treats the other as an acquisition or a hindrance. War springs from this so-called relation, but this state of affairs, experienced as a right, must be the foundation for our attempts at building peace. In other words, assuming that war, not peace, is natural, that human nature cannot survive on what nature provides, and that in our attempt to escape nature we have nothing to rely upon *except* what nature itself *has* provided, we must use nature to artificially create a power that does not exist by nature, that is capable of stopping us from harming one another.

When each of us, acting against our natural condition, gives up the use of our natural right in respect to others, we voluntarily annihilate our power, annihilate our right; and because natural right is war, the complete annihilation of natural right is the end of war. For this cease-fire to persist, a natural passion must incline all to respect it. That natural passion is fear—in this case, fear of recovering a natural right. The right or power of the state, formed by transferring every individual's right to a single person or assembly, is so unimaginably strong and so persuasively mighty compared to the power of any individual that the desire to challenge it practically disappears. None will attack another, because anyone daring to do so would be crushed by the full might of the state, created for and making laws to this end.

So peace is born from a double fear: first, the fear of other humans that causes all to calculate that it is to their interest to escape the wretched condition imposed on them by nature and, second, the fear that causes them to obey the laws—fear of the state's awesome resources, which they themselves have granted it. For the sovereign power's deeds have no *author* other than all who have given over their birthright to the state, by their natural right and for their personal benefit.

Has the contract abolished nature, so that civil peace is established for good? In a certain sense, yes. What is artificial, what cannot be found in nature, opposes nature. Hence, life flourishes in political communities that curb the anarchy of desires and present ambition with attainable goals. Fame, medals, public office provide licit targets for glory's aim. The desire to harm may be taken out in competition or backbiting, even in slander, but it will rarely kill. Civic peace is so necessary that it must be considered, according to Hobbes, the condition for civilization.

But nature never disappears. Even in a community at peace, not only do vanities and ambitions clash, though bloodlessly, but cheaters exist who do not respect law and try to escape its sanctions; and what is more important, human institutions are all inherently frail and liable to collapse, whatever precautions we take in their creation. People diminish themselves because they fear death, but they do not thereby gain perfect trust in the state, any more than in their fellow humans. Otherwise, why would they bolt their doors, why would they travel armed, why would they lock chests in their own homes,[64] when in theory the laws protect them from any sort of assault? Are these not signs that under the gloss of civility human nature seeks only a chance to do harm the minute it can do so without immediate danger?

Hobbes devotes a long chapter in each of his three great political works to the causes of sedition.[65] There we find the reasons republics are destroyed. These reasons arise from a mistaken calculation in the design of the state, so that the passions are allowed to flourish, or else they result directly from individual passions' having somehow regained their natural strength. Civil peace has become a reality, but a fragile one. War is far stronger because it expresses nature. Therefore war regains all its rights when the state fails in its purpose, when it no longer guards the safety of those who created only that they might live in peace.

In any case, a contract between states is unimaginable. Nations live in a more or less open state of war among themselves, without hope of a permanent peace. Hobbes believes that no accord between states is possible because there is no supranational power that can coerce compliance. And these uncontrollable foreign wars can set off civil war in a state too painfully affected by its defeats. For what choice have those whom a common authority no longer protects except to take up their natural weapons again?

So war is indeed inherent in human nature. One of the philosophers most intent on finding the path to peace—and who undeniably shows its possibility, if also its limits—is forced to such painstaking analyses because the primary threat weighing on humans is war; it is so deep in their nature that it must be their fate. Hobbes has not tried to deceive himself. He does not consider the war of each against all to be the forge of humankind's greatness and growth. On the contrary, he finds war to be the expression of a nature that we must recognize for what it is, that gives us no cause to rejoice, and that must be turned from its natural course in order to save it from itself.

Hobbes's description of human beings is meant to define their essence. The state of nature, which we experience at times of civil war, is the set of traits that constitute the human essence—not at the beginning of history, not in a past so distant that it no longer has any conceivable relation to us, but as it defines humans in every time and place. We realize it is logical to begin with the analysis of this irrefutable reality that, once it *exists*, destroys by its own action the existence that manifests it. This explains why men and women, against their own essence, have always pursued an existence in political states. The state allows them to stay alive, in accord with their natural inclination, but not in accord with the means that this tendency would naturally grasp. As soon as the existence of human beings actualizes their essence, it is endangered by the elements of that essence, it is betrayed to war and plighted to death.

Each of us bears these traits, however painful it is to acknowledge, and though they make up our being, we know how to operate to our own advantage the mechanism of opposing movements. But it is difficult work, its success uncertain; and even when it attains its end, we need only observe ourselves without complacency to recognize beneath our "virtues," as we call the habits society imprints, the far deeper gravings of nature. In periods of crisis, what remains of the repeated training, of the socialized reflexes that owe nothing to nature?

In the dedicatory epistle of *De Cive*, the phrase *homo homini lupus*[66] [man (preys like) a wolf on man] expresses the wretchedness of a state in which desire is the desire for life, fate is violent death, and skill is the power to calculate a peace that is necessary but as precarious as are all human plans and accomplishments. At least we know where we stand. And certainly the most foolish dream—because only its opposite is likely to come true—would be to believe that the human race has a calling to peace or that the species could one day live in perpetual peace. As for Hobbes, he was never tempted to examine what he would have considered chimerical speculations.

CHAPTER 4

Freedom and War

Desire, with its fierce greed, draws the design for the human being's fate. Within political communities, it yields to the authority of legislation that restricts desire's endeavors even while supporting them. Whether political society is natural to humans or results from a contract, the peace it provides calms and restrains the aggressiveness of desire, so that desire is compelled to accept peace as a necessity. Yet the human is still a warring creature; hence peace remains fragile, even when it seems most certain. Our civilizations' most dazzling enterprises need peace and stability in order to flourish, but the loss of the latent disequilibrium owed to the tangle and clash of desires would destroy them. Vast projects of expansion and conquest are essential to them; they make opportunities for desire's creativity, even as they expose it to the risks of annihilation intrinsic to every hostile offensive. Machiavelli and Hobbes have shown in noteworthy fashion that war is as inherent in us as is the desire without which no human being exists. But we are left with a paradox: Although indispensable both to desire's survival and its gratification, war betrays what it serves; the ills and miseries resulting from war make life so precarious that it seems little better than death. To Machiavelli and Hobbes, the suppression of war did not appear either possible or beneficial. Granted that peace is desirable, it would not only be utopian to believe that it could last forever, but on the contrary, it would assuredly be disastrous if it did. Desire and war are so closely entwined that if one disappeared, the other would as well. We therefore have no alternative but to consent to this mystery, desire, in which life and death, essential war and necessary peace are bound together.

Certainly, we might also view war very differently. Instead of insisting on the evils of war, however obvious, we could highlight war's positive aspect as creator of the human. Humankind separates itself from animals only through warfare, and we can go so far as to say that renouncing war would mean renouncing humanness. Without war, humans would not be humans. We must, then, study war not as destiny but as destiny's opposite, freedom. Freedom is the truth about humankind, and freedom works and grows within desire by means of war. Hobbes's philosophy considered war bred of desire to be our destiny. The Hegelian analysis of desire and war is as far from Hobbes's pessimism as freedom is from determinism.

War is the *acting*, the *making* from which the human being is born. Freedom's appearance and development are mediated by war; its blossoming into deeds, by peace. But protecting freedom's creative flourishing requires, once again, war. War is what has gradually drawn humankind from the grip of the determined routines and repetitious scenarios into which it is always tempted to fall back. If freedom is truly the authentic nature of humans, then war is freedom's oft-used instrument, peace being the breathing space needed for a rebirth of human activity, so long as it brings novelty and is marked by creativity. The alternations of peace and war are thus meaningful without being automatic. We have still to understand war's role in the making of humans and their history. For we are not concerned with struggle in general. All animals fight for what they need to survive; all fight to defend their physical life. Humankind is not an exception, but it would be but one species of animal among others if it fought only for such utilitarian purposes as these. Just as our biological life is an element of the tangible world, so are the external objects we crave, such as food and sexual partners. These elements are controlled by laws of nature and their actions determined by them, each in accord with its own character; and the movements that an observer might take for deliberate acts—the bound of a stag crossing a brook to reach a doe, the struggle of a lion trying to drag a gazelle from the grip of another predator—are in reality nothing but inevitable reactions to precise, discoverable causes. Nothing new is ever added to the selfsame repetition of behaviors that constitute the natural reality to which humankind's animal existence belongs. Whatever its battles, an animal remains an animal all its life. It is a thing of nature; it is a being, part of an order to which it submits unconsciously and that it does not attempt to alter. An animal never escapes the natural order, in which its life goes on without meaning or value to the animal. It is part of that order, moreover, without knowing it. It is characterized by determined movements that preserve its biological life. Once its needs are met, it lives in peace—in other words, in the calm of sleep and the inactivity that follows satiety.

In speaking of the human's animal nature, it would be wrong to speak of a "state of nature" in the sense that the social contract philosophers use the term. They describe the essence of beings who are human from the start, even though their existence has departed so far from their essence that the latter may have become unrecognizable. According to Hegel, the creature placed in the state of nature is not human or, more precisely, is not yet human. *Nature* is a term applicable only to the animal that will make itself into a human, though it was not one when first set on earth. Like any animal, it consists of nothing more than a biological life characterized by the natural and spontaneous movement that expects only continued existence in space; it is unchanging in its simplicity, its individuality, and its independence, indeed its autonomy, in respect to all other creatures. Hegel points out that natural movement tends to perpetuate itself without alteration.

An animal is sentient. The human animal, like all others, *senses itself,* but is not *conscious of itself,* for no animal is able to step outside itself and so become conscious of itself. It does not think; it does not conceive of itself: It senses. It is feeling, though it does not yet feel that it feels. Knowing nothing but the immediate moment, it begins as pure passivity. In speaking of "the nature of the *animal,*" Hegel says that "the actuality and externality of immediate singularity is countered by the *intro-reflected* self of singularity or the *subjective* universality which is *within itself.*"[1] He continues, "Above all [the animal nature] has *feeling* . . . for as the existent ideality of determinate being, it is the individuality which is immediately *universal* in determinateness, and abides by itself and preserves itself in its simplicity."[2]

For this animal, to sense itself is to sense its lacks and needs. An animal is the presence of a need, the absence of the object of satisfaction. Its movement is a tendency to go toward what it lacks. Need is its immediate experience, hence its sentience is the immediate sensation of a state of lack.[3] At this stage, the final end of the living being is inward, is *itself.* This end purpose must not be taken to involve consciousness of self; an animal is the final end it experiences, just as life as such is its own end, immanent and immediately inherent.

In so far as *need* is a connectedness with the *universal* mechanism and abstract powers of nature, instinct is merely an internal stimulation which is not even sympathetic. . . . Instinct maintains a practical relation in the face of inorganic matter; its stimulation is accompanied by the show of an external stimulation, and its activity is partly formal, and partly a real assimilation of inorganic nature.[4]

The living being is defined only by its ability to live, its tendency to self-preservation. The human creature as it is initially, simply as a living being, is nothing but an animal moving about in the space delimited by its needs, the natural objects that satisfy them, and the movements that mechanistically link needs with their objects.

The desire that drives the animal of any species to seize an object nature offers is, then, experienced as a feeling of lack, an interior lack of the object of need that is itself exterior to the animal, other than it. The animal has an inclination to assimilate the object of need into its own substance, into the biological life that, before the need is satisfied, is deprived of a necessary part of itself until the need is satisfied. The sense of self we call need is a mere dim awareness on the part of a biological existence suffering from the absence of a needed object. Feeling a need is, indeed, the act of a consciousness, but not of the consciousness that is conscious of itself. The animal is the most summary, the most rudimentary state; it is a living individuality, because it has independent embodiment, but it inclines only to self-preservation. The animal that will become human is also expressed in its simplest form. Essentially passive, it is in a relation of reciprocal possession with any exterior object it acquires. Does it drink water? It becomes the water, automatically integrating it with its individuality. "The instinct of the animal seeks and consumes food," Hegel writes, "but thereby brings forth nothing other than itself."[5] For this reason the human animal lives in a relationship of externality vis-à-vis other elements in nature and does not distinguish itself from them. "The process begins with the *mechanical seizure* of the external object. Assimilation itself is the enveloping of the externality within the unity of the subject."[6]

To find an object, seize it, assimilate it, make it one's own reality is, according to Hegel, to negate it as external reality, to transform it into animal reality. Moved by the desire to stay alive, the animal self negates the natural nonself, food. But though it is an action that transforms an object, negation does not transform the self. It persists as a natural self in an endless cycle of need and satisfaction. Although the hare negates the grass as in eating it, although it destroys the grass as grass, the hare still remains an animal destined by the laws of its nature to repeat the act anew with neither change nor progress. The frequent conflict of an animal with another that comes between its prey and its aroused desire is not war. It is one of the turns of events in the seizing of an external object suited to satisfying a need. When the struggle ends and the conqueror is gratified by control of the disputed object (be it food, mate, or hunting territory), no change has occurred in the mechanism of nature nor in either of the animals.

Because humans are first of all animals, they, too, desire natural objects and negate them by transforming them into themselves. But if they did not go beyond this desire and this negation, they would remain animals, living creatures confined to their separate individualities. The radical difference between the human animal and all other animals is that the human *creates itself* rather than *being created* by the cycle of need. So it leaves nature, but it is equipped only with its natural constitution in natural relationship to the object available for its satisfaction and with the potential to enter into relation with another natural constitution, another animal-human. To leave nature is to renounce it and distance oneself from it. The only form of renunciation possible to a natural being is to abandon, at least temporarily, the natural tendency to stay alive and to direct all the inherent energy geared to the satisfaction of natural needs toward a nonnatural object—toward what is *empty* of natural objects, toward a nonbeing, a no-thing. The negation of need is the first distance from nature a living being can establish. The object longed for is no longer given by nature, and in the world as it is given, the only thing empty of objects is desire itself. The human animal desires food as any animal would, but it becomes human only to the extent that its desire negates food as an immediate target and aims instead at the same food-desire manifested by another human animal—which behaves in the same way.

In other words, what comes to matter to each one's desire is less possession of food—that is, negation of it as prelude to its assimilation— than the possession—the negation and assimilation—of another's desire. To desire to possess another's desire is equivalent to negating a nothing-ness (desire) that negates another nothingness. From this "negativity that negates" (a nothingness), which comes into play when two human animals meet, there arises a confrontation, a struggle for recognition of something with no natural objective reality. What matters to each is that its desire be *recognized* in its claim to superiority over the other's. Mere animals would fight to survive, whereas the animals fated to develop into humans, as Hegel puts it, fight to have their desire acknowledged triumphant over another's. The stake counts for so much that each risks its animal life, and for literally *nothing*, for *prestige*, for the imposition of its desire on the desire of a chance opponent. Risking life in disdain of safety, risking it for a thing without being, hence for something with no existent being in nature, the animal-human leaves the natural order and the determinism of the natural laws that automatically drive it to protect its life. By this act, it liberates itself from animality, it makes itself human, that is, free from the total determinism of natural needs. Nature no longer constitutes all that matters to it. The desire to seize another's desire will now be what it *values*. Value replaces natural objects. The negation of another's desire propels humans into combat, separates them from preservation of them-selves as natural beings, gives them over instead to an unreality—value. They so prefer it to their biological life that they are ready to die for this thing-without-being rather than for the life-sustaining gifts of nature. To risk life in order to take from another a nothingness, an absence of natural object—to take, that is, the other's desire to be recognized in its own desire—here is the origin of humanity.

The human is the only animal able to tear itself from nature's hold, to escape natural determination, to be free. We create our freedom through war, which is initially and at its root individual. We effect our genesis ourselves by the necessary means of war, waged not in the intent of satisfying a natural need through simply taking a natural object from another, but as an activity that negates another's desire, as a demand for recognition of ourselves and our desire. Any object thus acquired will be no more than the *sign* of the submission enforced, however useful it may be otherwise. We see how ludicrous and false it is to believe that peace is humankind's essence or primary goal, when the rise of human as freedom and self-consciousness depends upon war. To obstinately focus on the ills unquestionably caused by war is to fail to understand that humans would never have come into being without it. If we are forced to recognize another's desire, we bestow on the other, by the very act of recognition, the certainty that we are conscious of ourselves. The war that mediates freedom is not war for survival but war to impose one's own worth. By showing another that we are not attached to life as an animal would be, we present ourselves as self-conscious.

> This presentation is a twofold action: action on the part of the other, and action on its own part. In so far as it is the action of the *other*, each seeks the death of the other. But in doing so, the second kind of action, action on its own part, is also involved; for the former involves the staking of its own life. Thus the relation of the two self-conscious individuals is such that they prove themselves and each other through a life-and-death struggle. They must engage in this struggle, for they must raise their certainty of being *for themselves* to truth, both in the case of the other and in their own case. And it is only through staking one's life that freedom is won; only thus is it proved that for self-consciousness, its essential being is not [just] being, not the *immediate* form in which it appears, not its submergence in the expanse of life.[7]

In the contest, we each try in this way to stop the other from desiring what we desire, to make the other renounce this desire, and to make the other submit to our desire. Becoming nondesire of a thing, we each become desire of the other's desire and fight to the death to gain recognition of this worth, that is, of what we are worth to ourselves. *Anerkennung,* "recognition," gives us recognized consciousness of our own value and, in addition, consciousness of the affirmation we receive through another's forced consciousness of us. It is through the opinion of others that self-consciousness is born; humans cannot achieve this distance from themselves and this recognition without others. Of course, each must first fight and win.

The notion of self-consciousness is not an immediate notion. It requires mediating acts. The animals that will make themselves human must first live in contact with one another so that their desires may come into conflict. Even at the level of purely biological life, human reality must not be isolated, or human beings will not be brought forth. Humans become human only when living close to others and contending with them. A fight with an animal, however dangerous, or an action involving high risk, as scaling a mountain could be, would not reveal one to oneself. The only humanizing struggle is that of one human animal against another. We again meet war's specific feature—that in it humans must risk both their own lives and others' in order to live as humans, to live free. In Hegelian anthropogenesis, the requisite relationship with others is obviously not a relationship of love. Far from it! The formative contact between humans is based on rivalry—not hate so much as a kind of scorn. The stake is no longer a disputed prey, as it would be among animals, but the *opinion* another holds of us. By animal logic, this would be merely grotesque, or rather this would not be at all. To an animal, values are nothing; all that counts is the object in its primary reality. Humans, on the contrary, cannot attain the humanity they fashion unless they prize *recognition* above survival. To be human will be to prefer opinions and inventions to the real objects of nature. Human reality is social reality; that is, society is human because it is a gathering of desires desiring one another as desires.[8]

We must observe, however, that in the fight to the death from which the human will be born, the notion of "human" splits into two opposite notions determined by the way war is waged by each adversary. If neither of the two combatants fears death at any point in the struggle, it must end with the death of at least one of them. This makes recognition and the advance to humanity impossible. Therefore, one of the two locked in struggle must in some unforeseeable and nondetermined way suddenly regain fear of the death they both face, whereas the other continues to defy it. Finally, the victor must overcome an intoxication with success to concede to the vanquished the gift of life. The victor is he who preferred his values to his life; ready to die for a no-thing, he would never have given up the fight. He would rather die than remain an animal, rather die than not become human. The vanquished began the contest in exactly the same state of mind. And then he became afraid—afraid of death by the hand of one he had himself been determined to kill. So he asks for mercy on his life, his animal life. He submits by recognizing his adversary's supremacy, accepting his desire, and agreeing to serve it.

So humans are never originally and merely humans. War separates humans into unequal individuals. The lords are those capable of risking their lives for their values; the underlings are those who fail, from fear of death and the one who might inflict it, to maintain a distance from their animal lives to the very end of the struggle. There is no basic definition of a human being applicable to all, only definition by *behavior*; it varies according to whether it applies to those who had no fear of death or those who fell to their knees, begged for life, and acknowledged the other and the power over life and death that the other had won. Hegel conceives of lordship and servitude very differently than does Aristotle. The latter saw a complementary relationship between master and slave that was intrinsic to the *nature* of each. The master is born suited to command, the slave suited to obey. Consequently, the master protects the laboring slave as he would protect an organ of his body. Each is fulfilling his function in the best interests of the family the master is responsible for. Spared economically productive tasks, the master is able to play his part in the life of free men, which is to say, to concern himself with the affairs of the City.[9] Neither family nor City figures in the relation of lordship and servitude that Hegel describes, but only two individuals without natural complementarity, without inborn hierarchy of aptitudes, battling each other for individual conquest of supremacy. War inaugurates a human's power over another, legitimate power, because it is the expression of the human's emergence. Having escaped the mechanical sameness of primitive urges, the lord is free. His power sets him apart. Individuals are not equal. To make themselves human, humans must control humans. By risking their lives, by conquering their animal fear of dying, they have won the power to dominate others. The first relationship between humans that is born of war is the relationship of lordship and servitude.[10] Unless there is war between one nonnatural desire and another, there can be no humanity. This is the price of the human *self*. The human being is born of war much more surely than of flesh-and-blood parents. The life-and-death struggle to possess a thing without being is the source of beings whose future lies in negating themselves as natural beings so that they may transcend themselves in the destruction and assimilation of another negativity negating other natural beings. This dialectical process is inseparable from war.[11]

Certain points brought out in this analysis are all the more important insofar as humans' future partly mirrors their genesis. The lord's reality is proved by the dominance of his speech. He alone has the power to say "I"; this word of his represents the affirmation and recognition of self-consciousness by itself. Saying "I" allows the lord to say "you" to the underling, but there is no word in response, as the underling does not have the *power* to speak. Neither lord nor underling can say "we." The lord's "I" stands alone, initiating no exchange, no dialogue, only a relationship of domination and obedience totally without reciprocity. Regarding the negation that suppresses the desire of the vanquished while sparing his life, Hegel writes, "Through this [experience] there is posited a pure self-consciousness, and a consciousness which is not purely for itself but for another, i.e. is a merely *immediate* consciousness, or consciousness in the form of *thinghood*."[12] The lord indeed receives recognition, but "a recognition that is one-sided and unequal."[13] When he feeds on another's desire, as his own desire had wished, the effort of fashioning himself into a human—that is, into freedom and speech—is not a happy task. The lord's "essential nature is to exist only for himself; he is the sheer negative power for whom the thing is nothing. Thus he is the pure essential action in this relationship."[14] But though the lord's humanity is mediated by one whose retreat from combat has left him dependent on nature (and through whom, therefore, the lord now controls nature's gifts), he is not recognized by humans capable of risking their lives to create their own self-consciousness. "The unessential consciousness [i.e., the underling's] is for the lord the object, which constitutes the *truth* of his certainty of himself."[15] With only a dependent consciousness to recognize him, the lord "is, therefore, not certain of *being-for-self* as the truth of himself. On the contrary, his truth is in reality the unessential consciousness and its unessential action."[16]

Albeit the first form of war is the condition enabling the human as such to appear from among the animal species, it does not accomplish enough. It is not peace, however, that will allow humans to actualize their truth (that is, autonomous self-consciousness). Once again, it is war, though of a different kind, that will fill long years of history.

The human who was capable of risking his life by negating his natural motivation to stay alive was born to freedom by negating its absolute opposite, need. He thus shattered the determinism defining the situation of the human animal. He replaced the merely sensed repetitive cycle of the lack and assimilation of natural objects with a new situation, unprecedented in the natural order. By so doing, he transformed his own reality. A thing of nature tied to a space, he made himself that which *becomes other*, he made himself *history*. Time is specific to man. It is the unpredictable succession of actions that transform the human being and the human being's world. From this point of view, human history cannot be other than the history of human wars. Only animals have no history, for they do not know the struggle to the death for recognition.

The lord can live at peace with the underling for a time, and he can force the underling to work for him, that is, to bring forth from nature whatever is necessary for his own gratification and the underling's biological sustenance. He leads a life of enjoyment. He enjoys the underling's opinion of him; for in recognizing the victor as his lord, the underling simultaneously recognizes himself as underling of this lord, whose values he is subject to and whose needs he is required to satisfy. The lord is forever separated from nature by the underling's *work*, of which he passively enjoys the results but without experiencing *Befriedigung*, "fulfillment." Though he is the *source* of language, change, time, and history, the lord is not recognized by another self-consciousness; in this contradictory situation he will not *make* history. Not he but the underling will be the channel of history.

The work the underling is obliged to do is in fact, like the lord's, an activity both negative and creative. The underling does not leave nature as he found it; he transforms it so that it produces what it would not have produced if left to itself, to meet the needs of two or to satisfy the demands of a lord whose tastes tend more toward wine than water, more toward cooked dishes than raw meat. The underling becomes increasingly distant from nature. If he remained a purely natural being, he could not succeed at his work, and then the risk of death would reappear. By working, the underling transforms himself, educates himself. Humans do not grow like plants; they create themselves through *Bildung*, a process that simultaneously molds, educates, and refines. The transformation of nature by human beings transforms the humans in return. Humans are what they *do*. In the underling's case, a *technician* evolves whose abilities will be indispensable to the lord in his idleness. Granted, his work is performed according to the lord's coercive will, and its basic character is apparent: Accomplished as it is under submission and constraint, it is not natural, nor does it yield products that are natural. It is primarily a physical struggle with the *space* that it transforms, and it progresses through *time* according to a schedule that controls its principal stages. Consequently, although a servile activity, work mediates between the underling and nature. Therefore the one who failed to escape the order of nature through combat is able to do so in his turn by a process totally different from the lord's. Forced to distance himself from nature instead of staying immersed in it, he, too, makes himself freed. "The *truth* of the independent consciousness," Hegel writes,

> is accordingly the servile consciousness of the bondsman. This, it is true, appears at first *outside* of itself and not as the truth of self-consciousness. But just as lordship showed that its essential nature is the reverse of what it wants to be, so too servitude in its consummation will really turn into the opposite of what it immediately is; as a consciousness forced back into itself, it will withdraw into itself and be transformed into a truly independent consciousness.[17]

Fear of dying, equivalent to fear of the lord who was accepted as such in order to avoid death, dissipated the self-consciousness that sought to be recognized; but work has enabled it to perceive what it is. "It is in this way, therefore, that consciousness, *qua* worker, comes to see in the independent being [of the object] its *own* independence."[18] His fear is destroyed in and through *Bildung*. "In fashioning the thing, he becomes aware that being-in-self belongs to *him*, that he himself exists essentially and actually in his own right."[19]

Having become "freedom within servitude" and contemplating a lord who lacks the skills and intellect required by tasks he does not himself do, the underling quickly grasps that he can resist this inert lord, trapped in his enjoyment. The underling has become indispensable to a lord who can do nothing by himself; he has acquired technical skills that give him such a wide margin of superiority over his lord that he will easily be able to overcome him in order to become in turn the lord.

Though created by the lord, history is made by the underling who works and gains new powers that allow him to attack his lord and easily win the unequal contest. For the war that the underling has given himself the capacity to win is an intelligent war, reasonable because waged by reason. The underling leaves nothing to chance. Already accustomed to applying means he was forced to create to the achievement of another's ends, he calculates the most effective moment to use those means to his own ends: to forcibly invert the hierarchy and take over the lordship. Though there is little doubt that the underling will be victorious, the struggle the underling initiates lacks the prestige of the lord's original combat. The underling risks his life, as must happen in any war, but he risks it as little as possible, protected by instruments of his own making. When the underling becomes lord, he forces his erstwhile lord to be the worker, though the former lord is soft from the leisure that made his life worthwhile. In reversing one historical state of affairs, the underling creates a new one; it, too, will be eliminated, but not in recurrent fashion, although it could seem so. Although each war initiated by the worker in order to assert himself at the expense of his lord may be negation of servitude and of the power of the lord whom the underling replaces, it is not merely a cycle of destruction and recurrence, a sterile repetition. Each historical situation not only follows another but also differs from it: It is a negation of the preceding one and simultaneously a transcendence and preservation of its true essence, now lifted to a higher level. This *Aufhebung* is the process through which human beings make and transform themselves, negating what they are in order to make themselves other than they are and at the same time preserving and further elevating accomplishments they have gained.

But we are forced to admit that historical progress is dependent on war. Without it, consciousness and freedom would become mired in stagnation and insipid satisfaction. Two events are necessary. History opens with the risk of life in the war for a thing-without-being. There the lord transcends his biological existence. This is followed by the underling's becoming conscious of his powers. He then wages war against his lord, who, having triumphed in the first war, has enjoyed life and now wants to continue living. History is not a mere chain of occurrences isolated from what has gone before; it is not an irrational succession of scenarios. In what seem to be random victories or defeats, history is being changed and continued. History's unfolding is the progress that takes place through the varying relation of lord and underling, thanks to the mediation between humans and nature established by the risk of life or human toil. Although gripped by our passions, we notice only their mad fluctuations, which appear to be the cause of the churning incoherence of successive situations. We do not discern any reasons that history should have meaning. We do not recognize the work of freedom until it is finished. Then progress is understood to be rational, as in fact it is.

It is characteristic of humans ever to widen the distance between themselves and nature. The radical and first distance, creator of our humanity, is established by risking life and affirming the self as value; the distance grows through work and its inevitable technological production, requiring thought and invention. This twofold distance that begets what is human in our species depends on an unchanging condition—war. History, then, is the reality of human beings who have been creating themselves by negating and transcending what they are. History is intrinsically dialectical. Dialectic is the true nature of things.[20] So humans become conscious of themselves in their freedom, attain knowledge of themselves in their truth—as a process of becoming and self-creation, not as a mere sequence through time, waiting for time to lead them to their deaths.

If each moment of history enriches humans and brings them partial knowledge of what they are as beings different from all others, we may wonder whether this process will continue indefinitely. Or will real satisfaction of the particularity within the universal occur, will humans become really human, or in other words will there be an end of history in peace? Does the struggle to the death, the struggle at the risk of life, whether in civil war or foreign war, have an end? According to Hegel, *Aufhebung* inaugurates a progress in consciousness that gives human history its meaning. Each historical sequence is understood as a moment of new consciousness accomplished by means of war. What progresses and is transformed as it progresses contains in its very movement the actualization of future becoming. Now there is a type of war seen in history that breaks out at the moment when the dialectic of lordship and servitude must be transcended, because the historical form of lordship has become devoid of effective reality. In 1789 the French ancien régime existed, according to Hegel, in name only. Its reality had peacefully succumbed to the blows the *Aufklärung* [Enlightenment] had dealt it. The lords have become *nothing*, whereas the underlings have become masters of skills; there is thus no need for them to wage war. They are emancipated de facto because they no longer have lords, but because their "freedom" was not gained by risking death, it is empty, an absolute void. Hence this freedom—absolute freedom, because now without obstacle—is not creative. Having nothing to negate, it transforms and transcends nothing. Consciousness "is conscious of its pure personality and therein of all spiritual reality, and all reality is solely spiritual; the world is for it simply its own will, and this is a general will."[21]

In lectures later published as the *Philosophy of History*, Hegel shows that "the Will is Free only when it does not will anything alien, extrinsic, foreign to itself (for as long as it does so, it is dependent) but wills itself alone."[22] Although this freedom of the will is the foundation of all right and is "that by which Man becomes Man," this abstract will, which "in willing itself, is nothing but an identical reference to itself,"[23] has no defining content. How can reality be given an abstract principle, a "will of all *individuals* as such,"[24] that finds no object it can oppose? Insofar as each of us is absolute freedom, we can will in our particular will to *realize* absolute freedom. The process continues until a single individual, "the One of individuality . . . an individual self-consciousness,"[25] overcomes others and becomes real. This individuality, too, is a void. It attains reality only by abolishing the void, that is, by the suppression of individual wills in a manner that is totally arbitrary (because there is merely emptiness to be suppressed). Our name for this is the Terror. (Hegel has in mind the phase of the French Revolution known by that name.) The Terror can be nothing but death. It is the form of absolute war that occurs between factions attempting to rise at each other's expense. This battle to the death is not carried on between *lords* and *underlings* (for none remain), but it lets those who have never had to risk their lives—former underlings, effectively emancipated and free, but having an *empty* freedom—obtain *real* freedom through experiencing the danger of death. The Terror may be described as the most pointless of all struggles, as it is a battle against no freedom but an empty one; but at the same time it is necessary to the humanization of the conflicting revolutionary factions. For this reason, the faction that briefly has the upper hand destroys not only those who symbolize the former lords but the other revolutionary factions as well. The realization of absolute freedom, moreover, cannot be other than a "*fury* of destruction," because universal freedom, which is a void, a nothingness, "can produce neither a positive work nor a deed; there is left for it only *negative* action."[26] The Terror, correctly defined, is purely negative; there is no *Aufhebung* in it, no transcendence and preservation. It is a total war, the most horrible of wars; for in the eyes of the revolutionary government—a government in name only, as it is illegitimately claimed to be one by a mere *faction*—each individual will, because it is absolute freedom, is necessarily "suspect." The war would also be total destruction if it were not destroying itself. Meanwhile, *"being suspect . . . takes the place, or has the significance and effect, of being guilty."*[27]

Hegel knew of the factional struggle between Girondins and Montagnards, the consequences of the latter's success, and the dictatorship of that "singular self-consciousness," Robespierre. The tumbrels of suspects drawn to the guillotine were the realization this man gave to his absolute freedom. "Robespierre," says Hegel,

> set up the principle of Virtue as supreme [virtue as an abstract principle, or freedom, within the subjective will], and it may be said that with this man Virtue was an earnest matter. *Virtue* and *Terror* are the order of the day; for Subjective Virtue, whose sway is based on disposition only, brings with it the most fearful tyranny. It exercises its power without legal formalities, and the punishment it inflicts is equally simple—*Death.*[28]

The Committee of Public Safety, the Committee of General Security, and the Revolutionary Tribunal, in the name of the Law of Suspects of 17 September 1793, put to death "even infants in swaddling clothes."[29]

Actual history had taught Hegel that the masters of the Terror also ended up on the scaffold. The philosopher explains the necessity of their fate. Regarding the victorious faction, "in the very fact of its being a faction lies the direct necessity of its overthrow."[30] Once it has usurped universality, every faction that has seized power is doomed to disappear because it is only an individuality. Representing none but itself, it cannot long claim to act as if it were universal. Its power is corrupt, for a pseudo government is now claiming to represent all freedoms. Nevertheless, the Terror is a sort of pause in history. Every consciousness, revolutionary or not, has felt terror of dying and thus known itself for what it is, a nothingness. "The *terror* of death is the vision of [absolute freedom's] negative nature."[31] In other words, human beings' truth when they succeed in defining themselves as absolute freedom cannot be other than death, for absolute freedom is also absolute negativity. It is violent death, the kind of death that realizes the absolute freedom exercised by the dictatorship of those who won freedom in the battle of factions and who cannot possibly constitute a true government. The experience of the fear of death reveals to consciousness that absolute freedom is not its truth. Humans want to live. This does not imply, however, a return to evasion and servile behavior. In the struggle against the tyrant,[32] there is no cowardice, no relinquishment of values, no desire to rule in his place. By means of war against the destructive faction, we win the life that we have recognized and affirmed as good and defended as such against those who would have negated it for their own advantage. The issue now is not our original humanity but the conservation of values acquired over time and their transcendence through new forms of life where lordship and servitude no longer have meaning because they no longer have a function. Once having transcended the abstraction of absolute freedom—thanks to our fear of death and to the death of the tyrant (who furnished the guillotine)—we make real and actual the form of civil society that preserves our lives and keeps us free: the modern state.

The state is, according to Hegel, the actualization of the self-consciousness that knows itself and is recognized by others, for "the State is absolutely rational inasmuch as it is the particular self-consciousness once that consciousness has been raised to consciousness of its universality. This substantial unity," Hegel says, "is an absolute unmoved and in itself, in which freedom comes into its supreme right."[33] So all wars, from the death struggle the human animal needs in order to make itself human through those that make human history not "a tale / Told by an idiot, full of sound and fury, / Signifying nothing,"[34] nor yet a dull cycle of eternal beginnings, but the actualization of Spirit—all these wars, then, are for the purpose of the dialectic reversal of the absolute negativity, absolute freedom, into an absolute positivity: the state.[35]

Is the state the state of *peace*? Servitude disappeared through terror; can consciousness in and for itself be affirmed thereafter without war? If so, war would only have been the condition enabling the appearance and flowering of peace. Whether in the form of individual combat, civil war, or battle abroad, war, however necessary, would not be eternally essential to a human being in perfect self-consciousness, a human being whose abstract concept has become the reality of absolute Spirit and who—to the rhythm of wars—reaches the end of that temporal flow of events we call history. From that moment on, war, too, would seem to cease having a function.

As "the actuality of concrete freedom," the state lives in peace within its borders, for "concrete freedom consists in this, that personal individuality and its particular interests . . . achieve their complete development and gain explicit recognition for their right . . . in the sphere of the family and civil society." This concrete freedom is achieved only in the state, because individual particularities have arrived at that moment in history when "they know and will the universal; they even recognize it as their own substantive mind; they take it as their end and aim and are active in its pursuit."[36] At that time in history when a civil society is living according to such an *interior public right* as manifests this union of the particular and universal, the concrete actualization of freedom has occurred; but to the extent that only a partial number of those comprising the civil society receive recognition, this actualization also remains partial. The struggle for recognition is necessary until enslavement has truly vanished. The civil society that in fact realizes concrete freedom is the modern state, and this term, in both its form and meaning, should be applied only to postrevolutionary societies, those, that is, in which public right is guarantor of each individual freedom as well as of the cohesion, the unity of those freedoms. "The principle of modern states has prodigious strength and depth because it allows the principle of subjectivity to progress to its culmination in the extreme of self-subsistent personal particularity, and yet at the same time brings it back to the substantive unity and so maintains this unity in the principle of subjectivity itself."[37]

Why and with whom would anyone fight, in a society that recognized and guaranteed the rights of all without one person's still having power over another? From another point of view, personal freedom is itself a principle of right when it recognizes itself to be a duty. "In the state," Hegel says, "duty and right are united in one and the same relation."[38] The accomplishment of duty is to everyone's interest, for when there is no conflict between the particular and the universal, each person receives recognition. "The *isolated* individual, so far as his duties are concerned, is in subjection; but as a member of *civil society* he finds in fulfilling his duties to it protection of his person and property, regard for his private welfare, the satisfaction of the depths of his being, the consciousness and feeling of himself as a member of the whole."[39]

Just as war is the means of attaining freedom, we understand that for the nation that actualizes freedom, peace will replace war as the means for attaining the free flourishing of each citizen. What is more, patriotism should be viewed as a state of mind both conscious of itself and satisfied with the nation's institutions. Hegel's definition does not, strictly speaking, apply to the military world: "Patriotism is often understood to mean only a readiness for exceptional sacrifices and actions. Essentially, however, it is the sentiment which, in the relationships of our daily life and under ordinary conditions, habitually recognizes that the community is one's substantive groundwork and end."[40]

Even in the state of right, nonetheless, legislation is to a certain extent compulsion, however well understood and internalized it may be. The passions are still alive, so the state's existence must still be protected. Hegel knows that "civil society is the battlefield where everyone's private interests meet everyone else's"[41] and that private interests and the passions that whet them may conflict with the superior interests of the state. Patriotism acknowledges, of course, that the state "maintains . . . particular spheres of interest together with the title, authority and welfare of these";[42] but the fact remains that internal peace must still be defended by "the organization of the state."[43] So within the modern state, its citizens have peace, a peace that is necessary for their welfare and their contentment, but a peace that is explicitly guaranteed by laws and maintained by enforcement of laws; otherwise precisely because of its freedom, civil society would succumb to civil war.

Individuals' interests that aspire legitimately to gratification are defended and upheld against whoever in the civil society might dispute them. In relations between people, the private individual's will is exercised; it grapples with the complexity of exterior relations in general, which reintroduces the contingency of its nature.[44] Therefore,

> to keep in view this general end [satisfaction of the needs of individuals], to ascertain the way in which the powers composing that social necessity act . . . and to maintain that end in them and against them, is the work of an institution which assumes on *one* hand, to the concrete of civil society, the position of an external universality. Such an order acts with the power of an external state, which, in so far as it is rooted in the higher or substantial state, appears as state-"police."[45]

In the *Philosophy of Right*, Hegel uses similar language to define the necessity and role of the police. "Its primary purpose," he writes, "is to actualize and maintain the universal contained within the particularity of civil society, and its control takes the form of an external system and organization for the protection and security of particular ends and interests *en masse*, inasmuch as these interests subsist only in this universal." In addition, "the public authority must also undertake the higher directive function of providing for the interests which lead beyond the borders of its society."[46] The state guarantees the civil society the realization of its goals and interests by keeping order among its different constituencies and defending it against "the sphere of contingencies."[47]

Now, with civil war contained, is foreign war still of concern to the state? When Napoleon entered Jena in 1806 after a battle quickly won, Hegel perhaps believed in the actualization of absolute Spirit and the termination of history in a real and definitive totality, the empire. To the author of the *Phenomenology of Spirit*, wars and revolutions had played their part; they would no longer have any function useful for the human being.[48] In 1818, when Hegel was beginning to teach philosophy of law in Berlin, Napoleon was a prisoner on Saint Helena and the French empire in collapse following the two surrenders of Paris, in 1814 and 1815.[49] Jena marked the end neither of wars nor of revolutions. Once again the realization of Spirit, of consciousness in self and for self, is the work of some nation other than the most recent. The *Philosophy of Right* is unambiguous: Albeit the state is the political form of actualized reason, actual states have a history that does not end with the reign of Friedrich-Wilhelm

III. "Rome and its fortunes, or the Decline of the grandeur of the Roman empire . . . is the presupposed end which lies at the basis of the events themselves, as of the critical examination into their comparative importance, i.e. their nearer or more remote relation to it."[50] In the same way, is the Napoleonic state not a moment in the development of the state of which Hegel can write the history as *an* end, because it has really existed and only what is past can be understood? "The owl of Minerva spreads its wings only with the falling of the dusk."[51] We cannot say, however, that any state is *the* end of history, or predict that a universal state would complete the actualization of freedom. The very notion of a universal state is contradictory. If internal war were to cease in every state while its institutions remained strong, the human being's freedom would still require war. To remain free, a person must have enemies to challenge. Conversely, if foreign wars were to end, freedom would disappear. More than one state is therefore necessary for freedom. A state reconciles the particular with the universal inside its own borders, where civil peace prevails; but outside its territory, it perpetuates freedom through life-risking war with other states. In this sense, we can say that history is genuinely completed in the *form* of the state, which is indeed its *end*, but that history continues indefinitely in the relations among states. If this were not so, it would be necessary to postulate a world state—which Hegel never does, because it would be contrary to the requirements of freedom—or else to allow a contradiction between the definition of the state as the actualization of objective Spirit and its definition as an individuality—a contradiction according to which the state "differentiates its moments within itself and develops them to self-subsistence," while at the same time it is "an individual, unique and exclusive, and therefore related to others."[52]

Then what are in fact the nature and role of war? The question concerns the meaning that human existence and the state (as conceived by actualized reason) would have if war were permanently replaced by peace. Hegel is very clear on this point in all his works. He is certain that given the nature of Spirit, reason, and freedom, wars must continue. Until the state becomes a historical reality, a people's spirit is embodied in some *form* of civil society at some moment in time, at some point in space, receiving and transcending in and through war a legacy from another place and an earlier time, itself fated to be negated and transcended in turn by another people. Thus is universal history intelligible, Hegel declares, and it moves toward a destination—the actualization of objective Spirit in the state. As he traced the dialectical movement of this development in the *Philosophy of History*, Hegel maintained that "the category which first presents itself in this restless mutation of individuals and people, existing for a time and then vanishing, is that of *change* at large."[53] From this truth that he has shown to be necessary, Hegel deduces that "the next consideration which allies itself with that of change, is that change, while it imports dissolution, involves at the same time the rise of a *new life*—that while death is the issue of life, life is also the issue of death."[54] This is the most general consideration. What meaning would man's world have if he were fixed, unchanging as stone, in the serenity of a life that would no longer transcend itself in a form other than it had taken? "For interest is present only where there is opposition."[55] This would be the world of boredom, of old age that quietly flickers out in a natural death. "Thus perish individuals, thus perish peoples by a natural death; and though the latter may continue in being, it is an existence without intellect or vitality; having no need of its institutions, because the need for them is satisfied— a political nullity and tedium."[56]

Still, when the spirit of a people dies upon reaching consciousness of what it is, and when, in the Hegelian image, "this fruit does not fall back into the bosom of the people that produced and matured it,"[57] it is because "the principles of the successive phases of Spirit that animate the Nations in a necessitated gradation, are themselves only steps in the development of the one universal Spirit, which through them elevates and completes itself to a self-comprehending *totality*."[58]

This is the same requirement we find at the conclusion of the *Phenomenology of Spirit*. Spirit is not actualized in its objectivity except as absolute knowledge at the end of history. But although the *state* is the last form of this actualization, the history of *states* must last as long as humankind so that man may remain man, may remain freedom. To say that universal Spirit is raised to a totality through the repeatedly transformed and renewed life that constitutes the history of the different peoples, and to say that the *state* is objective Spirit is not at all to say that the *states* will live in peace. Such a situation would surely be the end of history, but it would also be the end of time and the end of man as freedom.

Time originated in the struggle for recognition in which history began. Why did this struggle take place at one time rather than another? Hegel gives no answer, for at bottom the question springs from simple archeological curiosity. More at issue is the symbolic analysis of an abstract, essential necessity—time was a necessity because the animal capable of humanity was pursuing self-consciousness. Also at issue is the role that chance or contingency plays in human affairs, even when they have attained rationality.[59]

Time began with the human being and the human being's history. They will end together. When? It is as idle a question as that about their beginning. Self-consciousness culminates, is actualized, in the state; there, objective Spirit is absolute knowledge, the consciousness and knowledge of one who lives free throughout the temporal existence of civil societies that have attained the form and content of a state.

This is why "the state is the absolutely rational. . . . Since the state is mind objectified, it is only as one of its members that the individual himself has objectivity, genuine individuality, and an ethical life. Unification pure and simple is the true content and aim of the individual, and the individual's destiny is the living of a universal life."[60] We have arrived at the goal of history, its telos, the concrete actualization of the Idea that is "the absolutely eternal and necessary being of mind . . . the unity of objective freedom (i.e. the universal or substantial will) and subjective freedom . . . in self-determining action on laws and principles."[61] In the state, those who battled throughout history for what would satisfy their human desire—that is, for recognition—have reached their goal.

We have come to a limit that is finally real, actual in every way; yet for all that, at the end of the story (or, more accurately, at the end of history, as the definition of the state would have it), man is not a being born for peace. Hegel is very clear about this. At the time man emerged as freedom and while he was developing through historical forms that culminated in the state, we could say the human being could not exist without war; we must still say it in the state, and without self-contradiction. The state, for Hegel, is indeed the effective and efficient actuality of Idea, it is the form in which humans attain satisfaction—but humans will not accept simply any satisfaction. Human satisfaction is not mere pleasure, not a calm life such as only an animal can know. It is the very opposite. The political form historically known as the state is a totality, and in this sense it is of course a termination; for the individuals belonging to it—its citizens—are fully human within its bounds. But humanity, as Hegel shows everywhere in his writings, depends on risk. What separated one species from all others remains necessary to freedom.

In the article published in 1802 and 1803, "The Scientific Ways of Treating Natural Law," Hegel was already saying:

This second aspect of the bearing which the shape and individuality of one ethical totality has on another is what establishes the necessity of war. In war there is the free possibility that not only certain individual things but the whole of them, as life, will be annihilated and destroyed for the Absolute itself or for the people; and therefore war preserves the ethical health of peoples in their indifference to specific institutions, preserves it from habituation to such institutions and their hardening. Just as the blowing of the winds reserves the sea from the foulness which would result from a continual calm, so also corruption would result for people under continual or indeed "perpetual" peace.[62]

The theme of the health of peoples reappears in the *Phenomenology of Spirit*.[63] The necessity of war is proved at equally great length in the *Philosophy of Right*. Hegel cites himself when he reminds us that the "higher significance" of war is that "as . . . remarked elsewhere, 'war preserves the ethical health of peoples.'"[64]

War retains its role of molder and teacher. Anthropogenesis is ordained to last as long as the human race. Even in the state of recognition and reconciliation, humans are born endowed with passion on the one hand but, on the other, with another tendency inherent in mortality, the tendency to let themselves slip into laziness and apathy, which risk turning the state into the dreary dwelling of boredom and regression. Even if the perfection of the state has been forged in the course of history and if, thanks to the state, the satisfaction of its members has been achieved, there is still the need to prevent the loss of these indispensable products of freedom. In the concrete life of a nation, war keeps freedom alive. "This negatively absolute, pure freedom, appears as death; and by his ability to die the subject proves himself free and entirely above all coercion."[65] On the day that men in a state no longer wish to fight, whatever their reasons, they are no longer human, for they are no longer capable of freedom. In Hegel's brilliant phrase, "Their freedom has died from the fear of dying."[66] Every type of pacifism is refuted here before it appears. Behind the contemporary slogan "Better red than dead" would really lie hidden, in Hegel's view, the rejection of humanness. In his spirit, we might reword the phrase "Better a slave than dead," even "Better an animal than dead."

A human is defined by Hegel as nature-negating freedom, evolving in dialectical progress over the course of history. In this perspective, the state, the last stage of history's progress, cannot without contradiction—without, indeed, absurdity—be the gravedigger of freedom. This is why the state, while sovereign within its own borders and able to maintain freedom and civil peace because of its sovereignty, is at the same time an "individuality . . . [that] manifests itself here in the state as a relation to other states, each of which is autonomous vis-à-vis the others."[67] This "autonomy" of a state in respect to another is the sign that it has begun its participation in history. Abstract until it has developed into concrete autonomy, as it has in the modern state, it is nonetheless the necessary condition of a people's historicity. So it is also necessary that it be sustained. Then the negativity that is freedom turns outward, and although it is only manifested under contingent circumstances that are often hard to sort out, it is, according to Hegel, "that moment in the state which is supremely its own."[68]

The defense of autonomy cannot do without wars, even though treaties will frequently interrupt them, as expediency dictates. We must be quite clear that the state's "final end" is not to protect the lives of particular individuals or groups that make up civil society. On the contrary, it is they who have the duty of defending the state, even at the cost of their lives, because it is the place where life finds its highest meaning. The state is not a sheepfold, for in the final analysis the shepherd only protects the unwitting sheep in order to shear them and kill them; nor is it a kindergarten where safety measures are essential to the well-being of every child. Man is only man by risking his life. War is not the ultimate way to stay alive, as it was for Hobbes. Defining "the ethical moment in war," Hegel writes that "war is not to be regarded as an absolute evil and as a purely external accident, which itself therefore has some accidental cause, be it injustices, the passions of nations or the holders of power, etc., or in short, something or other which ought not to be."[69] As biological existence, everyone's life is contingent. (What grandmother might not have died as a child?) The contingency of the events determining it molds its fate, that is, its necessity. This is what it means to be finite. But this existence that obeys the laws of nature (which is no other than necessity) "is exalted to be the work of freedom, to be something ethical."[70] In other words, though our daily life consists in attachment to what is finite (life, possessions) and therefore to what is hollow, to detach ourselves from all that determines this life, from all the habits that keep us rooted in the soil where chance planted us, from the entire reality of our lives—this is freedom. Detachment is the risking of life.

A particular "class" in the state, "the class of courage," what we call a professional army, has the task of risking its members' lives in conflicts between states. But from a modern point of view born in the French Revolution and previously suggested by Rousseau, Hegel defines the citizens' duty at times of danger to the state as a whole: "If the state as such, if its autonomy, is in jeopardy, all its citizens are in duty bound to answer the summons to its defence."[71] So because free and receiving recognition within that political structure, the state, each citizen is obliged to risk life in war to remain free; for no one can be free outside the substantial reality of the nation. This is not the ordinary risk of life that everyone assumes simply by being human. Besides, anyone may risk life for anything—a thief or a murderer is courageous after a fashion. "The intrinsic worth of courage as a disposition of mind is to be found in the genuine, absolute, final end, the sovereignty of the state. The work of courage is to actualize this final end, and the means to this end is the sacrifice of personal actuality."[72] The courage of the citizen running the risk of dying for the autonomy of the state depends on the acceptance of such "extreme contradictions" as total obedience to orders and the most intense presence of mind.[73] Courage resides in this adaptability for the good of the state. "It is the positive aspect, the end and content, which first gives significance to this spiritedness."[74]

It is interesting to note that in the risk of life for the good of the state lies the attribute of war that permits the full development of freedom. At the first stage of humanity's genesis, a human individual left behind his purely animal nature by desiring another individual's desire and insisting that the other desire his desire in turn and recognize its superiority. In man's ensuing history, progress in technology is accomplished by means of progress in consciousness, and vice versa. By turns, humans and their wars are transformed. The invention of firearms, for example, has eliminated hand-to-hand fighting between two warring individualities. Now soldiers kill an unknown adversary from afar and are killed in the same way. There is no contact with or direct knowledge of the enemy on either side. Both parties to the conflict try to kill without passion. Courage is "the act not of this particular person, but of a member of a whole. Moreover, it seems to be turned not against single persons, but against a hostile group, and hence personal bravery appears impersonal."[75] For Hegel, "anonymous death" in defense of the state is the most significant manifestation of the risk of life; it is its crowning achievement in impersonal courage, the virtue of an exceptional person, who is the agent of courage without being its purpose. To defend the state is not to defend one's life; it is, on the contrary, to endanger it, not for personal benefit but for the highest value, exceeding the individual value of the one hazarding life, the universal value—the state. In this obliteration of the individual except as a support to the state, the "I" of our earliest speech, affirmation of emerging consciousness, has ceded to the "we" of the whole, in which the "I" finds its meaning through acceptance of its own disappearance. In Hegel's view, this is the highest expression of the actualization of freedom. It requires war. Therefore it is necessary, it is inescapable that states live as enemies. "If a number of states make themselves into a family, this group as an individual must engender an opposite and create an enemy."[76]

Because the state is "mind in its substantive rationality and immediate actuality," it is consequently "the absolute power on earth."[77] But as an actual individual, it inevitably has relations with other nations. This does not mean that these relations are comparable to the relations among private individuals that civil law controls. There is no court with the power to judge sovereign states. What would Hegel have thought of the projects of Bertrand Russell and Jean-Paul Sartre? They would have seemed quite simply senseless to him, because they failed to take into account the true nature of the state and its supreme autonomy in respect to other states. To play the "praetor to judge between states"[78] is to forget that there are no praetors for states because it is impossible that there should be. So states are "in a state of nature in relation to each other. Their rights are actualized only in their particular wills and not in a universal will with constitutional powers over them."[79] Hegel embodies this will in an individual subjectivity, the prince, and in particular the power to declare war.[80] The details of Hegel's constitution are of less interest to us than is the unalterable situation of the states. Whatever pacts they sign, whatever treaties bind them, whatever moral obligation they feel (in spite of their passions and vices) to respect certain tenets of the law of nations, they must still go to war to save the autonomy of their concrete existence.

Does this mean that peace is in itself an evil? Clearly not. Treaties exist to guarantee it. It is necessary for the satisfaction and development of civil society. "In times of peace, the particular spheres and functions pursue the path of satisfying their particular aims and minding their own business."[81] Hegel shows, of course, that

> it is in part only by way of the unconscious necessity of the thing that their self-seeking is turned into a contribution to reciprocal support and to the support of the whole. In part, however, it is by the direct influence of higher authority that they are not only continually brought back to the aims of the whole and restricted accordingly, but are also constrained to perform direct services for the support of the whole.[82]

Meanwhile, these forms of self-seeking exist, they threaten the state's internal peace; hence, it is not the least of the roles of successful wars to "have checked domestic unrest and consolidated the power of the state at home."[83]

War and peace, then, are inseparable moments in a people's life as well as in the life of a state:

> The fact that states reciprocally recognize each other as states remains, even in war—the state of affairs when rights disappear and force and chance hold sway—a bond wherein each counts to the rest as something absolute. Hence in war, war itself is characterized as something which ought to pass away. It implies therefore the proviso of the *jus gentium* [law of nations] that the possibility of peace be retained,[84]

as in the presence of ambassadors or the respect of noncombatants.

War is not an end in itself. No more is peace. Peace is necessary, but war is no less so, and it has far more influence than peace on the development of the human being. Hence, to want peace without agreeing to war, without understanding it as the necessary expression of freedom, is contradictory. A fortiori, philosophic thought concerning war should stop short of all dreams or abstract constructions of "perpetual peace," such as Kant's. It is not simply that these are chimerical expectations but that perpetual peace would be no more desirable than it is conceivable. It would swallow up the human being, human freedom, and human achievements, including the most exalted of them wherein humans create themselves as self-consciousness and as historical beings—the modern state, existing concretely in the multiplicity of states that are the forms of its actuality.

The highest actuality of human life is the state, of which Hegel was able to write the theory because it had effectively completed its historical development. To him, the state is the perfect form of civil society, for it is where human freedom is actualized. The state, objective Spirit, incarnates consciousness of self and for self.

"State? What is that? Well then, open your ears to me, for now I shall speak to you about the death of peoples."[85] To Hegel's thought, the state is the destination of a progress that the philosopher can understand only at dusk, when Minerva's owl takes flight; but Zarathustra, the man who blesses the rising sun, sick of his own wisdom, dances with life and denounces that new idol, the state: "the coldest of all cold monsters"; state, the work of destroyers, not of the creators, whom it catches in its traps; state, the liar; state, the robber; "state, where the slow suicide of all is called 'life'"; state that stinks with the foul smell of human sacrifices. But we can "break the windows and leap to freedom"; then in spite of the boasts and tyranny of the state, "a free life is still free for great souls," for "only where the state ends . . . there begins the song of necessity, the unique and inimitable tune. Where the state *ends*—look there, my brothers! Do you not see it, the rainbow and the bridges of the overman?"[86]

To be done with the state, to sing the song of necessity, which is the song of freedom—is this how we shall finally leave war behind? Does dancing with life mean living in peace? If we were to seek a systematic answer from Nietzsche's works, we would be disappointed. Nietzsche traps no lesson in the net of didactic discourse. Philosopher, poet, child, he coins baffling aphorisms, yet he draws those who can still hear with the ears of childhood into the dance of the future and of life. Life affirms, it does not exclude, it does not proceed by negation; and if its energy breaks forth in war more easily than it remains peaceable, it is the sign that it flourishes in the constantly renewed emergence of values that hold sway then break down in the face of the creation of others that ceaselessly appear. We think, we speak, of course. Nonetheless, says Nietzsche, "I should think that today we are at least far from the ridiculous immodesty that would be involved in decreeing from our corner that perspectives are permitted only from this corner. Rather has the world become 'infinite' for us all over again, inasmuch as we cannot reject the possibility that it may *include infinite interpretations.*"[87]

Nietzsche's judgments of war and peace bespeak the variety and abundance of the perspectives from which their value can be viewed. Is he so far from Hegel,[88] for example, when he exclaims, "It is vain rhapsodizing and sentimentality to continue to expect much (even more, to expect a very great deal) from mankind, once it has learned not to wage war"?[89] In Nietzsche's view, war is the torrent from which the spirit drinks, so that "such a highly cultivated, and therefore necessarily weary humanity as that of present-day Europe,[90] needs not only war but the greatest and most terrible wars (that is, occasional relapses into barbarism) in order not to forfeit to the means of culture its culture and its very existence."[91]

We could draw parallels between the role of war as Hegel often described it and what we find in this paragraph from *Human, All Too Human*, according to which "we know of no other means to imbue exhausted peoples, as strongly and surely as every great war does, with that raw energy of the battleground, that deep impersonal hatred, that murderous cold-bloodedness with a good conscience, that communal, organized ardor in destroying the enemy, that proud indifference to great losses, to one's own existence and to that of one's friends, that muted, earthquake-like convulsion of the soul."[92] Hegel had already discussed analogous themes, we recall, in, for instance, the *Philosophy of Right*. Whatever their differences, the two philosophers unite in their judgment of war as indispensable to humans and their civilization. War is not the path of a will absorbed in its own preservation. "The wish to preserve oneself is the symptom of a condition of distress, of a limitation of the really fundamental instinct of life which aims at the *expansion of power* and, wishing for that, frequently risks and even sacrifices self-preservation."[93] War, according to Nietzsche, is the exaltation and triumph of life. When "the esteem for war and the pleasure in war diminish," it is, he says, a symptom of a society's corruption, using the word in the sense a pathologist would.[94]

Taking another point of view, however, Nietzsche challenges himself. Because of the existence of war and hence of preparations for war, "year in and year out, the ablest, strongest, most industrious men are taken in extraordinary numbers from their own occupations and professions in order to be soldiers. . . . One may ask whether all this blossoming and splendor of the whole . . . is *worth* it if all the nobler, more tender and spiritual plants once produced in such abundance on its soil have to be sacrificed to this gross and gaudy national flower."[95] In addition, Nietzsche blasts with sarcasm "commands whose roar surrounds the German cities now that they drill outside all gates." The "military tone" and the "most immodest and distasteful" style of the officer class have contaminated music, literature, and, obviously, the emperor's speeches.[96] The Prussian officer whose vulgarity—copied even by young girls—he castigates does not represent a resurgence of "stages of *earlier culture*"; he does not show us "what we *all* were" and fear to be.[97] He has little in common with "the beast of prey, the splendid *blond beast* prowling about avidly in search of spoil and victory."[98] Neither is he the pure representative of "the kind of people who alone matter: I mean those who are *heroic*."[99] The army serves the state. The soldier is not the warrior.[100]

Then what is war to Nietzsche? Is there, beyond the diversity of his appraisals of war, something we can say of war and human beings other than that such contradictory opinions are irreconcilable? The reply is not made easier by the fact that whatever subject he turns to, Nietzsche's language is most often the language of combat. Looked at a certain way, everything becomes war. We could investigate war through a purely linguistic study and analysis of the vocabulary that either speaks explicitly of war or alludes to it in ways that are sometimes quite surprising. Although all writers frequently borrow metaphors from the vocabulary of war, even when dealing with the least-related subjects—a revealing fact in itself—Nietzsche's constant use of war language as something other than a literary convention, barely as a comparison or image, fills us with an awareness of war's indelible presence in the universe and human life. War inheres in all reality, in all our being, to such a degree that Nietzsche never refrains from evoking its actuality. Thus, when addressing the "higher men," Zarathustra says to them: "To my arms and my legs . . . I show no consideration; *I show my warriors no consideration:* how then could you be fit for *my* war? With you I should spoil my every victory. And some among you would collapse as soon as they heard the loud roll of my drums."[101]

In his vigorous attack on David Strauss, he denounces the gap between the university scholarship that shapes public opinion and what he considers true creation of culture. He writes, "After taking part in the grasping, agitated race of modern scholarship, how many could preserve the calm and courageous gaze of the embattled man of culture [*jenen mutigen und ruhenden Blick des kämpfenden Kultur-Menschen*], if, in fact, they ever possessed it at all—that gaze that condemns the race itself as a barbarizing force?"[102]

Two more examples among the many that we could choose illustrate well the predominance of this vocabulary. "The most common means that the ascetic and saint uses in order to make his life more bearable and entertaining consists in occasionally waging war and alternating victory and defeat. To do this he needs an opponent, and finds him in the so-called 'inner enemy.'"[103] In contrast, but equally to our purpose, in comparing Parmenides and Heraclitus, Nietzsche writes, "It was then possible for a Greek to escape the luxuriant richness of reality, as a simple jugglery of imaginary schemas, and to take refuge, not as Plato did in the land of eternal ideas, in the studio of the artist of the universe, there to feed his glance on the spotless and immutable prototypes of things, but in the corpselike and still peace of the coldest concept, the least expressive of all, being."[104] Here peace means death, nothingness, absence of movement and life. It would be pointless to add examples—we would have to quote all that Nietzsche wrote.

In actual fact, to attempt to grasp Nietzsche's ideas on war as the political conflict that sends groups of men to risk their lives in combat, we must understand the full richness of his vision of life. In spite of the reversals in his attitude, the multiplicity and diversity of his judgments, from his earliest works to his last, Nietzsche apprehended—or, more accurately, he sensed—what there is behind the appearance of things that gives them their depth, their multifaceted character, and, though it seems paradoxical, their lightness. What appears simple and orderly is superimposed on a swarm of forces that can be explained by neither Socrates' illusory final cause nor the scientists' causality, which Nietzsche had given up as a pious hope (though he had once hoped to lay the groundwork for a scientific understanding of life).[105] We must view war and peace from the complex variety of perspectives created by the sublime, cruel, and frightening aspects of a will to power that deploys its energy beyond good and evil, that does not judge except when it gushes forth as both ecstasy and pain for humans, unspeakable sufferings and triumphant joy.

Nietzsche is perhaps the philosopher who has been the most aware of the enigma of existence that no certainty can brighten, no respite ease, that possesses a stirring beauty owed to the innocence of the future. We should remember that Nietzsche did not practice the philosopher's trade in the too common retreat of thinkers who "present" a problem as if it were external to themselves and "soliciting" their mental efforts. And although he was capable of making experiments, as any scholar would be, he did not separate himself from the subjects of his experiments; he became the very emotions of jubilation and suffering as they asserted themselves in succession or simultaneity. "I have always composed my writings with my entire body and life: I do not know what 'purely intellectual' problems are."[106] As the philosopher is inseparable from life, so war is entwined in the fabric of life; it is neither an accident, a necessary evil, nor a means of preserving anything, and even less is it the consequence or punishment attached to a mistake; it is the life force affirming itself; it builds and destroys, because life in its abundance unceasingly creates worlds and annihilates them. In this sense, the innocence of the future belongs to war, despite the hideous upheavals it brings, despite the way it crushes souls and bodies in the exuberance and madness of the "springtime urge" that inspires it.[107]

We must, then, be wary of judging war by a fixed system of evaluation that would condemn it without knowing it for what it is, or that would find in it a death instinct, a yearning for nothingness, an attempt at total annihilation. War seems, on the contrary, the expression of the will of an instinct to dominate. It asserts itself against the other instincts just as it overpowers adversaries, necessarily involving life and death in the combat but supporting the victory of the life energy. Hence it is creating values even as it destroys together with the fairest lives, the old tablets of outworn values. Zarathustra is awaiting his time, sitting "surrounded by broken old tablets and new tablets half covered with writing."[108] He symbolizes the action that demolishes in order to create but that does not linger over a form it has invented. New tablets are always half inscribed. As soon as they are perfect and complete, they no longer represent values; they are pathologically rigid. Value resides in creative action, not in what is accomplished. This is why war is ambivalent. There is a war, we could say, that destroys so that the new may emerge; it is the powerhouse of life. There is also another kind of war.

There is nothing static, nothing final in the life that is always becoming. The warrior is able to risk his life by intertwining with it, marrying himself to its creative energy. A destroyer so that he may rush into the future, he is not afraid of being destroyed. He is not in the fief of the immutable values defined by traditional morality. Far beyond the good and evil that have lost all ideal reality and no longer exist as such, Nietzsche shows from his research into the history of the two concepts that originally the "good" man meant the man who fought. The good man judges himself on the basis of the power, the superiority he has won and continually risked in warfare. The warrior is thus the creator of language, which he originates by addressing himself in the positive action of name-giving, according to his own reality. He describes himself as "good" because he judges that his actions are "good," not because they must be measured against a universal criterion external to the deeds in question. On the contrary, the warlike deed is good because it asserts itself as the will to power inseparable from life. By his action, the warrior sets a "distance" between others and himself. It proves his authority, his lordliness: "It was 'the good' themselves, that is to say, the noble, high-stationed and high-minded, who felt and established themselves and their actions as good, that is, of the first rank, in contradistinction to all the low, low-minded, common and plebeian. It was out of this *pathos of distance* that they first seized the right to create values and to coin names for values: what had they to do with utility!"[109]

Nietzsche considers the most telling proof of this to be found in etymology. Referring to *duonus*, the archaic form of *bonus*, he assimilates *bellum*, "war," to *duellum*, which he derives in turn from *duonum*. "Therefore," he names the *"bonus* as the man of strife, of dissention (*duo*), as the man of war."[110] Whatever the validity of the etymologies Nietzsche cites, the meaning he attributes to them lets him draw his conclusions unambiguously. "The knightly-aristocratic value judgments presupposed a powerful physicality, a flourishing, abundant, even overflowing health, together with that which serves to preserve it: war, adventure, hunting, dancing, war games, and in general all that involves vigorous, free, joyful activity."[111]

Nevertheless, if these men "go outside, where the strange, the *stranger* is found, they are not much better than uncaged beasts of prey"; if they "go *back* to the innocent conscience of the beast of prey," if they become again "triumphant monsters who perhaps emerge from a disgusting procession of murder, arson, rape, and torture, exhilarated and undisturbed of soul, as if it were no more than a students' prank, convinced they have provided the poets with a lot more material for song and praise,"[112] then the meaning of war is not exhausted in "their indifference to and contempt for security, body, life, comfort, their hair-raising cheerfulness and profound joy in all destruction, in all the voluptuousness of victory and cruelty."[113] It is not the weak, crushed on their journey as the grass is trampled by our feet, or the lamb eaten by the wolf—it is not they who are the adversaries capable of creating in the masters "the noble mode of valuation" that "acts and grows spontaneously."[114] On the contrary, the confrontation with one who is like him, with the enemy worthy of respect, defines the warrior, who has "his enemy for himself, as his mark of distinction; he can endure no other enemy than one in whom there is nothing to despise and *very much* to honor!"[115] We meet this theme of the enemy as a *peer* elaborated in most of Nietzsche's works. "'At least be my enemy!'—thus speaks true reverence," Zarathustra says; "If one wants to have a friend one must also want to wage war for him: and to wage war, one must be *capable* of being an enemy. In a friend one should still honor the enemy."[116]

The enemy's function is thus defined; it is a moral function:

One has duties only to one's peers. . . . The capacity for, and the duty of, long gratitude and long revenge—both only among one's peers—refinement in repaying, the sophisticated concept of friendship, a certain necessity for having enemies (as it were, as drainage ditches for the affects of envy, quarrelsomeness, exuberance—at bottom, in order to be capable of being good *friends*): all these are typical characteristics of noble morality.[117]

The feeling of power that wants victory finds in the enemy's resistance the opportunity to show that it is an offensive force, indifferent to the consequences it brings upon itself. "And in all decent actions, are we not deliberately indifferent to the prospect of what may happen to us?"[118] "Abundant strength wants to create, suffer, go under."[119] We cannot, it seems, speak of life, of the highest type of life, unless we also speak of untroubled daring, of the need for conquest felt by independent, privileged souls, of the *elite*, rich with the future but heedless of their lives.

Conversely, most of the herd, the mass of those who submit, being incapable of enthusiasm and affirmation, wage another kind of war that does not involve armed struggle, for that is beyond their powers. Their concern is to protect themselves against the strength they hate or envy, to wear it out by methods that deny its value, to use cleverness to promote the opposite values. The good man is henceforth the one without power, the very one who *wills*, for his will to power still exists but can now be exercised only by rejecting and negating the values of life, its dynamism, and its ever renewed power of creation. Becoming is paralyzed, replaced by abstract values that are external to living beings and that they believe to be blessed with eternity. These values, fruits of *"ressentiment,"* become the standard of moral judgment. Then goodness, justice, love have no reality except as weapons of the weak, helping them "tame the wild beast" and keep it from doing harm by teaching it guilt. "The appearance of moral scruples (in other words: the becoming-conscious of the values by which one acts) betrays a certain sickliness; strong ages and peoples do not reflect on their rights, on the principles on which they act, on their instincts and reasons."[120] According to Nietzsche, the priestly caste whose form of existence exemplifies weakness is the historic cause of the slave revolt that begins "when *ressentiment* itself becomes creative and gives birth to values: the *ressentiment* of natures that are denied the true reaction, that of deeds, and compensate themselves with an imaginary revenge."[121] It is a passive revolt, to be sure, but its effectiveness is formidable. It is carried out for the sake of "'happiness' at the level of the impotent, the oppressed, and those in whom poisonous and inimical feelings are festering, with whom it appears as essentially narcotic, drug, rest, peace."[122] And their war without the name of war ends nevertheless in victory. Their "prudence" overcomes courage, their wickedness stands against carefree action as their "culture" against "nature." For "it was on the soil of this *essentially dangerous* form of human existence, the priestly form, that man first became *an interesting animal.*"[123] But in so doing he forged himself only "an ill-constituted soul."[124] "What today constitutes *our* antipathy to 'man'?" Nietzsche asks. "*Not* fear; rather that we no longer have anything left to fear in man; that the maggot 'man' is swarming in the foreground; that the 'tame man', the hopelessly mediocre and insipid man, has already learned to feel himself as the goal and zenith, as the meaning of history, as 'higher man.' "[125]

Eternal values also end by losing credibility; humans have invented them, God is their own chimera. The "reaction" to a discovery of this kind could not belong to a creative will. "This long plenitude and sequence of breakdown, destruction, ruin, and cataclysm that is now impending— who could guess enough of it today to be compelled to play the teacher and advance proclaimer of this monstrous logic of terror, the prophet of a gloom and an eclipse of the sun whose like has probably never yet occurred on earth?"[126] Nihilism is the most despicable form the will to power can take. It overthrows idols, but from a purely destructive urge in which it is mired, having affirmed nothing but nothingness. "Nihilism," Nietzsche writes, "is a symptom that the underprivileged have no comfort left; that they destroy in order to be destroyed; that without morality they no longer have any reason to 'resign themselves'—that they place themselves on the plain of the opposite principle and also want power by *compelling* the powerful to become their hangmen."[127] This is the time of the "last man," the one who remembers human happiness and so despairs of his solitude and moans, announcing the death of man.[128]

Nietzsche denounced the modern state, the state with the "absurdly fat stomach."[129] He never stops criticizing it roundly. It is the breeding ground of nihilism, the result of the degeneration of the masters and the triumph of the herd and its egalitarian ideals. Certainly, "decadence itself is nothing *to be fought;* it is absolutely necessary and belongs to every age and every people. What should be fought vigorously is the contagion of the healthy parts of the organism."[130] Hence he does not contradict himself when he writes in the same year (1888): "The maintenance of the military state is the last means of all of acquiring or maintaining the great tradition with regard to the supreme type of man, the strong type. And all concepts that perpetuate enmity and difference in rank between states (e.g., nationalism, protective tariffs) may appear sanctioned in this light."[131]

The stealthy war that the weak wage, using as weapons ideals that perpetuate inverted values, which slowly sap the strong of the energy to assert their own values and advance past the inverted ones without hesitation—this war, despite its necessity, is a bad war. When the decomposition has gone far enough, an armed struggle such as a revolution crowns the victory of those who never before had other than the negative strength to react in imagination, to destroy a man by denigrating the power within him of affirmation and self-transcendence, the will to power, whatever its consequences. It is true that "history shows: the strong races decimate one another through war, thirst for power, adventurousness. . . . Their existence is costly. . . . Periods of profound exhaustion and torpor supervene. . . . The strong are subsequently weaker, more devoid of will, more absurd than the weak average."[132] Still, they have created their own momentum, they have left peace to "the graves" and have seized "the eternally living."[133] To them, peace is not the "goal for the world" that would become a weakly "happiness of repose." The strong have only honored "even in peace the means to new wars" and have nurtured "a mode of thought that prescribes laws for the future, that for the sake of the future is harsh and tyrannical towards itself and all things of the present; a reckless, 'immoral' mode of thought, which wants to develop both the good and the bad qualities in man to their fullest extent, because it feels it has the strength to put both in their right place—in the place where each needs the other."[134]

In this sense does "man exist before man," as Nietzsche's often-repeated phrase goes. Man does not "exist" in the sense that he has a predetermined nature that can be captured in a definition. He is never at rest in his trajectory. So Nietzsche, in an impulse that transcends itself, muses:

Suppose the strong had become master in everything, and even in moral valuation: let us draw the consequences of how they would think about sickness, suffering, sacrifice! Self-contempt on the part of the weak would be the result; they would try to disappear and extinguish themselves. And would this be *desirable*?—and would we really want a world in which the influence of the weak, their subtlety, consideration, spirituality, *pliancy* was lacking?[135]

Hence Nietzsche never speaks of a war to be waged against the triumph of the weak—it would be reactive. If, as he reminds us, decadence is "nothing to be fought," we must at least as carefully avoid identifying the deeds of the will to power, instinctively creating forms and values, with the crimes or vices that create the opposite—sickness, weakness, the rotting of strength. We must make a distinction between the healthy badness of the wild beast and the "kind of evil that manifests itself as a decadent overrefinement and stimulus, i.e. as a consequence of physical degeneration (gratification derived from cruelty, etc.)."[136] We must distinguish between the "crime" of Cesare Borgia that constitutes *virtù*[137] and the "actions which are *unworthy* of us: actions that, if regarded as typical, would reduce us to a lower class of man."[138] Between them stretches the chasm separating the two forms of the will to power, that of the strong and that of the weak, that of the masters and that of the slaves. Nietzsche condemns a confusion that is "quite natural, although its influence has been fatal: that which men of power and will are able to demand of themselves also provides a measure of that which they may permit themselves. Such natures are the antithesis of the vicious and unbridled:

although they may on occasion do things that would convict a lesser man of vice and immoderation."[139]

War appears in the many masks the will to power wears. The battle that affirms new forms of life, joyous and cruel at once,[140] is the battle that lets man transcend himself. Whether an outward battle with weapons or the inner combat that is as dangerous and sometimes as deadly, it makes of man "a rope, tied between beast and overman—a rope over an abyss,"[141] for "man is something that must be overcome."[142] This is man's *duty*, dictated to him by no morality that is not higher than the herd's. It is a morality not descended from principles that give order and meaning to the world for all eternity. It is one that leaps forth from deeds and imposes the order of its creator as long as he is capable of creation. If war and battles are necessary evils[143]—if Nietzsche was right in saying that "if a temple is to be erected, *a temple must be destroyed:* that is the law"[144]— then we should not take peace to be a final state, letting humankind at last find its truth in the blossoming of its talents. In 1888, before retreating into the evening silence of his life, so like the solitude of Zarathustra in his pale morning light, Nietzsche draws distinctions among men once again and asks,

> Are you a man with the instincts of a warrior in your system? If so, a second question arises: are you by instinct a warrior of attack or a warrior of defense? The remainder of mankind, all that is not warlike by instinct, wants peace, wants concord, wants 'freedom,' wants 'equal rights': these are only different names and stages of the same thing. . . . In the case of the born warrior, there is something like armament in his character, in his choice of states, in the development of every quality: in the first type, it is the 'weapon' that is developed best, in the latter the armor.[145]

For Nietzsche, there was never anything but the weapon, for "thus alone— thus alone, man grows to the height where lightning strikes and breaks him: lofty enough for lightning."[146]

PART TWO

Utopias of Peace

History is a nightmare from which I am trying to awake.
—James Joyce, *Ulysses*

CHAPTER 5

Conjecture on Natural Peace

The reasons philosophers think human beings are made for war are numerous, profound, and mutually supportive. Nevertheless, these reasons have not always been persuasive in the past, nor do they persuade everyone today. Humans are in the habit of waging war; it is a reality we know and live, hope for or curse. But perhaps we have only a bad habit rather than an intractably bellicose nature.

In a general way, desire seems to imply conflict, but has it not simply chosen the shortest route to gratification, despite its being the most burdensome, indeed the most tragic one? Can we not find other outlets for desire? Can we not satisfy desire under conditions that would make war seem pointless, in fact repugnant, to Cities and their citizens, making them peaceful and peace-loving forever after? Voices have spoken and continue to speak in ever greater numbers demanding peace: not a *truce*, but *peace*, when at last we would lay down our arms in order to destroy them.

We can glimpse currents of thought in philosophy that account—some quite obviously, others more subtly—for the strength of our longing for peace. All, we must admit, partake of the utopian. It is not an adequate reason to ignore them. The strength of an indisputable desire for peace should not be dismissed as a weakness without consideration. Must peace perhaps also be "conquered" by means of a reorganization of society that would be humanity's greatest creation? Has humanity merely forgot that its true nature is more peaceful than warlike? Would not war then be only the hateful result of an "essential accident" affecting nature? And would not humanity's awareness of its authentic essence allow war to vanish, first within political communities and then between nations? If on the contrary humanity is evil, is this reason enough to believe that it is incapable of recognizing that peace is in its best interest? The expectation that war will be totally eradicated probably remains a pious hope; that does not prevent us from imagining nations internally structured so that peace is absolutely enforced inside their borders and that wars that have become too dangerous are minimized outside them.

We should begin our investigation of the conditions requisite for peace with a study of such clearly defined utopias as those of Thomas More and Tommaso Campanella. More writes of peace as a thing "whereof you ought to have a thousand times more regard than of war,"[1] whereas of war he affirms that Utopians "detest and abhor war or battle as a thing very beastly, although by no kind of beasts is it practiced so much as it is by man."[2] More and Campanella provide for civil peace but cannot promise peace beyond the borders of their societies. Utopias teach us that a human being is defined by reason yet is not spontaneously peaceable. That is why attempts at enforcing peace are so oppressive. Historical societies are expressions of human desire, which in turn defines humanity and its passions. Only laws that stringently regiment the community and are enforced by constant surveillance can initiate and preserve civil peace, because, according to the utopists, such laws are emanations of reason. All in all, their estimation of human nature is pessimistic: Human beings are not good by nature; their good behavior toward each other results more from measures legislated by reason than from any natural capacity of theirs that is strong enough to evolve peacefully through its own momentum.

Must we accept Hobbes's claim after all and admit that man is by nature a wolf that preys on man? When we begin from humanity's state of nature, do we always end with the ineluctability of war? We know how historical reality led Hobbes to seek the causes of war's occurrence in a human essence left completely untrammeled in its actualization until opposed by the creation of the state. But if, contrary to Hobbes's reasoning, which infers from war an essence defined by war's passions—if such passions were not originally in our nature, perhaps our nature was initially peaceable and became inclined to war, in spite of its original character, after it had evolved into a "second nature." In that case the investigation of humanity's state of nature would be highly important; new truth about the human essence might point the way to its regeneration through the deliberate placement of men and women in conditions that foster peace. Recognition of an essence characterized by traits opposite to those observed throughout history would set the stage for a return to true human nature by means of procedures so obvious as to be universally accepted. So Rousseau believed, at any rate. Even before him, however, the hypothesis that human nature was peaceful had received some attention. A short work from the sixteenth century is of particular interest to us, although it does not claim to be a treatise on political philosophy. In the simplicity of its ideas little troubled by proofs, Etienne de La Boétie's tract *The Discourse of Voluntary Servitude* allows us to observe the method demanded by the belief that human nature was originally free of political behavior, innocent in the original sense of the word—that is, incapable of doing harm—

because no violent urge had yet stirred within it. A human would then be, by nature, beyond good and evil, as Rousseau will claim, or fundamentally good, as La Boétie believes.

In fact, this text, written in 1553, "touched by the burning breath of Anabaptism,"[3] cares less about war as such than about denouncing the political regime that instigates war. Is this a pamphlet that masks an attack on the monarchy by an attack on tyranny in general? Is it actually anarchist, identifying all forms of government with tyranny? It is also known as the *Contr'un* [Against one], which seems to favor the first hypothesis, though the title is not La Boétie's.[4] Whatever the real intention of the work, what interests us is the description of the (peaceful) state of nature and its degeneration into a (warring) political state.

La Boétie's chief concern is to show the connection between peace and a human being's natural freedom. Freedom is the individual's independence of others, the individual's nonsubmission to others, resulting, La Boétie claims, in affection and brotherhood. Whether or not La Boétie is protesting the monarchy when he speaks of tyranny, we must admit that no politically instituted government, in fact no authority of any sort, could rationally accommodate such a status from the start.

The description of human traits that we find in La Boétie borrows from both classical and Christian thought on the sociable nature of human beings. But contrary to the traditional definition, his human is not a "political animal," and he makes no allusion to a spiritual purpose in creation. Human essence is entirely explained by reference to material reality, and the person is characterized as "God's agent," where God simply stands for the natural state, with no other intention or implication. It is very significant that the description is entirely legitimized, in contrast, by an appeal to the *rights of man*. "In the first place, all would agree that, if we led our lives according to the ways intended by nature and the lessons taught by her, we should be intuitively obedient to our parents; later we should adopt reason as our guide and become slaves to nobody."[5] Natural, because given to us by nature, these rights are indefeasible, inalienable—and yet alienated from us by the usual conditions of civil communities. Because they are what defines the human's nature, to be deprived of them is to be deprived of one's humanity.

What are they? How can we recognize them and formulate them? We need only follow nature's teaching, which is so plain that it is available to whoever is willing to seek the human's first reality. When we come into the world, we know that we have parents whom we must obey until we can care for ourselves. The resemblance of La Boétie's thought to one of the commandments of traditional morality is of no consequence, for the natural obedience of children to their parents does not entail any general precept ensuring that the latter will retain power once the former have reached adulthood and, even less, that political authority has a right to the same fealty as does parental authority. On the contrary, it is noteworthy that La Boétie speaks of the natural obedience of children and not of the natural authority of parents. Obedience, moreover, is individual, "each one admitting himself to be a model,"[6] and involves no general societal obligation; it is the child's inborn nature that teaches him this obedience, without any need of parental coaching.

Nature's second lesson is that every person possesses reason. "Some native seed" of reason lies in us all, which education either cultivates or inhibits. Hence, it appears natural to us to submit to governmental power because we are accustomed to do so. To believe, however, that such submission is necessary is an error, a mistake due to reason's having been kept from proper development. Instead of "flower[ing] into virtue, . . . unable to resist the vices surrounding it, it [reason] is stifled and blighted."[7] The passions are not natural to humanity. Refusing to enter the debate as to whether reason is innate or acquired, La Boétie simply declares that some natural grain of reason is present in each human being. He thus spares himself the difficulty of facing the thorny problem of evil on the metaphysical level. The writer does not allude to original sin. The unhappiness due to our emotions and the emotions themselves result from an education typically perverted by its origin in the political relationship of command and obedience that creates the category of enemy. Passions are not the unfortunate consequence of a fall from grace, of natural weakness, or of natural viciousness. Because the human being is rational by nature, none is subject to another. Each is free, meaning not dependent on anyone and not inclined to attack anyone, as no one by nature wants to subjugate anyone. The human being's natural state is therefore a state of peace. War is against nature. It is the odious product of the loss of liberty and of servitude, by which is meant submission to a political regime. "You bring up your children," La Boétie writes, "in order that [the ruler] may confer upon them the greatest privilege he knows—to be led into his battles, to be delivered to butchery, to be made the servants of his greed and the instruments of his vengeance."[8]

The freedom constituting human nature is inseparable from the equality our identical natures confer on each of us. "Nature, handmaiden of God, governess of men, has cast us all in the same mold in order that we may behold in one another companions, or rather brothers."[9] This original brotherhood is perfectly apparent. To fail to see it is to "play blind," and this is not allowed. La Boétie's discussion of original brotherhood, interrelating liberty, equality, and fraternity, is relevant to our interests, for it makes brotherhood the basis of peace. The differences among people—strength and weakness, youth and age, dissimilar intellectual capacities—make sense only as complements of each other. Nature has not planned to place us in this world as if it were a field of battle, and has not endowed the stronger or the cleverer in order that they may act like armed brigands in a forest and attack the weaker. One should rather conclude that in distributing larger shares to some and smaller shares to others, nature has intended to give occasion for brotherly love to become manifest, some of us having the strength to give help to others who are in need of it.[10]

The natural inclination of human beings toward each other is thus a feeling, an "affection," that is an expression of their independence, of that freedom that bends no one under another's yoke. Fraternal feeling transforms individual inequalities into universal equality that grants each the rights due a rational being; and "there is nothing a human should hold more dear than the restoration of his own natural right, to change himself from a beast of burden back to a man, so to speak."[11] To be human is first of all to be a brother to humankind. The typical political relationship of protection and submission yields to a purely social relationship of mutual assistance, essentially affective in origin. The brothers are all children of one mother, nature, who loves them equally. They love each other with a love that admits of no divergence of rank. Their differences do not inspire combat or a scuffle for superiority but mutual support in which the pluses compensate the minuses. In this way each is identical to all, regardless of particular talents. Peace, not war, is natural to humanity. Cain cannot sulk over some paternal preference that Abel enjoys. God has given nature all jurisdiction; nature is "God's handmaiden" and nature is "mother." God himself, seated afar, is for all practical purposes absent and without a relation to human beings. The father's law seems to have vanished. Cain, having no reason for jealousy or envy, cannot do otherwise than help his younger brother and, if need be, share with him.

All in all, there is nothing clearer than the rights that nature has given us. "This kind mother has given us a dwelling place, has lodged us in the same house."[12] This means that there is no right of ownership but that each has equal right to everything. Because the earth belongs to all, we each have the same right to whatever of its fruits we may need. None can declare himself the legitimate owner of land that is common to all. No child can keep his mother to himself; she has the same love for each, inspiring friendship, not rivalry and greed. Common occupancy and use of the earth are the guarantors of peace; when all have a common inheritance there are no quarrels about division of property, no struggles over ownership. The theme of the natural commonality of the earth will recur frequently in anarchist writings, but it will also reappear in works of liberal thought.[13] As La Boétie presents it, it seems to have a certain Franciscan inspiration that differentiates it from traditional ideas, whether classical or medieval. In this "universal brotherhood of the human race," the family disappears, though La Boétie does not say so explicitly, and with it the need for fathers to provide for their households. At the same time, we see the disappearance of the family's spiritual purpose (to be a microcosm existing, over and beyond its economic function, for the sake of a transcendent value) in favor of a purely worldly purpose having nothing to do with the struggle for life or war but revealing the true face of peace, as La Boétie imagines it.

Nature, he says, assuredly "has fashioned us to the same model so that in beholding one another we might almost recognize ourselves."[14] This statement is so extraordinary that it must be emphasized. Each is a mirror for each, presenting the other only with an image the self. The reason Cain cannot kill Abel is that Abel, strictly speaking, does not exist, any more than Cain exists as such for Abel. Each sees only himself in the other; each is the reflection of the other. All otherness vanishes. What could set one against another, or even place them in hierarchy? The other is "another self" and never "other than myself." Without mystery, without intrinsic strangeness, deprived of the opacity that separates persons even when each is intent on being as intimate and transparent as possible, unconscious—thanks to the mirror's effect—that they necessarily occupy different spaces, brothers do not even see themselves as partners in a harmonious dialogue. There is not, strictly speaking, an exchange of words; there is no groping for a common language. Spontaneously, each says the same thing as the other. This is the point La Boétie stresses, moreover. "Since she has bestowed upon us all the great gift of voice and speech for fraternal relationship, thus achieving by the common and mutual statement of our thoughts a communion of wills . . . she has revealed in every possible manner her intention, not so much to associate us as to make us one organic whole."[15] It is worth underscoring that communication becomes communion, a fusion of brothers on the maternal breast of nature, a communion of wills. This implies that speech does not affirm individualities but a totality, yearning with a single, same voice for the same state of blissful oneness.

In real societies, regardless of the natural feeling brothers may have for each other, they are not all born at the same moment. Not only do they have individual embodiments, but they are further individualized by time, which abandons them to inescapable ontological solitude despite their identical origin. Even identical twins must come into the world one after the other and are separate, however minutely, from each other. The most intimate sexual union never dissolves the distance between two beings to the point that they become the same. In the original brotherhood imagined by La Boétie, however, there is no longer even a question of union between human beings, but only of unity. Although individuals with different abilities exist, we find no principle of individuation to separate them;

humanity is an undifferentiated whole, a syncretism where no distinctions can be made, assuring thus both freedom and happiness. That no one differs in any way from another, such is the basis of freedom and, it follows, of peace.

That we are dealing more with simple declarations—supported, besides, by examples from the animal kingdom—than with a genuine proof and serious philosophic thought does not deprive the treatise of its importance. The work's profundity lies in its presentation of the old dream of oneness that haunts us all when we confront the difficult duty of finding ourselves, of straining to grow into adult humans capable of standing alone and so ultimately of entering into authentic unions. In each of us there lingers a little of this archaic longing for the peace of that symbiosis that lasted no longer than our earliest childhood—a carefree period, more than a genuine peace, when the world took responsibility for us, a period of retreat from the need to face the dangers inevitably implied by the presence of the other. If the other can be reduced to the one, the risk of any war evaporates. But are these still human beings?

To understand humanity, it is not enough, obviously, to declare that freedom and peace lie in equality and brotherhood. Our experience of history allows us to confidently declare the opposite. La Boétie is well aware of this when he asks, "What evil chance has so denatured man that he, the only creature really born to be free, lacks the memory of his original condition and the desire to return to it?"[16] In other words, What happened to make real life into the inverse of what our original essence should have accomplished? We find no satisfactory answer. "Men . . . consider as quite natural the state into which they were born."[17] They are born into servitude and do not realize it. Perhaps, but why? We will not find out. "Custom becomes the first reason for voluntary servitude."[18] Habit is of course second nature, but it must start with a single action; we do not learn what it was or why it was taken.

La Boétie still believes he has a solution to this problem of which we will never know the origin. There is a way to give up the disastrous habits that condemn generations to servitude and war. We start by becoming aware of them. This is the task of the *intellectuals.* Though we do not find the term in the works of the magistrate poet, the function is easily identifiable, as is the role the intellectual is to play.

There are always a few, better endowed than others, who feel the weight of the yoke and cannot restrain themselves from attempting to shake it off . . . and from remembering their ancestors and their former ways. These are in fact the men who, possessed of clear minds and far-sighted spirit, are not satisfied like the brutish mass, to see only what is at their feet, but rather . . . recall the things of the past in order to judge those of the future, and compare both with their present condition. These are the ones who, having good minds of their own, have further trained them by study and learning. Even if liberty had entirely perished from the earth, such men would invent it.[19]

These are the men who are astounded at "the spectacle of a million men serving in wretchedness, their necks under the yoke, not constrained by a greater multitude than they, but simply, it would seem, delighted and charmed by the name of one man alone."[20] They are capable not only of remembering humanity's true nature but of understanding how the pyramidal structure of the government guarantees the strength of the regime.

There are in the world, then, a very small minority of "older brothers" still aware of their human essence. Clearly, the political regime does not help them in their vital work of informing others. The populace itself refuses to accept them; it is "suspicious toward one who has their welfare at heart, and gullible toward one who fools them."[21] It is capable of shedding tears for Nero and sending the thinker to the stake. The necessary awareness, nonetheless, is easy to attain and requires no military feats. La Boétie never dreams of transforming society by spilling blood. He is satisfied to preach civil disobedience. As for a tyrant or ruler, "it is not necessary to deprive him of anything, but simply to give him nothing."[22] "If nothing is yielded to them, if, without any violence, they are simply not obeyed, they become naked and undone and as nothing."[23] He constantly reiterates this theme. "He . . . for whom you go bravely to war . . . has indeed nothing more than the power that you confer upon him to destroy you. . . . How does he have any power over you except through you? . . . Resolve to serve no more, and you are at once freed."[24] "Freed" means returned to a state of nature, to its unity, its peace. This is the only answer we can find here to the practical question—which La Boétie does not ask—of what will happen next, once the regime is destroyed and the bureaucracy dismantled. Will those in power accept disobedience without reacting? Are there not very effective ways of obtaining compliance from a population that is starving because of the general chaos? Only if nature turns into a good fairy and magically erases the difficulties of the transition from a political state to a reestablished state of nature.

We may wonder whether we haven't arrived at a typical utopia of peace by a new route. Instead of envisaging a state under the most stringent laws in some distant place—nowhere—in the peace of an egalitarian and brotherly communism of free people, imagination has us regress to our original state, our natural state, which assuages all longings for the life of bliss in harmony with nature, without another rending the perfect union of the child with its mother—an original state of peace. "The author," Henri Baudrillart comments, "seems imbued with the naive illusion that mankind can live without laws or leaders while realizing a paradise of innocence and bliss on earth."[25]

There is a desire that corresponds to such an illusion—the desire of the infant experiencing objects of satisfaction as part of himself. Strangely, this form of fusional possession is also, at bottom, the desire of the adult in our own societies. But nature has withdrawn. In its place are an endless variety of stimuli to greed, provoking rivalry and, inevitably, recourse to war. That is what history is really like, as we experience it and as it has been seen to be since time began.

There is also a method that suits the belief in original peace, providing fantasy its springboard for the leap beyond history. This method is "conjecture." Surely not the least of the merits of this little work is its use of a word destined to a rich future. We will find it in Rousseau and again in Kant. In their works, the conjectural method will produce political rules of conduct with claims to logical justification, but the rules will not be the same because they will derive from different conjectures and will be intended for different purposes; nevertheless, the three approaches are united by close methodological kinship. For our purposes, we must try to understand the significance and justifications of the conjectural method as it struggles with the problem of the status of war and peace.

La Boétie's little work has detained us because of its unsophisticated demonstration of the method at work. "Let us therefore understand by logic, if we can, how it happens that this obstinate willingness to submit has become so deeply rooted in a nation that the very love of liberty now seems no longer natural."[26] We know that war, in La Boétie's view, is due to the loss of natural freedom. Far from being the necessary implement of freedom (as will later be the case for Hegel, for example), neither is war the offspring of freedom nor yet the child of instinct. Although La Boétie writes under the influence of a civilization that, despite its incipient dissolution, is still Christian, he does not take freedom to mean the capacity for choice. We do not choose between good and evil, obeying divine command or rejecting it. If men and women are estranged from nature, it is because of a "misfortune" that remains unnamed. La Boétie's conjecture does not bear on the reason man has become thus "denatured," as he puts it; it bears on his natural attributes: the freedom of one human being from another and the equality of human beings, realized because of their brotherhood. These are the necessary conditions for the original peace that we have the duty to recover: "Let us therefore learn while there is yet time, let us learn to do good."[27] Civil disobedience is the obligation of whoever wishes to recover peace in all societies of the human race. The conjecture that declares man to be naturally sociable and peaceable ends, with no depth of proof, by enjoining anarchy. Although a solid foundation is wanting, for that very reason the threads joining conjecture to conclusion appear more clearly: Every conjecture is expressed in the *conditional* mood of the verb, every description in the *indicative*, and every duty in the *imperative*. In a treatise with aims that are more polemic than philosophical, La Boétie clearly signaled his shifts from one mode to the other but without justifying them. His successors made an infinitely more solid use of the method La Boétie had ingenuously sketched, by conjecturing an abstract human creature, removed from all the conditions of real life, then calling upon the historical human to perform a task derived only from their concept of a hypothetical human. Their approach has been so important in history that history has taken up their way of thinking. A belief in peace before history or peace after it—the attempt to understand war and peace to the advantage of the latter, expecting definitive peace within social and political communities or among states—is only today beginning to weaken, as must any belief in a political system with even the slightest utopian element when we finally discover that, in the final analysis, it has been an illusion.

CHAPTER 6

Original Peace
and Civil Peace

Experience teaches us much more about war than about peace, even though the misfortunes of war, which can be only too often observed, bring us to desire peace. Is peace nonetheless bound up with human nature? If we reject the utopia of a La Boétie, who sees each as the most intimate brother of his fellow, can we discover through philosophical inquiry a state of peace that determines our essence before our existence? Knowledge of this kind may be the guiding thread that we must hold fast if we are to find our way, under present, actual conditions, to a genuine civil peace and, as far as possible, to international peace. To the extent that human nature is in fact peaceable at its origin, there is a chance that we will accept the return to primordial peace as a duty. If, on the contrary, human nature is, as Hobbes thought, basically combative, then we comprehend that we are trying to make the existential situation peaceful—that is, endurable—by creating institutions to impose at least temporary peace on those who could not possibly survive without relief from the ceaseless war of each against all.

In one way or another, all the social contract philosophers have invoked a state of nature for humanity and have pointed out its features. Though it is Locke who describes it as the original life of the human race, the state of nature plays the identical role of benchmark for all, however different— even contradictory—the attributes assigned to it. The question is always how, on the basis of an acknowledged essence, we can account for our actual existence and set it right. But, as we have seen, if for Hobbes, the logic of essence shapes an existence made wretched by a state of war, for La Boétie and Rousseau, the logic of essence would have brought about a blessed and peaceful existence if nothing had obstructed it.

La Boétie is silent as to the reasons persuading him that peace, and not war, typifies a being created by nature within a brotherly assembly. Did uncritical acceptance of biblical tradition bias his conjecture? Probably. Rousseau, in contrast, defends the conjectural method much more astutely and extracts every ounce of what it has to offer. We find in him a clear awareness of the problems involved in forming a hypothesis and deducing indisputable conclusions from it. At the same time, he makes explicit the passage from conditional to indicative and then to imperative. Not only does he avoid obscuring it, but he goes on to justify it. There is no appeal to historical evidence. Rousseau knows that it can bring him no incontrovertible information about the essence he seeks. The reader is clearly warned, "Let us therefore begin by putting aside all the facts, for they have no bearing on the question."[1] Rousseau is not going to reason from historical facts, whether reported or directly observed, to other, new facts that can be induced as the antecedents of those accepted as true. "The investigations that may be undertaken concerning this subject should not be taken for historical truths, but only for hypothetical and conditional reasoning, better suited to shedding light on the nature of things than on pointing out their true origin, like those our physicists make every day with regard to the formation of the world."[2]

Here is a form of investigation in which hypothesis is called to play a basic role in helping us understand the nature of things, that is, the nature of human history as we know it and live it. From the hypothesis about the character of our origins, we should be able to deduce why so much of history is given over to war and to the disasters it brings even upon the victors. This is why Rousseau is not contradicting himself when he goes on to say, "O man, whatever country you may be from, whatever your opinions may be, listen: here is your history, as I have thought to read it, not in the books of your fellowmen, who are liars, but in nature, who never lies."[3] History is the set of unfolding events that we have finally illuminated, thanks to acts of hypothetical and conditional reasoning that enable us to understand original essence.

The method is defensible for two reasons. On the one hand, religion "does not forbid us to form conjecture, drawn solely from the nature of man and the beings that surround him concerning what the human race could have become, if it had been left to itself."[4] This means that we are neither impious nor indulging in fantasy when we investigate the kind of existence that must follow logically from a reconstruction of the original character of human essence. The method is in fact analogous, on the other hand, to the one used by physicists, and it is especially for this reason that it is justified. How do physicists proceed in order to explain the origin of the world on the basis of what they know of its present structure and laws? They have no way of running an experiment. They therefore work through hypotheses that are acceptable according to how rigorously they are related to what is known to be true. A hypothesis can be considered verified (and thereupon loses its hypothetical character) when it accounts for a significant number of apparently unrelated facts and at the same time does not contradict any law that has already been proved. It thus plays the role of general explanatory principle, a basis for logical connections among facts that formerly had no apparent relation or meaning.

In the seventeenth and eighteenth centuries, the method of the natural sciences was applied to history, and political philosophy did not fail to take advantage of this use. The concept of a state of nature, a hypothesis destined to be transformed into a logical principle for understanding history, came into favor because of the interest in a rational explanation for the creation of human societies. In Rousseau's conclusion to the first part of the *Discourse on the Origin of Inequality Among Men*, in which he has defined the human being's natural attributes, he applies the conjectural method to the beginning of human history, at the same time justifying it yet again:

> I admit that, since the events I have to describe could have taken place in several ways, I cannot make a determination among them except on the basis of conjecture. But over and above the fact that these conjectures become reasons when they are the most probable ones that a person can draw from the nature of things and the sole means that a person can have of discovering the truth, the consequences I wish to deduce from mine will not thereby be conjectural, since, on the basis of the principles I have just established, no other system is conceivable that would not furnish me with the same results, and from which I could not draw the same conclusions.[5]

Here is a clear summary of the place of the hypothesis in the scientific method, of its heuristic value, and of its legitimacy. At the same time the domain of the hypothesis is specified: It includes and makes sense of history.

We must nonetheless be aware that physicists' hypotheses regarding the structure of the universe contain no value judgments. They have a role solely in research and in explanation. They make sense of phenomena by relating them to each other, but the system that they help construct implies no evaluations. Facts as such are not good, bad, useful, harmful, desirable, or frightening. They *are*; and the physicist's entire task consists in finding facts and understanding causes and effects. Physics is a purely descriptive science. Whether we subsequently decide to protect ourselves against the series of facts or to put them to use is not as such a problem for physicists.

The conjectures of philosophers have a very different character. They spring from value judgments regarding the present condition of society, and they also become the source of value judgments about society's future condition, even when philosophers try to avoid such a usage, as do our modern social scientists. Rousseau judges, for example, that the history of mankind—at least until the "social contract," which he has not yet described in 1755—is the deplorable fruit of the degeneration of human nature. He states very plainly, "It remains for me to consider and to bring together the various chance happenings that were able to perfect human reason while deteriorating the species, make a being evil while rendering it habituated to the ways of society, and, from so distant a beginning, finally bring man and the world to the point where we see them now."[6] The value judgment is easily discerned. History, which to Rousseau means the history of the progress of reason, is simultaneously the history of the birth and spread of evil.[7]

War is one of the most fearsome forms that evil takes. Does it result from the development of reason? Can anything be done about it? To learn Rousseau's answers, we must begin with the hypothesis by which Rousseau, having first consulted the facts, arrives at the truth about humanity's essence—which its existence has probably never expressed. For, as Rousseau admits, he is seeking "understanding of a state which no longer exists, which perhaps never existed, which probably never will exist, and yet about which it is necessary to have accurate notions in order to judge properly our own present state."[8] The normative role of the state of nature could not be put more clearly.

Let us inquire into the sources of Rousseau's hypothesis and into his reasons for asserting that our original nature was peaceful. In speaking of how he came to write the *Discourse on the Influence of Learning and Art*, he often told how overwhelmed he was when, during a visit to Denis Diderot, he learned of the contest on that subject sponsored by the Academy of Dijon. His whole being was shaken, to the point of illness, at the vision of what humanity had been before it had been shaped by society and history.[9] Rousseau always taught, in fact, that an individual can only know what he has first experienced. Exceptional beings, miraculously preserved from depravity far from city life, owe it to a temperament still attuned to nature's voice (which the Savoyard priest discerns in that "divine instinct," conscience) that they have experienced the defining human reality within themselves in its original purity. Is Rousseau among them? Answering his critics in a note to the *Discourse on the Origin of Inequality*, Rousseau ironically exhorts them to recapture their "ancient and first innocence." "Go into the woods," he tells them, "and lose the sight and memory of the crimes of your contemporaries," for to them "the heavenly voice has not made itself heard." Has Rousseau heard it? Of course—although he writes with seeming modesty, "As for men like me, whose passions have destroyed their original simplicity forever, who can no longer nourish themselves on herbs and nuts, nor do without laws and rulers," they will scrupulously obey the laws, "but they will nonetheless despise a constitution . . . from which . . . there will always arise more real calamities than seeming advantages."[10] Even though mired in the filth of historical societies, does he not sense the criteria by which they should be judged? It is apparent that we cannot speak of the conscience in respect to human beings in a state of nature. The conscience, as its name hints, is a kind of consciousness. Though it is not primarily a form of thought, it nevertheless requires something more than mere sensation. Yet through it, those who indeed can hear its voice find their way back to their essence, beyond the aberrations of egotism, the envies it gives rise to, and the conflicts that inevitably follow upon it.

The question remains, What does Rousseau mean by the proposition that human nature was originally peaceful? Is humanity fundamentally predisposed to peace? The second discourse, the *Discourse on Inequality*, contains a much richer and more nuanced description than we find in *Voluntary Servitude*. By nature, the individual does not live—Rousseau considers this an essential point—in conditions that lead to confrontation. The state of nature is in fact a state of dispersion, where a human being comes into contact with others only by chance and not out of need to do so. We know that Rousseau's chief theme is *solitude*.[11] Humans are born virtually alone, they live alone, they die alone, and this situation is their joy and good fortune.[12] The chance meeting of a male and a female assures the survival of the species, without a pairing, a family, either setting the stage for the sexual act or resulting from it. Once weaned, the child easily does without its mother; their separation elicits no anxiety. Solitude is serene because all are dimly aware that on solitude depends their most valuable possession—independence. This is the fundamental meaning of the word *freedom* as Rousseau uses it. "Man is born free," he proclaims at the beginning of the *Social Contract*. We must understand this to mean that the natural state of a human being is to be independent of other human beings. Solitude guarantees independence much more surely than does Locke's natural law that lays upon all the moral obligation to respect the natural freedom of each.[13] Natural law, as we understand it in Rousseau, has no direct bearing on the (anyway nonexistent) relations among individuals. Though totally beyond our awareness, it drives us to instinctive self-preservation, accomplished without harm to any other, because the state of dispersion assures tranquility and an adequate, if frugal, living.[14] Under such conditions, how could a war break out? What sort of troops could it have, what sort of stakes, what sort of rewards?

Certainly Rousseau's description, emphasizing the solitude that underlies his definition of essence, is more an analysis of the negative conditions of peace than of a genuine propensity for peace. Fights between individuals do occur. They can never involve more than two protagonists, it is clear, because the solitary life excludes the possibility of social organization. What is more, the fights are short and without consequences. "Savage man, when he has eaten, is at peace with the whole of nature and the friend of all his fellow men." We see that friendship consists simply in not starting fights. "Is it," Rousseau continues, "a matter of disputing his meal? He will never come to blows over it without first comparing the difficulty of winning with that of finding his sustenance elsewhere, and as pride does not enter into the fight, it is ended by a few fisticuffs; the victor eats, the vanquished goes off to seek better luck elsewhere, and all is pacified."[15]

Aside from the rare occasions when two individuals put their lives at risk by engaging in physical combat, the peaceful state is the norm in a state of nature that knows no need of inventions nor even of the slightest alteration of nature. If we strip humankind of all the artificial devices that it has been obliged to contrive over the course of time and if we do not claim for it any supernatural endowment, we are left with what the human being is in his essence—an animal "satisfying his hunger under an oak tree, quenching his thirst at the first stream, finding his bed at the foot of the same tree that supplied his meal; and thus," says Rousseau, "all his needs are satisfied."[16] In this description, Rousseau is not so much mentally reconstructing what the human race might have been at its initial appearance on earth as he is evoking the discovery made by our inner sensibility when it almost miraculously happens to be left to itself, to its proper task of guiding the intellect, undistracted by the endless calculations that it has been continually making in partnership with the passions. So the solitary being is content with little. "Twenty steps into the forest" suffice to distance him from one who is such a freak of nature as to try to subjugate him, in the event of a chance meeting.[17]

When it takes the form of serene meditation, the same inner sense leads us to another principle that is prior to reason: Human beings have "a natural repugnance to seeing any sentient being, especially our fellow man, perish or suffer."[18] What Rousseau calls "the force of natural pity" is what "tempers the ardor he has for his own well-being."[19] This is by no means an impulse that inclines individuals to each other or leads them into a social existence that would end their solitude. As a beast turns aside to avoid trampling another beast that has fallen and cannot rise, so a person, Rousseau repeats, has "an innate repugnance to seeing his fellow men suffer. . . . The pure movement of nature prior to all reflection . . . which, by moderating in each individual the activity of the love of oneself, contributes to the mutual preservation of the entire species."[20]

This is the impulse that Rousseau will mention again, in rebuttal of Locke, when he comments on the writings of the Abbé de Saint-Pierre in the short work entitled, *The State of War Is Born from the Social State*.

If natural law were inscribed only on human reason it would hardly be capable of directing most of our actions. But it is also indelibly engraved in the human heart. It is from the heart that natural law speaks to man more powerfully than all the precepts of philosophers. It is from there that it cries out to him that he may not sacrifice the life of his fellow man except to save his own, and that even when he sees himself obliged to do so, he cannot but feel a sense of horror at the idea of killing in cold blood.[21]

In humanity's primitive state, natural law—of which we are unconscious—incites each to preservation of self but does not incline any to kill another. The voice of law speaks through our every deed, without need of our being distinctly aware of it. In historical societies, it cries out within the hell of passions and wars, but its call is quickly drowned out; nearly always inaudible, it still continues in the emptiness and dark of hearts that have forgotten the truth of humankind.

Pity and dispersion complement each other admirably to secure the peace of a creature whose reason is not yet active because nature originally provides for all its needs—very simple needs, it is true, but the only vital ones. This "ingenious machine,"[22] the human being, differs from other animals, however, by its ability to choose behaviors that are not rigidly repetitive. But in the state of nature, that an individual "contributes, as a free agent, to his own operations"[23] is of no consequence except for finding a new food when a familiar one is lacking, without, though, producing any. To trap a hare rather than to pluck a fruit is not the same as inventing cooking, plowing a field, sowing and harvesting wheat, or raising rabbits. Freedom of choice does not separate the human being from nature and its motherly nurturance. At one with nature, the individual owns it entirely yet owns nothing; for nature belongs to all, although without their knowledge. The utopists saw in deliberate, organized common ownership a protection of peace. Rousseau believes that peace is native to us because each of us unwittingly owns everything, no one having the idea of enclosing land, deciding to say, "This is mine."[24]

So peace is no more threatened than is the original state given us in a naturally stable equilibrium. "Since the state of nature," Rousseau says, "is the state in which the concern for our self-preservation is the least prejudicial to that of others, that state was consequently the most appropriate for peace and the best suited for the human race."[25]

What history calls war—that is, the clash of two armed forces for conflicting purposes of ideology, economics, geography, religion, or pure prestige—cannot happen unless the more or less well understood interests of each side are put into words. Even political doublespeak, alienated language par excellence, is a form of speech, and speech in general is far from always being communication, the attempt to understand another. The language of politics especially proliferates every type of verbal perversion. Lies, boasts, threats, righteous indignation, insult, abuse, slander, all kinds of foul insinuation become arms in the cold war, precede the killing war, accompany it—and too often conclude it by treaties resonant with reasons for future wars. It is not natural, Rousseau believes, for humans to speak. We need only a cry, unechoed by another's, for expressing any physical distress. No one says "I," no one says "thou." There is no "we." The dangerous attack that the pronoun "they" may suggest is unknown. Consequently, there is nothing imaginary either. The past is not burdensome; the future not frightening. We have known no hostility against which we must learn to defend ourselves; there is nothing alarming on the horizon that we must prepare against. Rousseau says in regard to original man: "His imagination depicts nothing to him; his heart asks nothing of him. His modest needs are so easily found at hand . . . that he can have neither foresight nor curiosity. . . . His soul, agitated by nothing, is given over to the single feeling of his own present existence, without any idea of the future, however near it may be."[26] He has, then, neither idea nor image nor even a suspicion of death. Knowing to what extent war plays on death's fascination and terror, we easily grant that the person without cognizance of death can know nothing of war either and so is living in peace.[27]

Caught in an eternal present, the human being is the happy, sturdy child of a generous mother who gives him *fellows* without requiring that he treat them as *brothers* and without his having to fear—or hope—that they will become his enemies. As early as 1775, Rousseau says of pity what he will again say several years later:

> With passions so minimally active and such a salutary restraint, being more wild than evil, and more attentive to protecting themselves from the harm they could receive than tempted to do harm to others, men were not subject to very dangerous conflicts. Since they had no sort of intercourse among themselves; since, as a consequence, they knew neither vanity, nor deference, nor esteem, nor contempt; since they had not the slightest notion of mine and thine, nor any true idea of justice; since they regarded the acts of violence that could befall them as an easily redressed evil and not as an offense that must be punished; and since they did not even dream of vengeance except perhaps as a knee-jerk response right then and there, like the dog that bites the stone that is thrown at him, their disputes would rarely have had bloody consequences, if their subject had been no more sensitive than food.[28]

Without sexual rivalry, which exists no more than do disappointment in love or surges of vanity from any cause, there is no occasion for personal war and, it goes without saying, none for international war. On the contrary, it is peace that is the essential state of a being who is exactly as independent as all others of the species. Freedom and equality are not part of humanity's awareness, but they are never in conflict with each other. What does it matter to anyone to be stronger than another? The natural distribution of beings who have no need of each other, who hardly encounter each other, who do not speak together, and whose "desires do not go beyond [their] physical needs"[29] simultaneously secures their mutual independence, that is, their freedom, and the mutual equality of their situations. Rousseau stresses the autonomy of all individuals, their self-sufficiency, their lack of dependence on all except nature, which provides them with every necessity of life. "Since the bonds of servitude are formed merely from the mutual dependence of men and the reciprocal needs that unite them, it is impossible to enslave a man without having first put him in the position of being incapable of doing without another. This being a situation that did not exist in the state of nature, it leaves each person free of the yoke, and renders pointless the law of the strongest."[30]

We understand, in addition, that when there is nothing to produce, reason is not needed. It is not yet awake. It remains in a state of potentiality—or "perfectibility"—that cannot be realized without the concept formation and communication that both require and define speech. It would anyway be pointless, because everything is provided. Having nothing to defend and nothing to desire, why would free and equal individuals begin wars? Why would peace not be natural to them?

> Wandering in the forests, without industry, without speech, without dwelling, without war, without relationships, with no need for his fellow men, and correspondingly with no desire to do them harm, perhaps never even recognizing any of them individually, savage man, subject to few passions and self-sufficient, had only the sentiments and enlightenment appropriate to that state; he felt only his true needs, took notice of only what he believed he had an interest in seeing; and . . . his intelligence made no more progress than his vanity.[31]

Such is Rousseau's conclusion as he sums up the traits of the human's essence and illustrates them by the description of an existence that never was but that accounts for the *logic* of the manifestation of the essence. Only a heart returned to its primal purity can lead the one fortunate enough to hear its message to discover the original reality of nature's children, whom civilizations have so perverted that "the human race, vilified and desolated," has sunk to "the most horrible state of war . . . battles, murders, reprisals that make nature tremble and offend reason, and all those horrible prejudices that rank the honor of shedding human blood among the virtues."[32] We recall the passage in which Rousseau, commenting on the writings of the Abbé de Saint-Pierre, paints an unforgettable picture of war: "I see a miserable people groaning under an iron yoke. . . . I see fire and flames, deserted countryside, pillaged villages. . . . I hear a terrible noise. . . . Before me is the panorama of murder—ten thousand slaughtered men, the dead piled up in heaps."[33] Compare the scene depicted here to the silence, the sylvan happiness, the peaceful simplicity of the natural human being.

How did a being born for peace, living in solitude and innocence, reach the opposite situation, as even the earliest remaining evidence bears witness? The answer is simple: Ownership destroyed our primitive equality, imposing the law of the strongest through the subjugation of the weak, whereas the rich thought only of increasing their wealth by warring with one another. Undoubtedly. But the question remains *how* we exchanged the satisfactions of our dispersion, the ignorance of thine and mine, for society and the ownership of both necessary and superfluous goods. Rousseau addresses this problem. Unlike La Boétie, he gives the reasons existence has not evolved in accord with its essence. They are many and, all in all, somewhat vague, but their character is important. Without actually saying so, Rousseau clearly absolves humankind of the stain of original sin. Humanity has no responsibility for its own downfall. The actual events matter little; what counts is that evil came from without, that it broke in on the calm and happy harmony that should originally have united the human being and nature. In other words, though in essence made to live peacefully in separation, independence, frugality, and an equality of condition that allowed of no disputes, human nature always lacked the material, geographic, climatic, and other conditions that would have ensured it an existence congruent with its true being. The environment, as we would say today, was not favorable. A nature suited to the truth of human beings was lacking.

Nonetheless, Rousseau never blames nature. It is no more guilty of evil than is humanity. He does not share romanticism's ambivalence toward nature. He could never have written, "We call you mother, yet you are a tomb."[34] What seems a misfortune to humans is merely lawful determinism to nature. "When the earth is left to its natural fertility and covered with immense forests that were never mutilated by the axe, it offers storehouses and shelters at every step to animals of every species."[35] But there have occurred what Rousseau calls "those singular and fortuitous combinations of circumstances . . . which might very well never have taken place."[36] He constantly evokes "new circumstances,"[37] "different risks,"[38] "the chance coming together of several unconnected causes,"[39] "various chance happenings."[40] He refers to "nature's obstacles . . . differences in soils, climates and seasons . . . barren years, long and hard winters, hot summers that consume everything,"[41] thunder, a volcano.[42] He rarely goes into more detail, but the scale of factors that are always external clearly is meant to teach us less about the power of the cause of evil than about its indifference to human nature. "Great floods and earthquakes surrounded the inhabited area with water or precipices. Upheavals of the globe detached parts of the mainland and broke them into islands."[43] In general, evil is always the outcome of "some fatal chance happening that, for the common good, ought never to have happened."[44]

This enumeration of some of Rousseau's expressions underscores the author's intended point: If humanity's existence has not manifested its peaceful essence, humanity is not to blame. In its essence, in fact, freedom is only each one's independence from any other. It is not defined by the acceptance or rejection of any prohibition or divine law, nor by recognition or rejection of the status of a creature submissive to the Creator or in rebellion against him, nor by obedience or disobedience to a moral law identified as the law of reason. But freedom is also, it is true, all the possibilities that an existence in accord with essence would not have needed to actualize. Perfectibility is primarily the capacity human beings have *not* to exist in accord with their essence, *not* to let themselves die like a diplodocus, deprived of conditions they should have had. Throwing off its lethargy, perfectibility creates an artificial environment that permits it to survive, though necessarily entailing, we must admit, other consequences: Because human contact has become necessary as the one condition indispensable to the growth of perfectibility, what might have been only natural history becomes history—the disastrous history of human societies whose life is internal conflicts and wars.

Although it is because of external circumstances that essence cannot be realized in complete accord with its attributes, we must not therefore infer that the peace inherent in essence results from the *goodness* of human nature under conditions of solitude. Rousseau does sometimes speak of the "goodness" of the primitive human, but he writes much more convincingly that "men in that state, having among themselves no type of moral relations or acknowledged duties, could be neither good nor evil, and had neither vices nor virtues. . . . Savages are not evil precisely because they do not know what it is to be good."[45] We can more accurately say of natural man, then, not that he is good but that he is innocent, in the original sense of the word. He does no harm to his fellow because in the circumstances of the state of nature he is incapable of inventing evil. Peace is the fruit of an indifference and ingenuousness that contain no impulse to evil. Evil, in contrast, is an intention; it implies awareness and an active reason. If Rousseau happens to speak of original humanity as good, it is because its innocence is so far from the depravity of human history that it can be referred to as goodness, though strictly speaking it is merely peaceful neutrality.

Men and women, then, have never had the chance to live the peaceable life that Rousseau describes in the second *Discourse*. The value of his conjectures on the unknown beginnings of the history of human societies—their prehistory—lies in that they make quite apparent the innate repugnance humans feel for communal life, its restrictions, and its toil. As soon as external pressures no longer prevail and survival is momentarily ensured, the group scatters, each returning as best as she or he can to what best suits her or him—independence, leisure, and peace. It took centuries, perhaps hundreds of centuries, before outward conditions forced men and women to join into groups, to form the stable communities in which we now live.

Throughout what some have called a philosophy of history,[46] Rousseau analyzes the progress of reason and of the social forms it gives rise to; he shows how perfectibility, a mere potential of no use in the state of nature, develops and functions in order to adapt humanity to circumstances that would otherwise forbid it all hope of survival. Reason is the capacity of humans who—in contrast with animal races that have died out because of the inflexibility of instinct—modify for their use what they are given. In this way they profoundly alter (sometimes to their own disadvantage) situations that would bring them only an unreliable subsistence or inexorable death. Reason awakes, as Rousseau demonstrates, with language, that is, when individuals gather together.

We might expect that the improvement of reason, at first necessarily technical, would not be prejudicial to peace. It is true that humans will not be living in accord with the basic traits of their essence, but perfectibility, the seed of reason, is natural. Why does reason's development put an end to peace and bring about our ever more terrible wars? It is because people, now conscious and able to reason, learn to observe one another and make comparisons once they are in permanent contact. "Each one began to look at the others and to want to be looked at himself, and public esteem had a value."[47] In place of the natural self-love that drives us only to stay alive, there is a passion. Like all passions, it can only develop through the joint action of reason, imagination, and memory, which transform a simple urge by giving it self-awareness. "Self love [*amour de soi*] is a natural sentiment which prompts every animal to watch over its conservation. . . . Pride [*amour propre*] is only a relative, artificial sentiment born in society, a sentiment which prompts each individual to attach more importance to himself than to anyone else, which inspires all the injuries men do to themselves and others."[48] It is even more out of self-love than fear of deprivation, born of the ability to imagine a future, that people try to get *not* what survival requires but what distinguishes them in the sight of others and hence in their own sight. Anxiety over seeming less esteemed, desire to be more esteemed—here is the origin of humans' struggle with one another to have the signs of a superiority that, though illusory, will create the value of life, at the risk of life, throughout history. To seize land, which by nature originally belonged to all, to seize more than is needed for the satisfaction of natural requirements, to commerce in the fruits of the earth, to acquire objects without practical value, then to dwell in cities in luxury and ostentation—these are enterprises demanding the submission of many individuals to the one who encloses a plot of ground and wants to keep and enlarge it.[49] Domination and boundless vanity on the one hand, poverty and envy on the other—the conditions of war are ingrained in the social state. When a person or group succeeds in gaining control, overpowers others, and uses them as pride and the passion for domination dictate, civil war and foreign war are manifesting reason's growth, made inevitable by circumstances beyond humanity's control.

In this way Rousseau can show that humanity is innocent of its own ills and yet say that "most of our ills are of our own making, and that we could have avoided nearly all of them by preserving the simple, regular and solitary lifestyle prescribed to us by nature."[50] The tragedy is that, although not to blame for its disappearance, we were not able to preserve it. With means that nature gave us in a latent form, we have had to invent what nature did not require—reason. Departure from a state of nature was forced on humanity by nature itself, by its inability to sustain us; no original sin, as we have said, drove us from the paradise that, given our essence, should have been our existence. Still, although perfectibility as an essential quality is guiltless, does it develop in such a way that it is tantamount to an original sin once natural self-love becomes that artificial perversion of itself, pride? "Madmen who continually complain of nature," exclaims Rousseau, "know that all your evils proceed from yourselves!"[51]

If we except a time we have no memory of but that Rousseau calls "the veritable youth of the world,"[52] history is a history only of evil, culminating in wars linked to the aspirations and inventions of reason. It is in this sense that humanity is the cause of evil without being guilty of evil, even though for Rousseau reason is identical to freedom; for reason is the capacity (of which only the seed, perfectibility, is given by nature) for emerging from the natural order and creating the specifically human order, the order of culture.[53] But like everything human, culture cannot be judged unequivocally. On the one hand, it is the formation of a world where human beings encircled by death can live and flourish, palliating nature's deficiencies and defying its threats while making use of nature in material and intellectual works unknown there. Yet on the other hand, culture is the accumulation of superfluities of every kind for which human beings kill each other.

What are we to think of the circumstances that obliged humankind to transform its nature in order to survive, at the same time making a frightful tragedy of its history? Humans were not, by nature, beings made for war. Have they become so, and is this irreversible? In speaking of perfectibility, Rousseau himself remarks that

> it would be sad for us to be forced to agree that this distinctive and almost unlimited faculty is the source of all man's misfortunes; that this is what, by dint of time, draws him out of that original condition in which he would pass tranquil and innocent days; that this is what, through centuries of giving rise to his enlightenment and his errors, his vices and his virtues, eventually makes him a tyrant over himself and nature.[54]

To be sure, no one could have affected the circumstances that made perfectibility's opportunities: Who is responsible for an earthquake? Should we be glad for those circumstances or deplore them? Rousseau gives his answer in the *Social Contract*. Speaking of the social, political state, he says,

> Although in this state [man] deprives himself of several of the advantages belonging to him in the state of nature, he regains such great ones. His faculties are exercised and developed, his ideas are broadened, his feelings are ennobled, his entire soul is elevated to such a height that if the abuse of this new condition did not often lower his status to beneath the level he left, he ought constantly to bless the happy moment that pulled him away from it forever and which transformed him from a stupid, limited animal into an intelligent being and a man.[55]

The "fatal chance happenings" denounced in 1755 have become the "happy moment" of 1762.[56] For by this date Rousseau believes he has found the remedy for the abuses of the new condition, in which reason's progress is "in appearance so many steps toward the perfection of the individual, and in fact toward the decay of the species."[57] Peace becomes a certainty within the City, thanks to the "social contract." As long as the contract holds, the individual, now a citizen, reclaims in large part the truth of his original nature and the advantages of the human condition in which, as we shall see, reason and freedom are the race's defining traits. Though the civil state is inevitable because existential conditions are incompatible with the human essence—"the human race would perish," Rousseau says, "if it did not alter its mode of existence"[58]—this state nonetheless poses a problem, which can be solved if we set forth its given elements clearly: The peaceful life depends on each person's independence from others. It has nothing to do with the brutal submission that results from the usual inequitable—though indispensable—contract that the rich force on the poor by promising them a misleading security in exchange for their obedience.[59] The independence that was natural in the original state of dispersion must be created in the environment of daily human contacts. But we must safeguard its existence by preventing anyone so tempted from taking advantage of an individual or group incapable of self-defense.

At the same time, the security of human beings who are free and equal in rights, as nature had made them, must be guaranteed by a convention, a "law" of coexistence, because nature no longer guarantees their security by scattering them. It is up to reason—natural in origin, artificial in its development—to find a form of political organization that respects humanity's true, original nature and at the same time gives it the happy historical existence it has never been able to have. Rousseau articulates the terms of a "problem"—the question that must be answered, the elements or givens that must be related in such a way that the solution appears as the result of unassailable logic. "Find a form of association which defends and protects with all common forces the person and goods of each associate, and by means of which each one, while uniting with all, nevertheless obeys only himself, and remains as free as before."[60] In other words, as it is necessary to give up the solitude that would have maintained our *natural* peace, we must find a way to provide for *civil* peace by preserving, in existence, the fundamental traits of our essence. Rousseau later formulates a second need—to establish as nearly as possible a state of affairs that provides for "small states to be given enough force to resist the large ones."[61]

Rousseau showed that the societies that have evolved over time are indescribably chaotic associations in which technical reason has created every instrument of enslavement and war, because its purpose was initially dictated by the urgency of accidental situations that overwhelmed the human race, then by the passions spawned within human relationships. It is out of the question to hope for a return to the beginning of history: "Peace and innocence left us forever, before we had tasted their delights."[62] But instead of letting history plunge down its own dangerous path (which could not have been other than dangerous because reason was still only a potential), armed with a reason now fully developed, we can try to discover what sort of political organization, though "manufactured," will yet be able to respect natural traits. "I suppose that men have reached the point where obstacles that are harmful to their maintenance in the state of nature gain the upper hand on . . . the forces that each individual can bring to bear to maintain himself in that state."[63]

The problem that reason must resolve is this: In nature human beings are free and are equal to every other because each lives in solitude; each knows only a state of peace. It being agreed that by definition the social state eliminates solitude, how can it preserve freedom, equality, and peace? True, Rousseau is more interested in freedom than in peace when he states the problem of the *Social Contract*. But civic peace will be a direct consequence of the solution. A caricature of peace already exists in the one-sided contract between the wealthy and the impoverished, the mighty and the weak; it is a poor peace, unstable and above all degrading because it fails to take nature into account.

Reason is now advancing toward the solution, being careful to remember that we have only our natural strength and freedom to preserve us; these are our "natural rights," defining our human essence but proving illusory in our existence. We cannot struggle alone against a stream in flood, a forest fire, the ocean. Because our rights do not come to our aid, we have all learned that it is in our interest to fashion a common strength; but to avoid slipping back into the evils of the past, when the many put their strength and freedom into the hands of the few, all group members, without exception, must give up everything they have, for what each possesses suffices to save none. "The total alienation of each associate, together with all of his rights, to the entire community" initially preserves natural equality; "each person gives himself whole and entire, the condition is equal for everyone; and since the condition is equal for everyone, no one has an interest in making it burdensome for the others."[64] Put another way, when each person is stripped of everything, no one can do harm to anyone, for all are equally deprived. Before the contract, there is indeed a group of unequal individuals. They differ in their resources, whether in physical strength, in moral force, or in possessions. What each gives up, then, is in fact not the same, and it is precisely this inequality that has caused problems in actual societies. But by the contract's enactment, equality is reestablished on a formal plane equivalent to the essential order that had proved unsuited to concrete existence.

So freedom is then saved by equality, because in equality no one commands, no one obeys, and all are independent of each other. "In giving himself to all, each one gives himself to no one."[65] We can mark two stages in the recovery of freedom. The first is negative—it is the stage of "total alienation of each associate, together with all his rights, to the entire community."[66] This is indeed an act that abolishes freedom and does so through freedom's opposite, alienation, which is prerequisite to establishing equal circumstances. The second stage is positive. "In giving himself to all, each person gives himself to no one"[67] and in consequence is no longer dependent on anyone. It is true that the individual is no longer dependent only on himself, either. In these two steps, freedom is transformed; absolute but futile, natural freedom has become civil freedom that, though limited, is guaranteed.

Now, we know that each person's will inclines by nature to individual interests. Each person wants above all to remain independent in full particularity. But at the moment of absolute self-abnegation that we call the contract, freedom and equality are the motivation—and simultaneously the creation—of every human will. They are its inevitable cause and effect. A person who is party to the contract is by definition a will that is stripped of its particularity and is, as such, universal and necessary, for the inverse would imply a contradiction. In this sense, the will of each must be the same. Both universal and necessary, the will of each is the general will. And because it is characterized by the same attributes as reason, the general will is identical to reason and cannot be identified with the set of all passion-driven, particular, and contingent wills.[68] We understand from this why will is inalienable, unmoved by passing whims, indivisible as the sovereign power it gives birth to, and incapable of error. We also understand that it cannot be the sum of those patchworks, individual wills, and that when their characteristic "pluses and minuses" are removed, nothing remains within general will except pure universality and the necessity of a will that is identical, in respect to this very trait, to reason.[69]

In transcending individual persons, the general will also expresses the unity of a "moral and collective body"[70] that it in fact creates. This body is collective because its members number as many as those who have a voice in the group. It is moral because it does not have the properties of a physical body. It does not exist naturally; it is the product of convention; it is artificially created by a will commanding an act of reason. From this act, it "receives . . . its unity, its common *self*, its life and its will."[71] It is not a "natural person" but the very opposite of that, a "public person," which can be said to be a fiction in the natural domain but real in the domain of will, whose work it is. As a member of the sovereignty, a human can no longer return to his individuality nor to the disappointments it inflicts or undergoes. The human is part of the moral body that "by the mere fact that it exists, is always all that it should be,"[72] for the inverse proposition would lead to contradiction. From this it follows that it is legitimate for each to be forced "to consult his reason before listening to his inclinations."[73]

A product of reason, the body politic or sovereign is also intrinsically the product of freedom (which it guarantees as well), as it is not the work of nature. Consequently, the forming of this moral body, this public person, not only makes will identical to reason but freedom identical to them both. Rousseau does not theorize about this. He is content to point out a certain number of implications, among them (particularly interesting from our point of view) those that concern civil peace and the continuation of war among nations. Rousseau's attentive reader, Kant, will not forget this triple identity and will justify it masterfully.

Let us note that in this process, reason, originally forced to fill a technical role by the threatening situation that called it forth, puts these same technical talents to work to find the solution to a problem, but at the same time reveals another aspect of itself. It is also—perhaps especially—ethical, as it shows the way to respect for human nature, opens us to the possibility of harmonious relations among people, teaches us the equal worth of all members of a community. As isolated beings, we lived within ourselves, in peace, true, but unaware of it. Now peace will ever after be the fruit of the freedom and equality that are recognized and defended by the law in the civil community.

Rousseau had already written in the *Discourse on Political Economy*, also published in 1755, that "the most general will is also always the most just, and that the voice of the populace is, in effect, the voice of God."[74] Ethics and politics converge to such an extent that "it is necessary simply to be just to be assured of following the general will."[75] The precept is clarified in the Second Essential Rule of Public Economy: "Do you want the general will to be accomplished? Make all private wills be in conformity with it. And since virtue is merely this conformity of the private will to the general will, in a word, make virtue reign. If politicians were less blinded by their ambition, they would see how impossible it is for any establishment whatever to act [unless it acts] in accordance with the laws of duty."[76] In 1762 the same thought appears not only in the *Social Contract* but also in *Emile*. Rousseau asserts in fact that "those who want to treat politics and morality separately will never understand anything of either of the two."[77]

I will not go into the details of how the body politic functions and is governed. I will restrict my study to the principle of "the sovereignty of the people," the sole possessor of the right to legislate and consequently unable, as a moral person, ever to injure any member of the social body, for no one does harm to himself. Humans are no longer subject to other humans; they need not be so in the political state any more than they are, in essence, in the natural state. But whereas by nature the human being is subject, like any animal, only to the laws of determinism, the willed, free, rational creation of political society makes him subject to the "State of Law"; and so Rousseau can say that "to be driven by appetite alone is slavery, and obedience to the law one has prescribed for oneself is liberty"[78] (it being understood, of course, that one has prescribed one's own law as a partaker in the universal will, not as an individual will). The liberty in question is much superior to mere natural independence. Granted, independence was an unbounded right, but it was quickly restricted by the weakness of the individual relative to obstacles he encountered. Freedom, in contrast, is no longer license to do anything whatsoever, but it is guaranteed. Within the bounds of the law, each can do as he likes with his own person and belongings. Above all, freedom is moral. Political freedom alone "makes man truly master of himself" by making it his duty to respect others. It is through the political creation that the moral person emerges. Natural man, the "perfect and solitary whole," gains "a partial and moral existence," for "each citizen is nothing and can do nothing except with the concert of all."[79]

Rousseau makes plain his belief that political life necessarily mediates ethical behavior. "This passage from the state of nature to the civil state produces a remarkable change in man, for it substitutes justice for instinct in his behavior and gives his actions a moral quality they previously lacked."[80] By the logic of the system, we must admit that if anyone willfully damages the civic peace by not doing his duty as a citizen, it is tantamount to denying his human status and treating himself and others as nonhuman. As a result, "whoever refuses to obey the general will will be forced to do so by the entire body. This means merely that he will be forced to be free."[81] This paradoxical utterance might allow us to believe that it is possible to drive a human being into freedom. This is apparently its intent. Let us nonetheless remember that the logic of a system is one thing; how it is interpreted when applied is quite another.

Civil peace is therefore secured when reason resolves the problem that existence presents to those who recognize humanity's essence. It is not an accident, however, that the Social Contract and Emile appear in the same year. There is no contradiction between the practical reason that is both will and freedom in the first work and conscience, the "divine instinct," in the other. If Rousseau is capable of imagining the terms of the social contract and resolving the difficult problem (so badly grappled with by others) of the transition from the state of nature to the civil state, and if he can imagine, articulate, and resolve the problem through intellectual speculation, it is because of his having listened to the voice of nature within him, as any sensitive being could have done. "Thank heaven," the Savoyard priest exclaims, "we can be men without being scholars."[82] The rights and duties that correct speculation discovers in the human order are instinctively known by an unperverted sensibility. But as we have already noted, though conscience is a natural voice,[83] it is not conscience, properly speaking, until it can be recognized as such. It needs language, it needs human intercourse in order to be heard. Perfectibility must, therefore, at least have begun its passage from potential to action. Still, conscience is muffled, inaudible, and ineffective in societies in thrall to pride. That is why its presence is felt only by the very few who are simple enough and pure enough to keep to the kind of life that is not overwhelmed by the passions' tumult. The Savoyard priest, Emile's tutor, probably

Monsieur de Wolmar, too—and Rousseau—were lucky enough to be of their company.

When alert to nature's voice, everyone, even the humblest, can sense the truth of the social contract: It brings to human beings who have necessarily congregated (despite their first nature) a way to be true to nature by shifting it, unavoidably, into the artificial—but no longer fatally horrible—environment of political life. Politics mediates ethics, but the converse is also true.[84] If his conscience had not spoken to him, restoring his reason to its true purpose, Rousseau could never have humanized the political community by uncovering the logic of the transition from the state of nature to the civil state.

We must not delude ourselves, however. The contractual state is not for everyone. Actual societies are too corrupt; their habit of servility too long ingrained; their territories, governed by complex representative mechanisms, too vast for them to have the ability or even the desire to reform. The only civil peace they have known has been either coerced or ephemeral. "There are peoples who, do what you may, are incapable of being well governed, for the law has no hold over them, and a government without laws cannot be a good government."[85]

Can we nevertheless apply the social contract in real life? Is Rousseau's discovery condemned to remain mere theory? Rousseau, we must admit, is not optimistic. His judgment of history is stern. We can take the *Discourse on the Origin of Inequality* to be a philosophy of history, but its controlling theme is the increase of humanity's degradation as brought about by the progress of reason. Its final pages are disheartening; they offer no prospect of salvation for human societies. Contrary to what we usually expect in a philosophy of history, in Rousseau reason's advance brings about the race's deterioration. To Rousseau, history is far more the story of freedom's loss than of freedom's achievement. Reason, of course, can resist nature, and in this sense we can say that reason is freedom, but reason is primarily "freedom to do evil," which is simply another name for passion. The words *degeneration, depravity,* or their synonyms flow constantly from Rousseau's pen. The text admits of no misunderstanding: The development of reason leads to "the most frightful state of war"[86] and to servitude, with no return possible. All misfortunes, remember, hardly start through the fault of humans, who are in the grip of the cruel need to survive at any cost.

Although the *Social Contract* could not have been created until reason had matured enough to understand a problem and try to solve it, we would be utterly wrong to interpret the work as some sort of end purpose of history made possible by eons of catastrophes that left humanity no choice but to learn to think. It is not the permanently happy culmination of the process of history. What is more, after it has been described by one who has thought hard about the logic of the transition to the civil state, the social contract cannot be applied to most actual societies; such was Rousseau's conviction, at any rate, however much his readers believed that they could change the world by giving all societies freedom and peace. According to Rousseau, a little country still in a semiprimitive state, like Corsica, or a large country that had not been damaged by civilization, like Poland, could perhaps benefit from successfully instituting the contract. The rest were lost:

> Just as an architect, before putting up a large building, surveys and tests the ground to see if it can bear the weight, the wise teacher does not begin by laying down laws that are good in themselves. Rather he first examines whether the people for whom they are destined are fitted to bear them. . . . Once customs are established and prejudices have become deeply rooted, it is a dangerous and vain undertaking to want to reform them. . . . [A people] can make itself free so long as it is merely barbarous; but it can no longer do so when civil strength is exhausted. . . . Liberty can be acquired, but it can never be recovered.[87]

When Rousseau asks the question, Which people is therefore suited to legislation? he hedges the response with so many conditions that he himself comments, "All these conditions, it is true, are hard to find in combination."[88] He has no illusions on the subject. The conditions for civil peace are not available to everyone, depending as they do on the quality of the political structure and the respect for freedom it is supposed to assure. From time immemorial, some external circumstances have even suppressed the occurrence of the right conditions. Influenced by Montesquieu, with whom he agrees, he considers that "since liberty is not a fruit of every climate, it is not within the reach of all people."[89]

Admitting the difficulties and supposing anyway that it might be possible to establish a nation according to the principles of the social contract, can we infer from its stable civil peace that a nation will be at peace with those surrounding it? The answer is obviously no.

In 1755, in the *Discourse on the Origin of Inequality*, Rousseau repeats Hobbes's reasoning. Nations are in a state of nature in respect to one another. This means that because they form societies that are distinct but incapable of surviving by themselves; because they are forced to engage in trade, business, and industry; because they are sometimes poor (or corrupt, for a nation's mere existence is a sign of the catastrophic development of reason in its individual members); they consequently try to solve their problems by a process that is identical to the one used by individuals who are forced to live in association before they have even poor civil law: They go to war.

In his discussion of the writings of the Abbé de Saint-Pierre, we find the same conviction. In theory, nature is abolished in a political society, but it "can be found where least expected. The independence that was wrenched from man has sought refuge in civil societies; and those great bodies, left to their own impulses, produce shocks whose terror is proportional to their mass."[90] In this whole work, the description of relations between societies, relations determined by the passions, brings to mind Hobbes's description of the state of nature in which he showed that the state of war shaped the relations of nation to nation. We are therefore not surprised to read that "according to me, the state of war is natural between sovereign powers."[91] Rousseau continues:"As individuals we live in a civil state and are subject to its laws; but as nations each enjoys the liberty of nature. The resulting continuing vacillation makes our situation worse than if these distinctions were unknown."[92] Rousseau puts little faith in the law of nations, which he defines as "some tacit conventions in order to make intercourse possible and to serve as a substitute for natural compassion."[93] He judges it totally incapable of preventing "the national wars, battles, murders, and reprisals that make nature tremble and offend reason, and all those horrible prejudices that rank the honor of shedding human blood among the virtues."[94]

There is no lack of causes for war between nations. One is the vanity of princes, by which Rousseau means not the sovereignty, that is, the general will, but a king, a term he readily equates to *despot*.[95] Another is the disproportion between the area of a nation and the size of its population—"the proximate cause of defensive wars" undertaken in an attempt to fend off neighboring peoples who invade lands that are poorly guarded or that produce enough to feed more inhabitants. The problem of sustenance becomes easier to solve when a nation realizes that adjoining land is more fertile than its own territory, which cannot provide for its burgeoning citizenry, and that it need do nothing more than take it over. It follows that "the proximate cause of offensive war" results from the lack of sufficient goods in a country whose subsistence depends on imports.[96]

Other causes reside in the nations themselves, which prefer "to make a great splash, to be impressive and formidable, to influence the other peoples of Europe."[97] They cultivate the arts, the sciences, commerce; they have professional armies, forts, military colleges; they know how to put money to work and make it grow, how to become wealthy. They also know how to maintain a dependent population by promoting "material luxury and the luxury of the spirit that is inseparable from it."[98] These nations—and we must recognize that in Europe they are the overwhelming majority—are scheming, greedy, insatiable, ambitious, servile, and deceitful, always "at one extreme or the other of misery and opulence, of license and slavery, with nothing in between," but they are counted among "the great powers of Europe," they represent "all its political systems," they are sought after as allies in all negotiations, they are joined by treaties, and there is no war that they do not have "the honor of being dragged into."[99]

Rousseau paints this dismaying picture for the Poles, because he hopes they will come over to his opinion and reform their constitution along lines inspired by the *Social Contract*. We can here repeat the question, though it cannot apply to the majority of peoples (as we now see only too clearly) but solely to those who could still resist the general degradation and who would be living in reasonably favorable material circumstances: Could such nations avoid foreign wars? Again the answer is no, for there are causes of war that seem to be beyond the control of any political structure, however rational. Even if we thoroughly understand that there is no one in the world who can exercise *natural* authority over any other, even if we prove beyond cavil that might is not right, that all legitimate authority can only result from a contract, and that the contract must have unanimous consent, thereby making the general will and the sovereign power identical, it remains no less true, as Rousseau himself says, that "all the peoples have a kind of centrifugal force, by which they continually act one against the other and tend to expand at the expense of their neighbors, like Descartes' vortices."[100] It falls on the statesman to seek the best dimensions for his nation's territory, striking the balance that, thanks to "a sound and strong constitution," will protect his nation against threats from without. Rousseau says nowhere, however, that the social contract state would escape the centrifugal force within its own borders. What is more, though he undeniably condemns wars of conquest waged from arrogance and a taste for acquisition,[101] we cannot say that he includes all wars in this judgment; he does not shrink from writing, "A little agitation gives strength to souls, and what truly brings about prosperity for the species is not so much peace as liberty."[102]

But the most obvious reason that the contractual state, an enclave among nations mostly too degraded to merit a good constitution, cannot be spared war is that love of country is the prime virtue of any citizen worthy of the name. Rousseau is in no respect the precursor of the "European mentality," much less a "citizen of the world." Passages indicating the contrary are numerous and clear. Because the human being cannot live as an isolated individual—as the "perfect and solitary whole" his essence would make of him if he could survive without betraying it— then he must live as a citizen, that is, as a patriot. This forbids him any nationality but his own and even any trait that is not typical of his nation. "Say what you like, there is no such thing nowadays as Frenchmen, Germans, Spaniards, or even Englishmen—*only Europeans*," he complains. "All have the same tastes, the same passions, the same customs, and for good reason: Not one of them has ever been formed nationally, by distinctive legislation." Although perhaps we cannot go so far as to invoke xenophobia, the individuality of states combined with the centrifugal force of their peoples can lead the contract state into war, defensive war in particular. The other nations, alike in their lack of a contract, are readily induced to attack each other for reasons already mentioned. Rousseau urges the schoolteachers of Poland to "keep [the Poles] from being absorbed by other people . . . by giving the citizens of Poland a high opinion of themselves and of their fatherland" so that they will have a natural dislike of mixing with foreigners.[103] Is this not perfectly consistent? By nature the human being is an individual and not a political animal. What he loses in the social pact, the nation created by it gains on his behalf; the nation must become an individual in order not to betray human nature, whose agent it now is. If each nation could be constituted according to the principles of the social contract, would its patriotism together with its love of independence bring it to end all contacts with its neighbors, and especially all hostile contacts? Rousseau does not posit any such hypothesis, for it is not realistic. Because of their passions, most nations are forever beyond all help.

Where the social pact is still possible, it "giv[es] each citizen to the homeland."[104] Speaking of the advantages that private individuals get from the social contract, Rousseau points out that "their life itself, which they have devoted to the state, is continually protected by it"; and he adds that, complementarily, "when they risk their lives for its defense, what are they then doing but returning to the state what they have received from it? What are they doing, that they did not do more frequently and with greater danger in the state of nature, when they would inevitably have to fight battles, defending at the peril of their lives the means of their preservation? It is true that everyone has to fight, if necessary, for the homeland; but it also is the case that no one ever has to fight on his own behalf."[105]

Still, he is only speaking here of everyone's properly understood best interest, which secures our safety by and within the community that protects our lives. Rousseau justifies his position with utmost logic. "The social treaty," he says,

has as its purpose the conservation of the contracting parties. Whoever wills the end also wills the means, and these means are inseparable from some risks, even from some losses. Whoever wishes to preserve his life at the expense of others, should also give it up for them when necessary. For the citizen is no longer judge of the peril to which the law wishes he be exposed, and when the prince has said to him, "it is expedient for the state that you should die," he should die. Because it is under this condition alone that he has lived in security up to then, and because his life is not only a kindness of nature, but a conditional gift of the state.[106]

This is what the logic of the contract requires of citizens, founded as it is on their essence and allowing it to be realized in their existence. The civil laws regulate the relation of the state to each of its members, "so that each citizen [may] be properly independent of all others"—here Rousseau alludes to the essential attribute of human nature—"and excessively dependent upon the city"—here we find the condition of the essential attribute's realization.[107]

We should not see any bloodthirstiness, any renunciation of natural pity, in the universal obligation to go off to war when the nation's well-being demands it. "War is not . . . a relationship between one man and another, but a relationship between one state and another. In war, private individuals are enemies only incidentally: not as men or even as citizens, but as soldiers; not as members of the homeland but as its defenders."[108] This idea that a person cannot be another person's enemy except out of depravity is so important for Rousseau that he extends it to nations. "Each state," he says, "can have as enemies only other states and not men, since there can be no real relationship between things of disparate nature."[109]

The requirement that all defend their country follows, then, from the citizens' best interests, as properly understood; but it is also a demand legitimately enforced by the state that guarantees respect for everyone's best interests. This is why Rousseau, unlike Hobbes, would not let the citizens decide when to take back their natural freedom if the state was no longer ensuring their safety. On the contrary, Rousseau condemns the crime of desertion very harshly. At the same time, calling on the authority of Hugo Grotius—and his own experience of life—he would not force anyone to remain a member of a nation that did not suit him. Any may take back his freedom and his goods.[110] Rousseau nevertheless feels the need to add a footnote: "On the understanding that one does not leave in order to evade one's duty and to be exempt from serving the homeland the moment it needs us. In such circumstances, taking flight would be criminal and punishable; it would no longer be withdrawal, but desertion."[111]

Rousseau goes farther: Defensive war is a necessity, it is a demand, it is above all a duty that is dictated by the very meaning of the word *contract* and by love of country. It would in fact be incomprehensible to make a unilateral contract. The person who enters a contract and who reaps its benefits makes a moral commitment. Coercion by the power of the whole is only necessary in cases of fraud. We must not forget that the contract is the fruit of reason and that unless depraved by passions, reason is the same thing as conscience. This is why a citizen is a moral being[112] and is capable "of sincerely loving the laws and justice, and of sacrificing his life, if necessary, for his duty."[113] In the *Considerations on the Government of Poland*, Rousseau confidently defines love of country as "love of the laws and of liberty."[114]

It is much to the credit of our era to have seen Rousseau as a political philosopher. But it has associated him with ideologies that he surely would have been astounded to have fostered. We usually forget his extraordinary panegyric of the homeland (from which the French Revolution drew inspiration). Its language reappears today in military speeches—which are not normally applauded, however, by admirers of Rousseau. Consider, for example, this passage, where Rousseau is sketching his reform of the Polish constitution in the spirit of the *Social Contract*. "I should like you," he says, "by means of honors and public prizes to shed luster on all the patriotic virtues, to keep the Poles' minds constantly on the fatherland, making it their central preoccupation, and to hold it up constantly before their eyes."[115]

The homeland, which is the solution reason gave to the problems posed by nature, is an entity we must be taught to love from the time we are in the cradle. Children must be educated with care, and adults must be surrounded by conditions that encourage this love. How do we make people love a contrivance? Although an emotion can be encouraged, it cannot be commanded. We can capture it for a time; we cannot force it to last. When love of country persists and impregnates the lives of all till it becomes the object of their greatest devotion, it is because good legislation has taken the most constant, attentive care to make the unnatural habitual; at the same time, and perhaps at a much deeper level, it is because what makes the legislation good is that it elicits each person's former natural, unconscious feeling of fusion with Mother Nature and displaces it to nature's necessary substitute, Mother Country.[116] Aristotle's citizen, the political animal, is born in the bosom of the natural communities of family and City. Predisposed by *philia*, a spontaneous feeling, to a natural relation with the first, he smoothly transfers his attachment to the other despite the difference in their purposes. Rousseau's citizen is confronted with difficulties that would be insurmountable without the artifice that annuls the conflict between nature and the unnatural fabrication, society. Although the family is called natural in *Emile* (whereas the political community is not), the logic of the *Discourse on the Origin of Inequality* vigorously denies any natural bond between human beings, thereby abandoning the solitary individual solely to relationship with a natural world that should have been there, but that, in fact, failed its children from the moment of their birth. The mother, nature, would have loved her offspring, if causes beyond her strength had not incapacitated her for nurturing them and at the same time concealed from them the truth about the original tie uniting them to the one who made them. But the love that nature should have inspired in them cannot attach itself to artificial objects. Out of all that people will one day invent, only one work will ever be worthy of their wholehearted love—it is that which will restore, within civil life, the essential reality that is theirs, but that they never had the chance to live out. The homeland, wearing no more than did nature a concrete human face, could therefore not possibly *enslave* them. It is only fair that they give their love and devote their lives to the one who bestows life.

In the *Discourse on Political Economy*, Rousseau demonstrates that love of country is "the most heroic of all the passions."[117] It is the source of all virtues. "Do we want people to be virtuous?" he asks. "Let us begin by making them love their country," for once aroused, it is a love that "a hundred times more ardent and delightful than that of a mistress, likewise cannot be conceived except by being felt."[118] We must induce citizens "never to consider their own persons except in terms of being related to the body of the state, and not to perceive their own existence except as part of the state's existence." So will they "come to identify themselves in some way with this larger whole, to feel themselves to be members of the country, to love it with that exquisite sentiment that every isolated man feels only for himself, to elevate their soul perpetually toward this great object, and thus to transform into a sublime virtue this dangerous disposition from which arise all our vices."[119]

The course of self-love could not be better portrayed. Natural in the solitary individual, it yearns only for fusion with a nature that satisfies its wants and keeps it safe. But nature, its mother, was never able to take care of her child. Left to rely on his own inadequate strength, he has had to live against his nature, to associate with strangers, and to develop pride. He was tragically routed down the wrong track, so to speak. The right route is indeed to renounce solitude, but for the sake of a greater "perfect and solitary whole," the homeland, which despite its artificiality is still capable of arousing the full power of a passion that, if also artificial, is nonetheless grafted on the only natural passion, love of self. Rousseau's human being, the nonpolitical animal, does not live, does not think, does not love, except through, for, and by the political nation that is his home country. Even when it does not turn the citizens to aggressive xenophobia, we may wonder whether such a consuming love, absolutely excluding the "stranger" (the word appears frequently in Rousseau's writings), does not risk becoming fanaticism. Rousseau reproaches religions for being the source of the kind of evil that leads to the worst wars. Are the citizens of the contract state not in danger of the same error Rousseau attributes to the pious?

In any case, the correctly conceived organization of the homeland is to be followed by the establishment of colonies—a legitimate enterprise, in Rousseau's view. He does not go into practical details, and he probably is thinking more of the ancient Greek and Roman colonies than of the colonial empires of the European powers. Whichever he has in mind, neither could be established without war, and on this point Rousseau is categorical; thus when the issue is how to reduce a coastal population, he says that "it is easier to unburden the country of surplus inhabitants by means of colonies."[120] If the Corsicans adopt the plan he is drawing up for them, they will be farmers and soldiers, for "all agricultural peoples multiply; they multiply in proportion to the product of their soil; and when that soil is fertile, they finally multiply to such an extent that it no longer suffices to support them; then they are forced either to found colonies or to change their form of government."[121] It is not very likely that Rousseau would prefer the second solution.

Their love of country must certainly explain Rousseau's admiration for Spartans, Romans, and the great legislators whose laws give birth to the political machine.[122] Great lawgivers are those who succeed in the seemingly contradictory enterprise of "alter[ing] man's constitution in order to strengthen it."[123] Moses, Lycurgus, and Numa "all . . . sought ties that would bind the citizens to the fatherland and to one another."[124] It is in the Poles' *hearts* that they must "establish the republic . . . so that it will live on in them despite anything [their] oppressors may do."[125] It is up to the constitution and laws to inspire in people "that ardent love of fatherland that is founded upon habits of mind impossible to uproot."[126] One of the best ways to succeed in this is to give up professional armies, which Rousseau denounces as dangerous and unpopular, and to make each citizen a soldier.[127] (We often find his writing inspired by the examples of republican Rome and Switzerland.)[128]

In addition to the advice on military tactics that Rousseau lavishes on the Poles, it is worth noting how insistently he returns to the idea that each citizen must join in the common defense, which is also the defense of himself, for as he knows and categorically states, peace can never be certain. "The most inviolable of all the laws of nature," he says, "is the law of the strongest."[129] We must not forget this phrase. It implicitly but very plainly establishes the distinction between this *law* of nature and the *right* of the strongest, which is not a law at all but an "inexplicable mishmash."[130] Yet despite this law invented for imposing a law that is always and everywhere a false law, despite this law, pregnant with future wars engendered by the instability inseparable from the use of force, the little nations still retain a hope of not being absorbed by the great, provided they have good institutions. Even Poland, in spite of the size of its territory, could strike fear into its formidable neighbors if, out of love of country, every citizen were always ready to fight. But in order to maintain patriotic spirit, Poland must honor frugality more than wealth and create an educational program to inculcate the tastes and customs proper to a people ready to put its country above all else.[131] "Is it indeed certain," Rousseau asks, "that money is the sinew of war? Rich peoples, in point of fact, have always been beaten and taken over by poor peoples. . . . Money, at best, merely supplements men; and that which supplements is never so valuable as that which is supplemented."[132] The passages condemning money contain some striking phrases. But they are not very realistic at the dawn of the industrial age, the first glimmers of which Rousseau in fact detested,[133] and all the more because, as he says many times, industry, like trade, is an extraordinary incentive for wars of conquest, whereas "tilling the soil makes men patient and robust, which is what is needed to make good soldiers"[134]—only in defense of their country, it is to be understood.

That rare nation that is founded on the contract, the only rational and just nation, must be constantly ready for defensive war; furthermore, the typical state of societies is inevitably a state of war; and, finally, the overwhelming majority of nations, driven by the ambition of their leaders, their love of luxury, their vanity, and the servility of their peoples, are alert only to the opportunity for an offensive war. What are we to conclude except that though "man is naturally peaceful and shy,"[135] humanity has no hope of peace? Perhaps it was not so much because his style was boring, crammed with digression, or too often opaque that the Abbé de Saint-Pierre could not win Rousseau to the possibility of establishing perpetual peace. In spite of declaring "the general and the specific usefulness of this project,"[136] Rousseau immediately pointed out "the obvious impossibility of its success." His critique is based entirely on real societies in which "on the one hand, war and invasions, and on the other hand, the progress of despotism mutually reinforce each other." How can we expect chance to grant "the happy agreement of all these . . . circumstances"[137] necessary to the realization of a plan that would require individuals in association—that is, beings of passion—to be reasonable?[138]

With impeccable logic, Rousseau adds a disturbing point. "The only way to make up for the failure of this agreement to come about by chance," he says, "would be to make it come about by force. Then it would no longer be a question of persuading but of compelling, and then what would be needed is not to write books but to levy troops."[139] To levy troops is, of course, to continue to wage war. The powers will never be able to agree; each must either protect itself or take the offensive. As has happened throughout history, "we see men united by an artificial accord coming together to cut one another's throats, and . . . all the horrors of war arise from the efforts that were taken to prevent it."[140] But is this all there is to it? Yes, beyond any doubt. We may still wonder whether the agreements reached as the result of war never hold some "divine surprise." Or to be more precise, can we not at least expect peace for nations that are governed by good constitutions resulting from a *revolution*?

We find no theory of revolution in Rousseau's works. It is not an inevitable historical process to which any people is, strictly speaking, compelled. In any case, a people worn out by unnumbered centuries of servitude can never expect freedom from a revolution, only a new master. We may then ask why we "sometimes find in the period during which states have existed violent epochs when revolutions do to peoples what certain crises do to individuals, when the horror of the past takes the place of forgetfulness, and when the state, set afire by civil wars, is reborn as it were, from its ashes and takes on again the vigor of youth as it escapes death's embrace."[141] If Sparta in the time of Lycurgus, Rome after the Tarquins, or the Netherlands and Switzerland had this good fortune, then it could be said of the Corsican people that it was "in that fortunate condition that makes possible the establishment of a good constitution,"[142] for the Corsicans had only recently emerged from a civil war to throw off the yoke of foreign governments, and their sense of equality and freedom had been reborn. Poland, "depopulated, devastated, and oppressed, wide-open to its aggressors, in the depths of misfortune and of anarchy, still shows all the fire of youth,"[143] because it had defended its freedom against a much more powerful aggressor. Whether we consider theirs a true revolution or a quasi-revolutionary state, the fighters of 1789 will believe, rightly or wrongly, that the inauguration of the state of law demands a radical break with the past. Rousseau is content to "examine facts from the viewpoint of right";[144] to him it is less a matter of "history and facts than of right and justice," and he examines "things by their nature rather than by our prejudices."[145] We must nevertheless recognize that any historical attempt to establish peace through law will succumb to the temptation of revolution, a soil that will seem indispensable to the germination of citizens. Does Rousseau really delude himself on this point? In his *Judgment* concerning the project of the Abbé de Saint-Pierre, he states that "whatever is useful to the public must be brought by force— seeing as special interests are almost always opposed to it."[146] Although civil war is the most horrible of wars, the one no people ever recovers from, the nations that believed in the *Social Contract* clung to the hope that it would lead to their rebirth. It is this especially that some of Rousseau's readers will comprehend.

If civil peace is initiated in the contract state, but war is still waged all around it—even against it or even, indeed, by it—are we justified in calling this sort of political vision a "utopia of peace"? We cannot, it goes without saying, interpret Rousseau as if he defined the human as a being made for war. Neither can we think that the human is or ought to be a being made for peace. We must nonetheless answer our question in the affirmative and state at least the most obvious reasons for doing so. The state of the contract Rousseau describes is an abstract, artificial construction based on the description of a human essence that accounts for certain tendencies that are indeed attributable to human beings but that are far from defining all that human beings are. Aside from imagining the possibility of imposing contract-based institutions from without on some people still barbaric, yet past the original state of solitude and silence, the contract remains a dream. (We would still have to leave out of consideration the character, the reactions, the *reality* of such peoples.) And would the legislation flowing from that initial unanimity, as well reasoned as anyone could wish it, suppress conflicts forever? At the most it might contain them. A human being is not God. In no respect is reason our complete definition, any more than our intuition is necessarily the voice of peace. The more unrecognized our shadow side, the more dangerously it asserts itself. Is this not what Rousseau himself implicitly acknowledged when, despite the perfect organization of Monsieur de Wolmar's little society, Julie feels her passion return so cruelly and finally sees no other refuge but death? And what are we to make of Sophie, the perfect wife of perfect Emile, brought up by a tutor who was a veritable "legislator"? She cannot refrain from deceiving her husband, a wrong so incongruous with the logic of this union that most editions have omitted the book's final chapter. And when Rousseau sits in judgment of Jean-Jacques, he sorrowfully admits, "After studying man all my life, I believed I knew men; I was mistaken."[147]

Rousseau's realism before the facts of history—which he never took to be progress toward peace but quite the opposite—will very rapidly give way to utopianism. He would not have wanted this, but by its very dynamism, his plan invites a successor. Faith in the human will identified with reason and freedom is about to be transformed into a duty of boundless universality. With all the vigor and depth that an apparently unassailable philosophical system gives him, Kant will be, even when unfaithful to Rousseau, his brilliant follower.

C H A P T E R 7

Perpetual Peace

Despite disagreements among their systems, the social contract philosophers all believed they had something to contribute to making domestic peace possible—the idea of a state governed by law and created by the human will. This state of law was intended to remedy a situation that had originally been wretched—or had become so—in which the individual lacked conditions for safety and even survival. These philosophers had to invent what they believed had not been given initially: the means for making human existence first possible and then beneficial and worthwhile. (Everyone was to interpret these terms according to personal leanings, within the boundaries of the law.) The state, an artifact drawing all its worth from humans, is established only for the sake of performing its mission. It must first of all safeguard the physical life of each member, that is, provide for the protection of every individual's body and everything the body needs to function in the best way possible. Bodily life, together with all the goods required for it, is our individual *proprium*, that which is our "own," our "property." It is an inalienable possession, as are additional, nonphysical benefits that allow each person's life to have meaning. Civil peace is the condition that makes possible the actualization of property rights and of meaningful ways of life. It is therefore, by definition, one of the state's purposes. The will that establishes the political state cannot be other than a will that makes laws; for by promulgating and respecting laws, we ensure the peace that is requisite for individual ownership of the most basic goods as well as of some less obvious goods (to engage in the arts or sciences, for example), and we avoid the abridgment of one person's rights by another. The state is the guarantor of the economic life of its inhabitants and of their activities within its borders, so long as they are obedient to its laws.[1]

Where the laws are silent, all have the freedom to do whatever suits them—follow a trade, go walking in the countryside, become absorbed in study, go window-shopping on a day off, travel, choose a marriage partner, and so on. Within the net of the laws there is freedom of action, because it is woven to be the sturdy support of peace. In theory, the nation as so conceived need not be a *planned* society. It should be a framework for the

137

activities of its creators, an encouragement, sometimes a brake, always a protection. Within a nation's borders, the inevitable conflicts of purpose come up against the fence of the laws and so are prevented from escalating into civil war. As for foreign war, defense of the nation is always its cause and aim, that is to say, defense of the properly understood best interests of the citizens, regardless of whether the war itself is one of defense or of offense.

On the basis of his own view of human nature, each social contract philosopher tried to give the state erected by the equal will of its inhabitants the structures that would best allow it to fulfill its responsibilities. Yet no constitution, however rigorously conceived to ensure civil peace, has ever claimed to eliminate foreign wars. In contrast, if a state is based on a good constitution, it is reasonable to imagine that it can meet challenges and surmount a paradox within its borders: On the one hand the nation must be like a dam or dike that contains the tide of human passions and limits the conflicts inevitably brought on by desire; on the other hand it must sufficiently encourage that desire so that the people's energy does not collapse into apathy or die out. The state overcomes the contradiction typical of desire by making each citizen equal before the law; it makes possible the competitive contact of human beings whose desire and whose most brilliant cultural creations are inseparable, but at the same time it formulates rules that eliminate death and slavery. Thus is conceived what will one day be called the "free society." A constitution legislated by all, either directly or by representation, has become the criterion for how to set limits on the violent passions of individuals in mortal competition while still not discouraging their desire. Domestic peace can be said to be identical to the reign of law because each person in the political community is its author, its defender, and its subject by the intermediary of the legislative, executive, and judiciary powers. These control the means of public sanction and must be separate in order to avoid the possibility of arbitrary actions.

But across borders there is no common power. Here reason is once more at the service of the passions. Here the conflicts that the state of right contained have every reason—in the other sense of that word—to continue. Nations can agree to humanize wars (warring powers find it worthwhile to put prisoners of war in camps rather than to kill them), but they cannot seriously claim that the war they have just started will be the *last* war. It is hard to see what might compel them to keep their word were the circumstances that inspired such a promise to change. All the social contract philosophers agree on this, holding the same opinion as the philosophers of antiquity and the Middle Ages, none of whom expected wars to disappear. Note that proposals like those of Grotius, who sought to establish the foundations of a *Law of War and Peace*, or those of Samuel

Pufendorf in his *Law of Nature and the Nations* did not intend to establish a definitive peace.

Despite historical experience, and at the same time because of it, the last (and not the most optimistic) of the great social contract philosophers breaks away from this view of things. He proclaims himself a believer in "perpetual peace" among nations. According to Kant, in fact, the conditions of genuine internal peace are the same as those for world peace, and anyone who has understood the truth behind the apparent disasters of history and humanity has a duty to cooperate in bringing it about. Kant has no illusions, however. In the *Idea for a Universal History with a Cosmopolitan Intent* of 1784, he points out the "excessive and never remitting preparation for wars" that nations engage in and "the resultant distress that every nation must, even during times of peace, feel within itself."[2] In 1786 he analyzes the beginnings of "the feud between men" and does not hesitate to confess that "the greatest evil that can oppress civilized peoples derives from *wars*, not, indeed, so much from actual present or past wars, as from the never-ending and constantly increasing *arming* for future wars."[3] He returns to the same idea in 1790 in the *Critique of Judgment*, where he pictures the distress and poverty that are bound up in war and the preparations for war, perhaps even more disastrous than war itself, that encumber peacetime.[4]

One of his most explicit passages definitely links "a *radical* innate *evil* in human nature" to the state of war: In *Religion Within the Limits of Reason Alone*, the existence of war is used to illustrate "a corrupt propensity . . . rooted in man." Kant gives two examples as sufficient demonstration. On the one hand, the philosophers who seek to prove that natural goodness determines human relations in a state of nature ought instead to investigate the cause of the "permanent warfare" among even the most primitive peoples, with cruelty, massacre, and bloody rituals observable everywhere. On the other hand, when we consider our own civilizations, we cannot escape being struck by "the international situation, where civilized nations stand towards each other in the relation obtaining in the barbarous state of nature (a state of continuous readiness for war) . . . from which they have taken firmly into their heads never to depart."[5] The conclusion seems inescapable: "The *philosophical millennium*, which hopes for a state of perpetual peace based on a league of peoples, a world-republic, even as the *theological millennium*, which tarries, for the completed moral improvement of the entire human race, is universally ridiculed as a wild fantasy."[6]

Kant has a clear and uncompromising view of the habitual relations among historical nations. He himself emphasizes the obvious logic of future events. Humanity has always waged war; there is no visible reason for it not to do so forever. The study of human nature, moreover, can only strengthen a thoughtful person's conviction in this regard. This analysis appears very likely to remain true until the disappearance of the human race, that is, forever. It is equally true that beginning from this same human nature as it developed through history, we can arrive at the conclusion that wars will surely cease. The idea of perpetual peace will become so real that all people will accept responsibility for it, grasping the necessity of ending war and at the same time recognizing, whatever their mental capacity, that they must work toward the creation of peace; for even the most ordinary mind is capable of seeing its duty.[7]

We must certainly begin by understanding how the state of affairs that we know, experience, and deplore originated. Why is history nothing but a heap of disastrous events? Why is war everywhere, either in its murderous actuality or in its constant anticipation, during which we train armies, fill our deadly arsenals, and consume immense human and monetary resources for baneful ends? We are admirably fitted, thanks to the faculty of thought, for steadily improving science and technology, but we appear incapable of drawing practical conclusions from history.

Nonetheless, when Kant ponders human nature, he initially finds it to have an original predisposition to goodness. The first condition for defining humanity is to state and describe this predisposition. In order to speak of "human nature," we must have three tendencies that are good in themselves. The first is to animality, which guarantees self-preservation, propagation of the species, and association with others of the same species by the instrumentality of self-love, simultaneously a survival instinct, a sexual instinct, and an instinct for community.[8] Although indispensable to humankind, this predisposition is not unique to it. It also makes possible the preservation of every other living species. Although it is not rooted in reason, the predisposition is good because it maintains life's good mechanical functioning, life's continuation, for human beings as for animals. By itself it provides for nothing except the harmonious continuation of a natural object. The second predisposition is peculiar to the human race. Its root is the aspect of reason that is capable of satisfying self-love only through comparison with others. Kant calls it the "predisposition to humanity." It originally seeks to affirm the equality of all but soon leads us to dread someone else's superiority and thus unjustly to claim for ourselves the dominance that we fear in others.

Onto these two predispositions, which, we repeat, are good in themselves, vices of all kinds are almost inevitably grafted—intemperance, jealousy, envy, and more; but these vices have not arisen *from* the original tendencies. Once they have emerged, however, Kant speaks of them in almost the same terms Hobbes used. If to his way of thinking they do not spring directly from nature, as Hobbes believed, they nonetheless nourish the natural fear of seeing others surpass us; they also inspire the defensive and offensive security measures that lead to war. "Nature, indeed," Kant writes, "wanted to use the idea of such rivalry (which in itself does not exclude mutual love) only as a spur to culture."[9] Why do dispositions that are good in themselves allow themselves to be invaded by what is alien to them? We pursue Kant's analysis to learn to what extent war can be declared inseparable from human nature.

A third original disposition—also good—is proper to the human species and defines its radical difference from all others. This is the predisposition to "personality," which Kant defines as "the capacity for respect for the moral law as *in itself a sufficient incentive of the will.*"[10] This natural predisposition makes possible the human's true nature, a nature that incorporates nothing into the "maxim" guiding the will but respect for the moral law as a basis for action. The two meanings of the word *nature*, very clearly defined by Kant, meet here. A predisposition is inborn, natural, as, for example, the natural tendency to self-preservation. But in itself the predisposition would not suffice to define a human if human nature, in the second meaning of the word, did not consist in free choice of respect for the moral law as its sufficient motivation. If this inborn predisposition could not be modified under any circumstances and so could not be grafted with vices, there would be no free will and its concomitant ability to choose without extrinsic determination the motivation of its voluntary decisions. A choice always implies that our freedom can *refuse* to let our innate respect for the law motivate our will. Freedom first appears, then, as freedom to deviate from nature's original goodness. Nature defined as freedom contrasts with nature defined as that which is inborn. They are incommensurable; the second obeys compelling universal laws that it never breaks whereas the first can impose on itself laws equally compelling and universal—and can also defy them.

Where does this power come from to choose, beyond the control of universal determinism, our actions and our lives? As early as 1781 Kant demonstrated in the *Critique of Pure Reason* that because freedom is not provable, it cannot be understood scientifically. He never again referred to the limits of speculative knowledge. In 1788 he proclaimed in the preface to the *Critique of Practical Reason* that "the concept of freedom, in so far as its reality is proved by an apodictic law of practical reason, is the keystone of the whole architecture of the system of pure reason and even of speculative reason."[11] He wrote the second *Critique* in order to justify this proposition. But Kant insists that "reason is not hereby extended, however, in its theoretical knowledge"; and he adds that "the only thing which is different is that the possibility, which was heretofore a problem, now becomes an assertion, and the practical use of reason is thus connected with the elements of theoretical reason."[12]

In 1793 he says that the origin of freedom is unfathomable but that freedom is the distinguishing trait of human nature. For human nature to be possible, it is necessary that human beings be free, but precisely because they *are* free, the *use* they make of their free will is contingent. The capacity for choice that we call freedom is the capacity to deviate from moral law and to include in the maxim that guides the will a motive other than perfect respect for that law, a law we receive from ourselves alone, a law grounded in our own universal reason. To say that a person is free is to recognize this propensity for evil, inseparable from freedom and in this sense both innate to persons and yet attributable to them, as persons can make choices. There is no contradiction—whether in favor of the moral law or unfettered by it, choice is still free. But choice implies that evil inheres in human nature, because acts of any type (whether in conformity to the law or not) can be selected without taking the law into account. Our inability to explain what allows an individual to make choices outside the law is due to the nature of freedom, which is itself beyond explanation. "A propensity to evil," Kant writes, "can inhere only in the moral capacity of the will."[13]

The human race can thus be *observed* to be the species in which every individual "is conscious of the moral law but has nevertheless adopted into his maxim the (occasional) deviation therefrom,"[14] but it cannot be *defined* as such, for if the propensity to evil were necessary to the definition, we could not hold a person responsible for it as if the person were free to choose it. Kant may thus speak of evil as rooted in all members of the human race. "We can," he says, "call this a natural propensity to evil, and as we must, after all, ever hold man himself responsible for it, we can further call it a *radical* innate *evil* in human nature (yet none the less brought upon us by ourselves)."[15]

We understand on the one hand that the principle of this inclination does not lie in the senses, which, being given by nature, are never bad in themselves. Natural tendencies are not subject to free choice. But the vices that are rooted in human evil graft themselves onto the natural tendencies and turn their needs into fearsome demands. So human beings do not make war, "that scourge of humankind,"[16] only out of an instinct to survive or to dominate others. They do so because, being free, they choose not to follow the moral law, the expression of practical reason and the very evidence of freedom within them; they choose instead to follow their fears, their ambitions, and all kinds of envies. These drives have become all the more insistent insofar as they have deformed the pure, natural inclinations, separating them from their mechanical purpose by inciting, thanks to reason's awakening, desires that are not based on predispositions and that actually impede their simple, harmonious action.[17]

In this complex analysis of human nature, as presented in *Religion Within the Limits of Reason Alone*, we can discern the reasons for war, and we can compare them with those presented in the short work that appeared in 1784, the *Idea for a Universal History with a Cosmopolitan Intent*. There Kant defines the human being by the antagonism he calls "unsociable sociability."[18] His terms are not analyzed with the same depth as in *Religion*, but the text is still informative. By nature we all bear contrasting predispositions that wrench us apart. They inflict on us a basic contradiction that inspires all that we *do*, never leaving us the leisure simply to *be*, like a plant or an animal. This split lies in the human core; it characterizes everything we undertake and experience. The social contract philosophers have sometimes included innate belligerence in their descriptions of human nature, as Hobbes did. Others have, with Rousseau, defined humanity by peace, proposing that by essence the human being was solitary. Sometimes war has been said to follow peace, as it does in the two states of nature Locke described and analyzed in the second *Treatise of Government*. According to Kant, conflict and division inhere in natural predispositions at their origin, and they are expressed in all the manifestations and works of human nature. "I understand antagonism to mean men's *unsocial sociability*," he writes, "i.e. their tendency to enter into society, combined, however, with a thoroughgoing resistance that constantly threatens to sunder society." Tendency toward society, resistance to it—in 1793 the first will become the "predisposition to humanity," inasmuch as the human being is a living being and a *reasoning* being. Aversion will be traced to the vices grafted onto this predisposition and, through them, to radical evil and hence to freedom.

Albeit the 1784 text does not make a point of these distinctions, the fact remains that the predispositions would not matter without freedom, which alone allows humanity to take the "first true steps from barbarism to culture,"[19] that is, to the opposite of what it is innately. This is only possible to the extent that what can be interpreted as a propensity or a revulsion operating between persons is primarily an internal conflict within each person's nature that is also externalized as propensity or revulsion. Every heart is marked by the clash between "same" and "other," between the need for and the rejection of otherness, between two tendencies that, working simultaneously yet in opposition, construct and dismember communities. For Kant, the person has a propensity for stepping out of himself, for shattering the self-absorption that confines him to the sterile sameness of his own company, and for "living in society," where his natural capacities will develop; "for in that state," Kant says, "he feels himself to be more than man."[20] Put otherwise, humans need humans in order to be human; our humanity, within us as free choice, is also outside us in the growth implied by freedom. It is through others that we endlessly progress in discovering freedom and self. But in contradiction to the urge to approach the indispensable other, there appears an equally strong urge to withdraw, to retreat into the self, as a unique subject hostile to all others. A person "has . . . a great tendency to isolate himself,"[21] to seek only his own company in order to affirm none but himself, in order to be the master of everything, expressing nothing but himself, conceding nothing to others. "He finds in himself the unsociable characteristic of wanting everything to go according to his own desires"[22]—to absorb into the "same" (the I-subject that denies the other the status of subject) the confronting unknowability of *otherness*, itself characterized by identical conflicting urges.

We see that, according to Kant, the human's nature is much more complex than it is as depicted by Rousseau. The innocence of the solitary being wandering in the woods in perfect independence is replaced by an essential conflict that because the individual is also free, generates all existential conflicts. And this freedom does not mean to Kant simply that the individual is in essence independent of any other but that, above all, each of us is capable of determining the goodness or badness of our own will. Internally torn, human beings cannot help but be ambivalent toward others, drawn as they are to live in community with others yet driven by predispositions to live only for themselves, to break off outside relations for the sake of their self-interest alone. The clearly stated description of human nature found in this brief passage suggests that for Kant the human being is above all a creature of desire. We have shown that desire prevents people from doing without each other, although at the same time it separates them from each other and pits them against each other in the intent to possess each other's goods, indeed to possess each other, for the human being is also a commodity that others want to acquire, want to control for themselves. The destiny of desire is indeed both to shape societies and to try to destroy them. Desire brings war, even though, paradoxically, desire simultaneously needs peace.

Such is humanity's *nature*, in work after work painted in the dark colors of the inner conflict that, when projected outward, directs the flow of history. From the time of humanity's state of nature, this intractability— part of the essence of that desire that constitutes the human being— threatens the peace that is born of the tendency to associate. Hence, for societies formed by this tendency, the unfolding of history means the existence of war—prepared for, predicted, or present—far more than it means that of peace, even though "man wills concord . . . wills to live comfortably and pleasantly"[23] and in the end cannot help but "overcome his tendency toward laziness, and, driven by his desire for honor, power, or property . . . secure status among his fellows, whom he neither *suffers*, nor *withdraws from*."[24]

Such is humanity's *history*. Perhaps people would be happy to be like the lambs they lead to pasture, but they must use the wolf's stratagems if they would attain to culture and civilization. But a human being can no more be compared to a wild beast than to a sheep from the flock. Neither is free. A human being is nature *and* freedom, the capacity for choice that is outside of nature, whether in compliance with moral law or in disregard of it. This radical evil cannot be rooted out, unsociability cannot be made to disappear. Just like evil, it must be transcended. How? At what point in history? These questions will not be answered until we have understood how the human—made "from such warped wood . . . [that] nothing straight can be fashioned [from it],"[25] something we cannot expect to be "perfectly straight [because it is] framed out of such crooked wood"[26]—is both victim and beneficiary of war, not only as an individual but as the member of a species not restricted to a single life span.

War seems indeed so bound up with human nature that it is hard to imagine what might bring it to an end. Let us recall, however, that war does not result from propensities but from what wickedness (the freedom to do evil) grafts onto them and perverts them with. Thus are born the passions, which Kant calls "a *disease* . . . an enchantment that . . . refuses to be corrected . . . a *mania* . . . for pure practical reason, cancerous sores . . . for the most part incurable, because the patient does not want to be cured."[27] This is why they can be imputed to humanity instead of to providence, which is another name for nature. "The philosopher," Kant writes, "cannot accept . . . prais[ing] the passions as a provisional arrangement of Providence, which would have purposely put them in human nature until the human race had achieved the necessary degree of culture."[28] Although the passions are truly diseases of freedom, they are not like physical ills except insofar as they attach themselves to the one who must endure them and who may even curse them, because "the unhappy man groans in his chains, which he cannot break loose from"; but we must not forget that "passion always presupposes a maxim, on the part of the subject, of acting in accordance with an end prescribed to him by the inclination. So it is always connected with his reason." In the most cruel enslavement, the person acting on passions always has made a choice contrary to reason. So the passions are "without exception, evil."[29] Now, we can only speak of "evil" in reference to a will that could have preferred respect for the law. We therefore manufacture our own unhappiness, even when we appear to be victims and pawns of fate.

Kant makes a penetrating analysis of passions. He shows how the (natural) inclination to freedom, the desire for vengeance, the desire to rise at another's expense become so many highroads to war, once they have turned into passions. Besides considering this dangerous slope that humanity has plunged down time out of mind and continues to descend today, take into account what humanity with its natural predisposition to reason has been able to produce as reason has developed. You will then understand why people have always waged war and why anyone expecting wars to stop would be considered mad; you will also understand why, from apparently contradictory points of view, which are nonetheless consistent with each other on a deeper level, the idea of perpetual peace will assert itself.

In the essay on universal history of 1784, Kant emphasizes the technical progress brought about by reason. As a mere natural predisposition, reason is fragile and must be cultivated in the individual before it can be effectively used; but it is in the species rather than the individual, whose life is much too brief, that we can expect reason to attain complete development.[30] Human differences, however, do not lead to wholesome competition but set one against another in ever more murderous fashion as the generations pass, for reason's progress results in improved technologies of destruction. Passions are armed with ever more sophisticated means of attaining their satisfaction, but the means turn against their inventors: Wars produce only horrible suffering. Reason could have foreseen this but made no attempt to, for in its first form it is technical.

In 1786, in the *Speculative Beginning of Human History*, Kant traces the development of reason. He uses for this purpose a procedure that we have already observed—conjecture, or *Mutmassung*. Starting from our present experience of nature, we can derive by conjecture what must have been the beginnings of human history, "if one presupposes that in their first beginnings these actions were no better or worse than we now find them to be, a presupposition that conforms to the analogy of nature and has no risky consequences."[31] It is a question, then, of discovering by analogy the "original capacities in the nature of man," and, reasoning from these, of understanding by what stages freedom and war developed. To begin with, Kant very clearly shows the first stage of this development to be something like nascent reason's detaching itself from the automatisms of instinct in the realms of both self-preservation and perpetuation of the species. So begins the history of freedom's development. It is the history of an animal species' separation from traits that would have characterized it as merely a natural object and, as such, subject to rigorously deterministic laws.

More as illustration, perhaps, than to justify his own conjectures, Kant will "use a holy document as a map," the second through sixth chapters of Genesis. The conceptual organization of the genesis of liberty is correlated with the events of the narrative, thus giving the latter a philosophical meaning; the "guiding thread," to use Kant's expression, that allows us to reconstruct by conjecture the first manifestations of freedom "follows precisely the same line as is sketched out in that historical document."[32]

Kant's interpretation of the texts he makes use of is obviously strictly secular. Between *natural history*, which is the study of all species living in blind submission to the instincts that preserve them, and our *human history* of inventions that, though subject to nature's laws, are in no way part of nature, there is a chasm that isolates the human race and sets it radically apart from all others. Even at reason's first dawning it discovers objects to satisfy the needs of instinct that instinct had not found. At the same time it profoundly transforms instinct itself. In human beings physical needs do not occur in a pure state because reason invents desires, that is, impulses to acquire objects of satisfaction that are not found in nature. The specifically human behavior introduced by reason is freedom to choose among objects devised by inventing new relations among things in order to placate new desires; behavior is no longer an automatic act to attain the natural appeasement of a natural need.

At this point human beings, influenced only by the results of their actions, create feelings that are unknown to nature and are contradictory. Self-satisfaction is humans' awareness of the distance they have put, unassisted, between themselves and nature. Reason's action takes the form of a mental state that is far different from the simple contentment inspired by the fusion of the needy animal with the fulfilling object; it is a turning inward, an act of thought that sets the value of the act of creation equal to, or even higher than, the value of the object created. Reason is consciousness of its own worth and is manifested as a joyous feeling of mastery and superiority that in one stroke reveals to human beings both their membership in a species unlike any other and their individuality. Thanks to reason's growth, human beings experiences the self as a unity both abstract and concrete, both intellectual and emotional. The unity is soon shattered. An opposing sentiment dilutes satisfaction—uneasiness or anxiety in the face of the unpredictability of choice and the lost hope of return to instinct's infallibility.

Reason is both source of power and threat of error, both humanity's weakness and its strength, each facet inherent in freedom of choice. Kant describes the sundering due to reason: "If only this attempt," he writes, "had not contradicted nature, it could, with luck, have turned out well enough, even though instinct did not advise it."[33] But the multiplicity of objects available to choice combines with the urging of desire to drive reason to technical inventions to replace the reliability of instinct; so reason must also become caution, even in the midst of its discoveries. The human species, as a result, is much more on its own than any other. There is a loneliness accompanying the exercise of reason that cannot be found in the world of determinism.

Can we not identify this duality characterizing reason as freedom of choice with the "unsociable sociability" of Kant's 1784 essay? Do not the trust that encourages one person to associate with another and the distrust that also exists between them suggest comparison to reason's hesitancy? Reason promises success but also failure; it summons us to seek out others in order to found stable organizations where it can flourish through cooperative action, yet it also impels us to withdraw into ourselves from suspicion of the superiority others might gain over us and use against us. The tie that binds us to nature becomes as ambiguous as the one binding us to other people; we challenged it the instant we felt it. Human beings need other humans to help them understand the causes of what is useful or harmful to them. When we discover by reason that we are power of choice, that we are freedom, then we must put our freedom to wise use. We must build a science of nature capable of assuring us of the outcome of our actions. In this science, we study ourselves as natural objects, but our creation of such a science demonstrates that we are outside nature. There is nothing instinctive in knowing nature and making use of its laws. The adaptation of an animal whose relations to all aspects of the natural world are unchanging is succeeded by research that, despite the richness of its results, can never provide for life with any certainty. This is why "unsatisfying satisfaction" is the mark of freedom from the very moment reason becomes manifest. Freedom lets a human race that is proud of itself and yet crippled find responses—no longer spontaneous and automatic—to the demands of its instinct for survival.

The truth of the human being will now be the separation from nature brought about by thought, a separation both fertile and dangerous, a source of self-admiration and a source of fear; for the other side of pride of creation is the worry that we are mistaken or have been tricked. As the human race is formed, a concept is also formed that has no meaning except for humankind—the concept of the future. When reason takes on the task of producing humans' means of survival, it tears them out of life in the immediate instant and sets them in what now becomes their true environment: the flow of time. Like all animal species, the human species cannot escape the natural periodicities of day and night, of the seasons, of everything that occurs in rhythmic alternations beyond its power to control. But this is not enough to constitute an awareness of time. Strictly speaking, it is the action of human thought that creates time. The past and the future acquire meaning through memory and forethought. Human life proceeds toward what does not yet exist, toward a future time that stretches beyond the limits of an individual lifetime. To be capable of leaving the present by conceiving of the present and of what follows it is to travel in thought beyond the self to where the future no longer directly affects the thinker. This is the future that belongs to descendants whose image is unknowable and whom we can envisage only as abstractions. "To make present to himself the future, often very distant time," Kant says, "is the distinguishing characteristic of man's superiority, for in conformity with his vocation he can prepare himself in advance for distant ends."[34] Reason thus removes the human being from total subjectivity, for though humans can imagine distant goals, these goals do not concern them directly. They are only *the idea of a history* that will be the outcome of future changes; they represent awareness of progress in ways of living and thinking that is beyond imagination and yet nonetheless certain.

Whatever interest we may take in the distant future, when we are no longer absorbed in the mere present moment, we imagine and dread the threats that weigh on our own and our children's future. Expectation is "the most inexhaustible source of cares and troubles, which the uncertain future arouses and from which all animals are exempt."[35] When we think beyond the moment we are experiencing, we discover we are mortal, as are all whom we love, as are all other humans. Death is far more a source of dread than of hope on the part of the only species that is aware of it, and according to Kant's analysis in this text, the individual self, confronted with its discovery of death, finds in it no transcendent meaning. Once more we come upon cause for ambivalence: Human beings make the history of their race, but history for them individually is the history of their disappearance.

Still, however disastrous war may seem for the individuals who start and continue it under the goad of their passions, the state of war that threatens their lives and destroys their accomplishments also has consequences that are *not* deplorable. To be precise, the extremity of misery that war always occasions demands of humans an attempt to create conditions of life different from those that would let war develop automatically. In other words, if we consider the nature of humanity, we may consider it natural, and hence necessary, that war should occur, together with all its train of wretchedness. And it is also natural and necessary to want it to stop. The invention of a civil state in which the passions are subject to laws is, therefore, both the product of a (natural) necessity and at the same time the outcome of free invention, because such a state does not exist in nature. As a first step, freedom responds to natural necessity by creating a political power capable of enforcing civil peace. Although this idea is good in principle, freedom does not immediately succeed in producing a satisfactory reality. Actual political communities include much that is irrational and arbitrary in their attempts at internal organization. Full awareness of the positive aspects of the results, as well as of their shortcomings, comes only at the end of a very long process requiring centuries for its accomplishment. War, the burden of preparing for war that weighs so heavily on times of peace, and the destruction and slaughter involved in battles, victories, and defeats are, paradoxically, the cause of this awareness. A generation has too short a life to experience more than the ups and downs of history. It cannot decode its meaning. It is only by means of knowledge accumulated by generations over a very long span and because of a necessity grown more urgent as weapons have grown more deadly that a time comes when what Kant calls the "establishment of a perfect national constitution" can be conceived and have some chance of being realized. Thus nature's pressure toward greater discord among people tends in the same direction as invention. Freedom, expressed in invention and goaded by necessity, initially becomes skilled at forming a nation's internal organization so that the arbitrary means always accompanying passion can at last be replaced there by rational means. Freedom later becomes skilled at managing relations *among* nations. When the nations have been in fact endowed with perfect national constitutions, they will be universally able to institute such relations as will leave no room for war.

Human beings, who are temperamentally inclined sometimes to laziness, sometimes to aggression, are in reality (but unknown to themselves) forced by nature to bring about freedom's supreme achievement, perpetual peace. This is the meaning of history, however hidden it may be by the facts of history, which are "folly and childish vanity and often even childish malice and destruction."[36] The purpose of the 1784 essay is to demonstrate how natural pressures have driven humanity to that expression of freedom, invention. It is as if nature acts with a purpose—to force humanity to create by itself, that is, of its free will, in slow progress through the chaos of history, a work that will only be apparent to fortunate generations far in the future, harvesters of the fruits of their predecessors' suffering. The ultimate importance of history is that it reveals the moral essence of freedom in the human race, even when generations and their individual members are more like devils than rational human beings. "A *pathologically* enforced agreement," Kant writes, can be transformed "into a society and, finally, a *moral* whole."[37]

Similar themes are developed in Kant's *Speculative Beginning of Human History*. We cannot deny that war is a plague. It is nonetheless true that fear of war "necessitate[s] . . . *respect for humanity* from the leaders of nations. . . . At the stage of culture at which the human race still stands, war is an indispensable means for bringing it to a still higher stage; and only after a perfect culture exists (God knows when), would a peace that endures forever benefit us, and thus it is possible only in such a culture."[38] The human race will eventually reach a moment when the laws a nation makes for itself will become perfectly rational, by which is meant necessary and universal, and when international relations can be based on similarly rational principles. The laws of nature are necessary and universal from the start; the laws of the human race take an enormously long time to become so. "The history of *nature*, therefore," Kant says, "begins with good, for it is God's work; the history of *freedom* begins with badness, for it is *man's* work."[39] Humanity only attains the same perfection as nature after the slow passage of eons. The actors in the drama of history either do not understand it at all or mistake its meaning. The generations fortunate enough to live at the end of history "should have the good fortune to live in the building on which a long sequence of their forefathers (though certainly without any intention of their own) worked, without being able themselves to partake of the prosperity they prepared the way for."[40] This kind of forward march of history toward an equilibrium that it can know nothing of along the way may appear "strange" or "mysterious." We might even think that it is unfair to the earlier generations, if we did not realize that history's progress must be understood as necessary. "No matter how puzzling this is," Kant writes, "it is nonetheless . . . necessary once one assumes that one species of animal should have reason and that as a class of rational beings—each member of which dies, while the species is immortal—it is destined to develop its capacities to perfection."[41]

Kant often refers to people as both reasoning beings and finite beings. Each individual can be said to be finite, not only because he is destined to die but because, despite his talent for reason, he often possesses a limited intelligence or else a morality that permits the worst of evils. The full development of rationality, by contrast, characterizes the species as a whole, which persists and evolves because unfettered by instinct. Albeit each individual is free and therefore called to a moral perfection that perhaps none will ever reach, the race's horizon is the perfection of political relations. This being the case, are morals and politics—Kant clearly distinguishes them—destined to converge? Or will they remain, on the contrary, completely separate? The answer will become clear as we analyze the conditions necessary for civil peace and for perpetual peace among nations.

In order to understand the qualities of the rational constitution thoroughly, we must begin by asking ourselves why it brings a definitive—that is, a fully satisfying—solution to problems that can be resolved only badly or not at all without it.

We can define an animal as we would any natural phenomenon. All that it is or can be and all that happens to it may be understood as the result of laws that have given it an unchanging nature. The human being is free. Although like any animal the human is related to the exterior world—to things or to other humans—the uniquely human type of relationship is not given but made. This is why it is not enough that we may legitimately investigate what our relations are in *fact*; we must also ask what they ought to be according to *right*. From this point of view, it appears that all human relations have, among other characteristics, a juridical one that is always present. A person as such never attains undisputed ownership of anything, even the direst necessities, where law does not reign. On the one hand, humanity has freedom; on the other, nothing can objectively be without an owner—for "freedom would . . . be depriving itself of the use of its voluntary activity, in thus putting *useable* objects out of all possibility of *use*."[42] Hence, the use anyone makes of freedom must "harmonize . . . with the external freedom of all according to universal Laws." Every object is therefore a "possible Mine or Thine," or, in other words, we have the right to "impose upon all others an obligation . . . to abstain from the use of certain objects . . . because we have already taken them into our possession."[43] The use of external objects and the distinction between "thine" and "mine" create "juridical duties" even in the state of nature. In Kant's words, "It is a juridical Duty so to act towards others that what is external and useable may come into the possession or become the property of some one."[44] If people were reasonable beings and never otherwise than reasonable, they would not have to leave the state of nature and create a political state to preserve the legality of their relations. Legality and morality would be indistinguishable. But such is not the case—far from it. By 1797, when Kant produced the *Philosophy of Law*, he had already written at length of how much the finite character of human nature, unsociable sociability, the penchant for evil, and the passions are generators of conflict. Every appropriation, however essential, is in question as long as it is the unilateral act of a single will, for no will can unilaterally impose an obligation on others. For ownership to be honored, it must be sustained by "an *omnilateral* or universal Will, which is not contingent, but a priori, and which is therefore necessarily united and legislative."[45] This will is not found in the state of nature, which knows only private wills. Acquisition in nature is "provisory"; only in the civil state does it becomes "peremptory." Although it is in fact natural to make use of the soil anywhere in the world,

> on account of the opposition of the free Will of one to that of the other in the sphere of action, which is inevitable by nature, all use of the soil would be prevented did not every will contain at the same time a Law for the regulation of the relation of all Wills in action, according to which a *particular possession* can be determined to every one upon the common soil. . . . But the distributive Law of the Mine and Thine, as applicable to each individual on the soil, according to the Axiom of external Freedom, cannot proceed otherwise than from a *primarily* united Will a priori. . . . This Law can only take form in the Civil State . . . as it is in this state alone that the united common Will determines what is *right*, what is *rightful*, and what is the constitution of the *Right*.[46]

Besides the duty to acknowledge that the will is endowed with a "juridical faculty" even in the state of nature, we have the duty to enter into the civil state in order to make this faculty effective.

It would be wrong to believe, however, that people are obliged to enter into the civil state solely because they make war against each other in the state of nature. It is not a *fact*, however significant, that gives rise to the civil state, but reason, where there is found a priori the *idea* that

> before a legal state of Society can be publicly established, individual Men, Nations and States can never be safe against violence from each other. . . . It is necessary to leave the state of Nature, in which every one follows his own inclinations, and to form a union of all those who cannot avoid coming into reciprocal communication, and thus subject themselves in common to the external restraint of public compulsory Laws. Men thus enter into a Civil Union, in which every one has it determined by Law what shall be recognised as his; and this is secured to him by a competent external Power distinct from his own individuality. Such is the primary Obligation, on the part of all men, to enter into the relations of a Civil State of Society.[47]

For all the social contract philosophers, the contract has, it goes without saying, a juridical character. In Kant's writings, even in the state of nature, which is not a juridical state because no criterion of distributive justice exists there, the human being appears as a "juridical animal," for however good we can imagine the state of nature to be, human reason nonetheless requires the creation of a state in which distributive justice can be established and maintained as the norm. Kant gives a rigorous definition of the state of right: "A State," he writes, "is the union of a number of men under juridical Laws. These Laws, as such, are to be regarded as necessary a priori. . . . The Form of the State is thus involved in the *Idea* of the State, viewed as it ought to be according to pure principles of Right; and this ideal Form furnishes the normal criterion of every real union that constitutes a Commonwealth."[48]

Granted that actual states are formally born of this idea, in practice they are only as good as they are able to be. The idea that creates nations is one thing, the reality of their historical existence quite another. They can be intended as juridical communities without corresponding perfectly to the intention. They maintain civil peace more or less adequately, guaranteeing compatibility of external freedoms by their laws, according to more or less satisfactory constitutions. Formally, the state contains three powers that are related to each other like the propositions of a syllogism, and they cannot be collapsed into one. By right the citizenry is the legislative power, as it is "the united and consenting Will of all."[49] In this sense the people are sovereign, and no monarch can legitimately legislate in their stead. We know that in fact reason develops over the course of history and does not display the full flowering of its predispositions at the outset. There is therefore very little chance that a genuine "republican constitution," the only rational constitution, should come into existence. People mostly live under different kinds of despotic constitutions. But the republican constitution, representing the "state of greatest harmony" between a constitution and the principles of law, is the type toward which all societies must evolve. Because it is the single rational form, we are obligated to it by a categorical imperative; and it is also the single form truly suited to safeguarding, in right and in fact, the civil peace.

Once the republican constitution has been established in every state, our duty extends to the entire world. Rational legislation within a state enjoins an *obligation* to have rational legislation among states. Although it will take an incalculably long time for peace to be definitively established by law, from the instant that the *idea* of it has been clearly conceived, peace becomes the next horizon that peoples must strive to reach.

Still, we can ask how an *idea*, however logical and seductive, can avoid being a fantasy and can somehow require its own realization.[50] Have we not come back to the dreams of the great utopias, or has Kant actually shown us how theory and practice could converge, as the idea is increasingly actualized in the course of history? It is necessary to get a clear understanding of what an idea is and of what we can hope from it.

In 1781, when he published the first edition of the *Critique of Pure Reason*, Kant precisely delimited the domain of our faculty of knowing. Any extension of the domain as he has defined it now becomes unacceptable. In science we can know only phenomena. From this perspective, everything that most intensely interests us but that is outside determinism is beyond our grasp. Kant nonetheless remarks that "our reason naturally exalts itself to forms of knowledge which so far transcend the bounds of experience that no given empirical object can ever coincide with them, but which must none the less be recognized as having their own reality, and which are by no means mere fictions of the brain."[51] Insofar as they synthesize sets of conditions with the unconditioned absolutes that unify them, ideas respond to a need on the part of reason. In this sense, we can say that the idea is, on the one hand, a necessary product of reason; on the other, the idea can only be considered legitimate if we remember that it can bring us no speculative knowledge and that we cannot make use of it in the domain of speculative knowledge. An idea's value, then, depends on its not contradicting the teachings of science—the idea of a dragon, for example, is contradictory[52]—and on its utility for practical reason. In other words, people have one and only one reasoning faculty; its speculative use is limited to knowledge other than phenomena, and its practical use is immediate knowledge of the moral law—the principle of universality—

in beings both free and yet dependent on their senses, their inclinations, and their passions. "What *use*," Kant asks, "can we make of our understanding . . . if we do not propose ends to ourselves? But the highest ends are those of morality, and these we can know only as they are given us by pure reason."[53]

This kind of passage clarifies the meaning, and hence the nature, of the perfect civil constitution, the constitution that, once inaugurated in a nation, assures its civil peace and that, when established in *all* nations, will assure perpetual peace among them. Kant's complex thinking is elucidated when we grasp that the human's sensual nature is not the cause of wars. Instinct would at most lead to passing confrontations between individuals, such as animals engage in, but never anything we could call war. Our passions, grafted onto our natural inclinations, are pathological because they are primarily free choices in disobedience to moral law. It is the passions that are the cause of wars. In addition, everything happens as if the history of our passions and their wars were unfolding in accord with a purpose—to drive us to awareness of misfortune and to its necessary abolishment. This purpose seems like the determinism of nature advancing toward a goal, and it becomes explicit in an idea of (nonnatural) reason, namely, that though each historical event is in fact determined, history nevertheless has a purpose. It is the creation of peace, that is, of the state of human beings' living *as if* they honored the moral law. What a free decision of humanity will probably never do—it would be utopian to expect it—will inevitably be incarnated in a legal structure that outwardly expresses, through the constraint of laws, the harmony of freedoms with each other.

In this way reasonable people, finite by nature, will be able despite their finitude to live together as if they were nothing but reasonable, in a network of relationships that bring them into contact yet not into conflict. Such is the idea of the perfect constitution that we are lead to by the *idea* of universal history, that is, of meaningful history; for just as reason makes technical progress generation after generation, it also progresses in the juridical sphere until it succeeds in conceiving a truly universal legality that eliminates war. To be sure, we are only speaking of an idea; but in following the notion of the progress of history—our guiding thread—the idea is justified because it is not contradictory. It is nonetheless not to be considered apodictic knowledge. There is no such thing as sensory apprehension of universal history. In the first place, then, the idea belongs to practical reason by its moral use. Human beings, who are free to decide the character of their will in accord with the dictates of reason, should do everything possible to speed the day of the perfect constitution and of peace. In the second place, the idea belongs to practical reason by its juridical use. No judge can know exactly what happens inside people when they choose behaviors, nor whether some self-serving motive has not tarnished the purity of their *moral* judgment. So the role of the statesman is to use *juridical* reason and, with rational laws, compel free wills that can always choose evil instead freely to prefer peaceful harmony. This *idea* is responsive in every respect to the demands of reason in matters of right.

To Kant, right is not the search for an order independent of human beings. On the contrary, right resides in the human universality of the law that freedom appeals to in its external use.[54] The ability that defines the concept of right, namely, the ability to bind others to a duty, develops out of the moral imperative—"which is undoubtedly a Law which imposes obligation upon me"[55]—and therefore out of the autonomy of the will-as-reason. It does not originate in anything except the immanence of reason. The creation and organization of the political community are the task of the human being, just as is the legal framework for peace that will put a final end to all forms of war.

Kant's thinking about war and peace did not change decisively during the years in which he published the books, articles, and essays that dealt either exclusively or incidentally with these subjects. From one work to another, he may highlight or change the order of different points, but his general intent does not alter. Although the theme of war and peace is not central to the *Critique of Pure Reason*, it lays the groundwork for it. "All our knowledge," Kant writes, "starts with the senses, proceeds from thence to understanding, and ends with reason, beyond which there is no higher faculty to be found in us for elaborating the matter of intuition and bringing it under the highest unity of thought."[56] Reason is indeed the faculty that gives us general principles, but its transcendent use—which would consist, as we have already noted, in the knowledge arising from conditioned objects to an unconditioned absolute—could lead only to illusion, despite the mind's inevitably endless repetition of this action. By contrast, the spheres of freedom and legislation, lying outside scientific knowledge, contain no illusions. Kant echoes the age-old wish that "sometime perhaps (who knows when!) may be fulfilled—that instead of the endless multiplicity of civil laws we should be able to fall back on their general principles. For it is in these alone that we can hope to find the secret of what we are wont to call the simplifying of legislation."[57]

As early as 1781 Kant expresses the hope that principles will be discovered someday—at an unknowable time in the distant future. Such a discovery is possible, despite the infinite variety in the laws, because of the variation among the circumstances under which they were drawn up. The different forms of laws depend on the obvious contingency of the different forms of constitutions that have promulgated them. In this sense, their diversity is comparable to the multifarious character of the objects of sensory experience. And although reason feels the need to make a complete synthesis of conditions, we would delude ourselves if we expected to find the unconditioned principle unifying the diverse objects of the phenomenal world; but we would not delude ourselves to expect to find the unconditioned principle unifying the civil laws. When we analyze codes of law according to the date of their appearance and the period of their use, we may attribute their variety and even their mutual contradictions to thousands of possible causes. From this point of view, it is not legitimate to look for the unconditioned principle of legislation. In contrast, when we consider civil laws in relation to freedom, they are no longer scientifically knowable. "The laws," Kant writes, "are only limitations imposed upon our freedom in order that such freedom may completely harmonise with itself."[58] This is an early version of the Kantian doctrine of the relation between law and freedom, which, if not fully detailed, is at least sketched in this passage. The function of civil law is to bring the external freedoms into harmony. In this respect, it is restrictive and coercive of what Kant will call later the freedoms for evil. At the same time, it brings freedom completely into harmony with itself, inasmuch as freedom-as-reason is itself (purely formally) a lawmaker. The law is of our own making. "We ourselves, through these concepts [of it], can be the cause."[59] We can then justifiably conceive of the possibility of discovering a unique principle underlying civil laws by attributing these laws to freedom as practical reason. It is reason that sees to it that there are laws, not a potentate or customs or anything else. That the *content* of the laws is not yet rational does not invalidate the idea that at some point in history we will succeed in conceiving the *form* of legislation in such a way that, because of the universality of their reason, its authors will not be able to legislate against their own best interests.

The importance of these few lines in a work little concerned with politics is, for that reason, all the greater. The passage establishes the status of the legislative domain and points the way to the *idea* of a perfect constitution. Such a constitution will not owe its legitimacy to any capacity for speculative knowledge about a world order that the laws would have to reflect, nor to some trait of the power that might decree them, such as age or military prowess. The unconditioned that is, by definition, freedom-as-reason *is* the principle of legislation in right, *can* become so in fact, and, finally, *must* become so, as the political writings will demonstrate. Reason has purposes, which it accomplishes as practical reason once it is alerted to the wrong use it could put itself to (as speculative reason) regarding principles. If we base our thinking on Kant, it is clear that a nation is duty-bound to a course that will let it move toward perfection, even though it cannot attain it. What that course should be remains to be seen. In 1781, before the political works had been written, we can already make out the broad outline into which the republican constitution and, later, the doctrine of peace will fit.

———————

Freedom is the very nature of humans. It defines the person as a being capable of self-determination and unfettered by any conditions except freedom itself. Kant sets forth the principles of his moral philosophy in the *Critique of Pure Reason*, then elaborates them in 1785 in the *Foundation for the Metaphysic of Ethic* and in 1788 in the *Critique of Practical Reason*. In this philosophy the *existence of reason*, taken as self-evident, gives *value* to the human being, thereby differentiating humans from all other living species. As we have seen, it is freedom that *obligates* a race that is unprotected from the arbitrary caprice of passions to leave the state of nature; and because it is reason, it is freedom that makes laws. Human beings make up the only species that gives itself laws. It imposes laws on itself and laws restrict it, because the human being "abuses his freedom" in his relations with his fellows. In Kant's words, "Man is *an animal that*, if he lives among other members of his species, *has need of a master*."[60] *Every* man—which excludes a priori the legitimacy of one person's wielding power over another. There is no legitimate control except the establishment of a perfect civil constitution in which the "master" would be empowered to "break [the person's] self-will and force him to obey a universally valid will, whereby everyone can be free."[61]

In 1784 Kant states the problem without, strictly speaking, proposing a solution. "The greatest problem for the human species, whose solution nature compels it to seek, is to achieve a universal *civil society* administered in accord with the right."[62] He says nothing about the structure of this society, but he expressly connects *"establishing a perfect civil constitution"* to *"the problem of law-governed* external relations among nations."[63] In other words, the political states that live in a mutual state of nature in which they enjoy "unrestricted freedom" in their relations and wage ever more ferocious wars, must resolve "to give up their brutal freedom and to seek calm and security in a law-governed constitution."[64] Kant says only that after the chaos caused by wars that threaten the integrity and even the existence of the nations, "finally—partially through the best possible internal organization of the civil constitution, partially through common external agreement and legislation—a state similar to a civil commonwealth is established and can maintain itself *automatically*."[65] It is obvious to what extent this constitution is left vague. There is to be a "federation of peoples" to protect and defend every nation, thanks to "a united might and . . . decisions made by the united will in accord with laws."[66] The *automatic* perpetuation of this community is not a contradiction of freedom. Nature and freedom join in making it automatic, because the laws possess the universality that their origin in reason demands. Nature automatically persists as nature. Because the universality of civil laws constrains everyone, both within states and between them, to respect the freedom of every other, person or state, the universal civil community will persist in peace, without need of any further progress.

This essay, the *Universal History with Cosmopolitan Intent*, gives scant analysis of the structure of the community that is to guarantee peace. What are its institutions? Who decides in cases of disagreement? In commenting on the work, Alexis Philonenko remarks that the "utopian stage" of Kant's thought begins with the Seventh Thesis of the *Universal History*.[67] The progress of history must bring the human race to live in peace, for the constitution that circumstances will have driven humans to create for themselves will be a constitution administering justice universally. In a world state? In the coexistence of states? The essay of 1784 does not let us draw any conclusions with confidence.

Nor does that of 1786. In the *Speculative Beginning of Human History*, an important element is made clear: When it extricated itself from nature, the human race discovered that it could make use of all living beings as means or instruments according to its will—with the exception of man. "This was early preparation," Kant says, "for the limitations that reason would in the future place upon him in regard to his fellow man and which is far more necessary to establishing society than inclination and love."[68] The step that consists in breaking free from nature and standing apart from any other species (which can be used because it is merely natural) is the step that makes every human being equal to all others. Without this "unlimited equality," no society could be formed. This passage, we note, is not concerned with the perfect civil society. A fortiori, equality will be one of the fundamental elements of such a society. Here Kant merely says that "only after a perfect culture exists (God knows when), would a peace that endures forever benefit us, and thus it is possible only in such a culture."[69]

The question of what composes a perfect society is not taken up in the *Critique of Judgment* either. The perfect society is evoked, however, as the "formal condition" permitting nature's attainment of its "final purpose," that is, of "the development of the natural capacities" of the human race.[70] The civil community is "that arrangement of men's relations to one another by which lawful authority in a whole . . . is opposed to the abuse of their conflicting freedoms."[71] Civic society is the condition of possibility of civic peace within a state, and therefore of "culture," the final end of nature. Culture is "the aptitude of a rational being for arbitrary purposes in general."[72] Over time it evolves, and as generation succeeds generation it develops the inclinations that nature planted as mere potentials. Unlike other natural beings, the human being is "the only being upon [earth] who can form a concept of purposes and who can, by reason, make out of an aggregate of purposively formed things a system of purposes."[73] In 1790 Kant writes that "though not for the determinant but for the reflective judgment," the concept of purpose has been justified "according to fundamental propositions of reason."[74]

At last Kant makes two observations that connect to the theses of his political essays. First, he says that once the civil constitution has been established—which is improbable because people are not "clever enough," nor are they "wise enough to submit themselves voluntarily to its constraints"—then there must still be "a *cosmopolitan* whole, i.e. a system of all states that are in danger of acting injuriously upon one another."[75] Here again is the same theme as in the *Universal History*, and still without any light being shed on this "system of states," no more, in fact, than on the makeup of the civic society. Still loyal to ideas he has already expounded, Kant adds that, in the absence of such a system, the ambition and avarice of people—and especially of their leaders—make history appear to be a jousting arena where states are made and unmade for no discernible reason within the melee in which the only constant is disorganization. That is, Kant repeats, unless war is "a deep-hidden and designed enterprise of supreme wisdom for preparing, if not for establishing, conformity to law amid the freedom of States, and with this a unity of a morally grounded system of those states."[76] Here again is war's role as a means nature uses to reach its ultimate end. Peace, however, is not claimed to be inevitable, even in the far distant future. It is only a possibility that would give meaning to "the dreadful afflictions with which [war] visits the human race, and perhaps greater afflictions with which the constant preparation for it in time of peace oppresses them."[77] Without mentioning war as the surest means to perpetual peace, Kant here terms war "a motive for developing all talents serviceable for culture to the highest possible pitch."[78] Without war, would the predispositions that become ever more conscious of themselves and so allow humanity to be no longer merely natural—would these predispositions suffice to make humans into free beings, developing and transforming themselves, instead of acting as mere automatons?

In 1793 Kant published an important article entitled *On the Proverb: That May Be True in Theory, but Is of No Practical Use*. There he details the union of the ends of nature and moral obligation for the realization of a "cosmopolitan constitution" guaranteeing a "state of universal freedom."[79] Nothing more than a "hope" is expressed here. The word appears frequently in Kant's writing. The improbability of the hope's fulfillment cannot be reduced, and yet as a moral project—"so to affect posterity that it will become continually better"[80]—this project becomes a duty "as long as [its] futility cannot be shown to be completely certain."[81] Taking as a starting point what he himself calls his "base of support"—and what base of support could be more sturdy than a duty?—Kant can clearly articulate a postulate that he transforms from hypothesis into obligation: In parallel with the evidence of *culture*'s constant progress over time, we must hope— to do so is a duty, because the impossibility of realizing the hope is not established—we must hope, then, that in spite of well-known appearances and facts, the morality of the human race is also improving through the effects of history. History, it is true, very obviously continues to disappoint our expectations; but though this hope cannot become a certainty, it is still compatible with the idea of a world shaped by a wise Creator and does not contradict the existence of rational choice by the free, if too clearly helpless, will within every person. "I will thus permit myself," Kant writes, "to assume that since the human race's natural end is to make steady cultural progress, its moral end is to be conceived as progressing toward the better. And this progress may well be occasionally *interrupted*, but will never be *broken off*."[82] We cannot now assume the certain moral improvement of all humanity to be the end result of this progress, for freedom will always be capable of choosing evil; members of generations as far in the future as we can imagine cannot "with certainty be conscious of *having performed* [their] duty altogether unselfishly."[83] Yet the idea of a better future for humankind is not fantastic, for the peace that will blossom within the various nations as a result of their civil constitutions will, by analogy, also flourish if all the world's nations are brought under such a constitution. Kant formulates the solution he has faith in as follows: "The sole possible remedy for this [international conflict] is a [state] of international right (analogous to the civil or national rights of individual men) based on public laws backed by force and submitted to by every nation."[84]

We now must specify the means by which nature and freedom will enable the human race to achieve its purposes in spite of human wickedness and the crushing facts of history. Religions have shown people that they are responsible for their own unhappiness. Their teachings have emphasized the importance of inner conversion as the only way to weaken the power of the passions enough that our original nature can approach (and perhaps attain) friendship, agreement, and peace both between individuals and between their societies. Kant knows all this, but he does not count on measures that have little chance of changing beings who are reasonable, of course, but finite. He does not mince words. "If we now inquire as to the means by which this eternal progress towards betterment can be maintained and perhaps even sped up, one soon sees that this immeasurably distant result depends not so much on what *we* do (e.g. on the education we give the world's children), nor on what method we adopt so as to bring it about; instead, it depends on what human *nature does in and with us so as to compel us onto a path that we ourselves would not readily follow.''*[85]*

Kant, then, hopes for humanity, and so for its members individually, a state of affairs that it is everyone's *duty* to try to hasten but that none will achieve, perhaps precisely because it is a duty. The goal will be attained somehow, in spite of humans, although for their good. Just as every person has the duty of entering the civil state but is forced to do so by the painfulness of the state of nature, so each nation and its members have the duty of living in peace with their neighbors but will also be forced to do so by the painfulness of history, the state of nature prevailing among nations. Kant has no confidence in humanity, but he does have unreserved faith in law. Genuine juridical relations produce peace between the members of a political community and between political communities; they are an essential expression of distinctively human reality, for "*the right* of men *under public coercive law*, through which each can receive his due and can be made secure from the interference of others . . . derives entirely from the concept of *freedom* in the external relations among men."[86] This is why "as an end that is an unconditioned and primary duty with respect to every external relation in general among men, this union is met with only in society, and then only insofar as it finds itself in a civil state, i.e. constitutes a commonwealth."[87]

An actual community of any sort entails a moral contract among its members, to the effect that each one, motivated by the wretchedness and insecurity to be endured in the state of nature, wills the limitation of his or her own freedom and the freedom of each other person "so that it is compatible with the freedom of everyone, insofar as this is possible in accord with a universal law."[88] People are *coerced* by nature, but because the civil state presents the only rational relation that could be formed among free beings, they are equally *obligated* by reason to accept it. "Reason itself—indeed, pure a priori law-giving reason, which takes no notice of any empirical ends . . . wills it so."[89] By definition, every civil constitution, by virtue of belonging to the juridical sphere, is founded on the *freedom* that characterizes each *human being* who is its member, on *equality* of all its *subjects* before the law, and on the *independence* of each *citizen* colegislator. The "original contract" that is synonymous with the general will of a "people collectively (since all decide for all, hence each for himself)"[90] is the defining feature of a republican constitution.

It is true that history has not seen this constitution realized. The principle of actual constitutions is nonetheless formally the same. (In constitutions properly called despotic, however, a single individual holds all the rights, which amounts to his doing as he pleases; and all the members are slaves, including the despot, who is a slave to his passions.)

Every place where we may speak of citizens, it is formally true (though at no time true in fact) that the union of individuals into a single entity has as its purpose "the *right* of men *under public coercive law.*"[91] The original contract does not exist in fact and does not need to: "Instead, it is a *mere idea* of reason, one, however, that has indubitable (practical) reality. Specifically, it obligates every legislator to formulate his laws in such a way that they *could* have sprung from the unified will of the entire people and to regard every subject, insofar as he desires to be a citizen, as if he had joined in voting for such a will."[92] Reason obligates, it does not coerce; this is why political states, though they have always existed, are far from having been "perfect constitutions." The idea of the original contract is the "infallible standard" of the legislator.[93]

We understand on the one hand that *by right* the sovereignty—that is, the legitimate power to make laws—resides in the people, who are *represented* in the person of the legislator. The chief of state must be "authorized to be the sole judge" of measures suitable "for *securing* the *state of right,* especially against the people's external enemies."[94] Whether the measures are popular or not, their purpose is solely to preserve the integrity of the state, and on this point everyone is, by right, in unanimous agreement. It is a matter of saving the "state of right," in conformity with its definition. Although the measures may prove ineffective, the law that prescribes them still conforms to ideal right.

On the other hand, no "right to resist" can have a coherent meaning within this kind of framework; it would be self-contradictory. Kant states without the least mitigation: "Thus, if a people should judge that a particular actual legislation would in all probability cause them to forfeit their happiness, what should they do about it? Should they not resist it? There can be only one answer: nothing can be done about it, except to obey."[95] The reason is plain and is tied to the *rightful* foundation or legitimacy of every nation:

> There is no rightfully constituted commonwealth without the power to put down all internal resistance, for such resistance would have to derive from a maxim that, if made universal, would destroy all civil constitutions, thus annihilating the only state in which men can possess rights.
> From this it follows that all resistance to the supreme legislative power, all incitement of subjects actively to express discontent, all revolt that breaks forth into rebellion, is the highest and most punishable crime in a commonwealth, for it destroys its foundation.[96]

Kant, then, rejects what Hobbes had allowed—the right of everyone to return to the state of nature if the political state no longer provides the safety that was the purpose of its creation. Kant by no means neglects this purpose. He simply subordinates it to the essence of the state, outside whose boundaries security has no meaning. Kant's definition of the state and the implications he draws from that definition are intrinsically legal because they involve our knowing and applying a law of practical reason that makes the civil state incumbent on everyone. In other words, *civil peace* is a duty. Having set forth the basis of civil peace, Kant is in a position to say that although nature forces us to make *perpetual peace* among nations, just as it forced all of us, because we are human, into civil peace, yet peace between states is, like civil peace, also a duty.

The hope that we see growing from one work to the next, this "sweet dream" of peace that only philosophers appear to harbor ("perpetual peace" being more commonly found in cemeteries than in history) is once more affirmed by Kant two years after *Theory and Practice*. But this time the natural and the moral conditions of peace are methodically analyzed as such, without becoming a subject for polemic as they had been for Hobbes and Moses Mendelssohn and were also, in the preceding essay, for Kant. Peace is conceived as the necessary conclusion of history and a duty that humanity must try to carry out. This is not new. Kant had long since expressed his faith in nature (the work of divine providence) and in human reason (whose work is the law). That they will be forever united in peace, a single purpose that illuminates and justifies each of them— this is the epitome of Kant's hope. The significance of the 1795 essay on *Perpetual Peace* does not lie, then, in any innovation but precisely in how systematically Kant expounds matters, much more so than he does in the *Philosophy of Law* in 1797, where he will recall the 1795 conclusions merely for the sake of completeness. Kant's commentators never fail to mention that the *Project for Perpetual Peace* was the first of Kant's writings to be translated into French (in 1796). It justified hopes—which in turn had probably strengthened Kant's own hope—of being able to see in the French Revolution, even more than in the British revolutions, the historic start of the realization of the state of right. The wars France had been fighting could be taken to be the great human catastrophes that were the necessary prelude to the inauguration of peace through law for the species. For in 1795 the French Revolution seemed over, Robespierre had been guillotined, and the peace treaties signed in Basel favored a country that seemed to have achieved the republican constitution; the idea of the perfect constitution would be realized. From Kant's perspective, this "historical progress" could, in the first place, be legitimized by a philosophy of history. Humanity had reached adulthood, or at least some of its members had. In the second place, the logic of the results of this progress should persuade other nations to transform their constitutions and, thereby, their relations.

Kant did not believe in what we would call today a balance of terror. He had written very clearly on that subject in *Theory and Practice*. "For an enduring universal peace brought about by a so-called *balance of power in Europe* is a mere figment of imagination, like Swift's *house*, whose architect built it so perfectly in accord with all laws of equilibrium that as soon as a sparrow lit on it, it fell in."[97] Nor did he think that history could be interpreted as a series of alternations of peace and war with no discernible meaning. This was the burden of the third chapter of *Theory and Practice*, directed against just such a position proposed by Mendelssohn. Kant, as we know, believed in the progress of the human race by means of the sufferings its history inflicted on it. Although for him the purpose of life to be studied was not happiness, as most of the Encyclopedists professed it to be, the theorists of the French Revolution, who had known nothing of Kant before 1796, took a friendly interest in a work that seemed to justify their ideas. This is all the more worth noting because Kant did not waver in his condemnation of resistance, revolt, and revolution. The *Philosophy of Law* dwells on this point at the conclusion of its proof:

> Resistance on the part of the People to the Supreme Legislative Power of the State, is in no case legitimate; for it is only by submission to the universal Legislative Will, that a condition of law and order is possible. Hence there is no Right of Sedition, and still less of Rebellion, belonging to the People. And least of all, when the Supreme Power is embodied in an individual Monarch, is there any justification under the pretext of his abuse of power, for seizing his Person or taking away his Life. The slightest attempt of this kind is *High Treason*; and a Traitor of this sort who aims at the *overthrow* of his country may be punished, as a political parricide, even with Death.[98]

In 1795 the most determined of the zealous regicides had nearly all perished on the scaffold, and the legal government of France was the republic. Now if the monarchists still attempted to resist, it was they who, according to Kant's logic, would become rebels against a "juridical state."

The *Perpetual Peace* is very formally organized. Was Kant mocking himself when he composed six preliminary articles on achieving peace, then three definitive articles, then added two supplements, followed by an appendix, also in two parts?[99] Or does the solemnity of such an orderly philosophical demonstration hide, beneath a form that lends itself to irony (the author's as much as the reader's), the seriousness with which he was justifying his hope? The importance of the work would tend to be proved by the repetition—and deeper exploration—of themes he had been discussing for several years and also in that the variations he will introduce in the *Philosophy of Law* will not noticeably modify what he establishes here. As soon as a translation appeared in France, moreover, the work's importance was accepted there. But has the philosopher not tried to answer death with life, the inevitability of wars with the possibility of peace, by ringing wars round with the unyielding rule of right, to which a solemn voice is perhaps fitting, speaking as it does the pure language of reason? Reason—how hard it is to discern behind the limitlessly varied disguises nature assumes in both the tangle of our passions and the confusion of our wars, though they work ceaselessly together to the same end! The question now at issue is whether peace is only possible in death. For if life is war, and war consists in killing and being killed, is life not in the final analysis the same as death? And is this not a contradiction?

Without going into the details of Kant's analyses, I will emphasize some points that he has fortunately clarified. Kant determines "juridically"— that is, according to nothing but pure reason—how that same reason can justify the *idea* of perpetual peace; for he is concerned exclusively with an idea, never with the deduction of a certainty. Although it may be rational to have articulated them, the six first or preliminary articles, we must admit, resemble pious hopes. If it is true, as Kant himself says, that not only do ruling powers like to make war,[100] but that war "appears to be ingrained in humanity,"[101] then it is hard to see how, in fact, we could possibly be certain that no unspoken intention to start a war is hidden behind a peace treaty. How do we restrain a nation that wishes to seize another? How are standing armies eventually to be broken up? How can a nation be induced to stop contracting debts to pay for future wars? Or another nation be prevented from forcible interference in the affairs of its neighbor? And how can we forbid a nation at war the use, despite the rules of war, of such means as will, alas, envenom the peace that follows?

In any case, such questions are not what is at issue for Kant, but rather to show, in these preliminary articles regarding perpetual peace, the foundation in right for such a peace. He is speaking morally, not pragmatically. We know that Kant does not count on morality as a basis for peace. Either the preliminary articles are a jesting way of showing that peace is actually impossible, or else they are meant to remind us of the rational behavior that necessity will force upon human beings, when history has driven them to renounce wars become so ruinous in every way that they must be given up.

The purpose of the six preliminary articles is to set forth the conditions indispensable to making and sustaining peace. Their negative approach— declaring what a state should *not* do—prepares the ground for the positive obligations of the three definitive articles, concerned respectively with civil law, the law of nations, and cosmopolitan law. Peace is the necessary consequence of respect for the three imperatives, and it is also their final purpose.

According to the first of the definitive articles, in order for peace to be perpetual, the civil constitution of each nation must be a republic. This would have been familiar to readers of Kant's earlier works, as would the statement that such a constitution "is the original foundation of all forms of civil constitution."[102] In other words, because there have been human beings and, simultaneously, political societies, such societies have been rightfully organized on the basis of the "original contract," the product of reason. The republican constitution possesses "a purity whose source is the pure concept of right,"[103] but never in history has it existed in its pure form, even though the actual kinds of government could not have come into being without it as their (rightful) foundation. For there to be peace, all states must (*müssen*—nature compels them) have republican constitutions in fact,[104] for the people by definition will never choose to endure the crushing burden of war when they have the power to decide for or against it. Kant considers the chief of state to be, according to right, the representative of the general will, but he expects nothing but self-indulgence from the chiefs of state who believe they own their nation.[105] As we would expect from the logic of his system, Kant attributes absolutely no sense of duty to them, unless it might be by accident. A monarch is not primarily God's agent for the good of those in his charge, not a *"minister Dei (a Deo per populum),"* as Saint Paul wrote in his letter to the Romans.[106] When the people, according to Kant, must give its consent "in order to determine whether or not there will be war,"[107] we can be sure that peace will be safeguarded "by virtue of [each generation's] self-love."[108]

It is the features of the civil constitution that make it mandatory. Even though they are not expressed here in terms absolutely identical to those of the *Theory and Practice,* the two texts do not disagree. *Freedom,* of course, is put forth as the primary principle at the origin of the republican constitution.[109] Kant insists on the outward, legal aspect of freedom. Although he speaks of the freedom that defines the human being, he is not concerned here with its arbitrary, untrammeled use, nor with its strictly ethical use. No state of right would be possible without respect for freedom, that is, for the rational choice—still a choice, even though necessity has compelled it—that each must make in favor of a state in which obedience to civil law derives from the primitive contract. By this contract, we each freely pledge to respect others' freedom and therefore to restrict our own in accord with the laws to which all consent. It is an act of reason; through it, we become both the lawmaking power and the object of our own legislation. This is why the state of right is fundamentally rational.

The next principle, fully consistent with the first, is "the principle of the *dependence* of everyone on a single common legislation."[110] If the legislation is founded on reason, it cannot be other than unique and common. Because reason has the properties of universality and necessity, it would be contradictory for it to be multiple and contingent. The variations among the positive laws that circumstances dictate do not deprive legislation of its uniqueness and commonality, as it remains formally the achievement of indivisible, lawmaking reason. Nonetheless, because freedom is the power of choice, it can always choose to flaunt the law, in other words, to bring back the state of war. Everyone is always free to choose evil. Nothing but dependence on common legislation can compel us to do otherwise, to respect, that is, our own freedom, inasmuch as it is the equivalent of reason within ourselves as within others. If people were reasonable, they would not need this restraint; uncoerced, they would follow reason in their choices and would respect the freedom within themselves and others. But they are not. It therefore matters little from what motive they obey the common legislation. The main thing is that they come to obey it as they would if they were still capable of freedom.

There is a third principle, that of *equality*. We have met it before, too. It is one of the hardest words to analyze, however, inasmuch as its history has been more obscured by the passions than clarified by reason. It is evident that we should eliminate the meaning this term had among the Greeks when it designated brothers of the same—sometimes mythical—stock for whom to be free was to be other than slaves or barbarians. The religious sense of the word is not appropriate here either. It does not pertain to those created equal to each other before God, equally sinners and equally redeemed by Christ's sacrifice. Kant, furthermore, readily acknowledges inequality of abilities. Women, children, and men who cannot survive without depending on others—these, too, are citizens, but "passive citizens"; according to Kant, they do not participate in civic life.[111]

Hobbes's philosophy has already provided a theory of the state of right, but what Hobbes means by equality is not identical to what Kant means. Recall that for Hobbes all are equal by nature because, whatever their differences (strength or weakness, intelligence or stupidity), each has the capacity to kill any other. Fear of dying is the equal condition of all, and everyone has equal opportunity to become aware of it. In the organized state, the law defends everyone equally by the use of the common force. The law can be said to guarantee each person equal security, so long as the individual respects it. What Kant means by equality overlaps with this concept but is much richer. "External (*rightful*) *equality* in a nation," he writes in a footnote, "is that relation among citizens whereby no citizen can be bound by a law, unless all are subject to it simultaneously and in the very same way."[112] This is also true in Hobbes's philosophy, but not for the same reason. According to Kant, mutual juridical obligation comes about because each individual in the state of nature is, despite its wretchedness, a free being, that is, a being defined by a reason capable of making laws. This high dignity of the person bestows on no one the power to subjugate another. Each is equally the source of law and equally subject to it. This is what is meant by the social contract. Security is not forgotten, but it is not the foundation right. Reason is not merely *ratiocinatio*. Kant had, in fact, remarked in a preceding note that "all men who can mutually influence one another must [*müssen*] accept some civil constitution."[113] The words *must* and *obligation* belong to the language of ethics, the source of obligations that are juridical and, consequently, political.

Note that though the earlier social contract philosophies differ among themselves, they also differ as a group from Kant's. It is not that ethics is absent from them but that it has another function. In Hobbes's thought, when the legislator declares what is just and unjust, he is, strictly speaking, inventing morality, a thing not present in the state of nature. In Locke, natural law indeed controls freedom, even in the state of nature, but as such it does not obligate us to the civil state. True, freedom obligates everyone to cling to life, but it is not invoked as the cause of our entering the civil state. The civil community becomes necessary because the passions are a threat to the individual's person and goods; it is less a moral obligation than an indispensable insurance: "The enjoyment of the property he has in this state of nature is very unsafe, very insecure. This makes him willing to quit a Condition, which however free, is full of fears and continual dangers."[114] As for Rousseau, he in fact thinks that man "ought constantly to bless the happy moment . . . which transformed him from a stupid, limited animal into an intelligent being and a man," though the moment is not one that he wanted; it is linked with physical catastrophes— "fatal chance happenings"—that have no moral import. Although the results of the contract are moral, its purpose is not, for Rousseau also thinks that "there neither is nor can be any type of fundamental law that is obligatory for the people as a body, not even the social contract."[115]

For the first time, at least for the first time with this much attention to practical philosophy, Kant defines a "perfect" civil constitution, the republican constitution, in a philosophy of history. He shows what juridical form typifies every constitution but shows at the same time which pure form must actually be realized in order to bring about peace.

The "general will" still had to be recognized as the origin, *by right*, of every constitution. Though a nation is always founded on the general will, it can be *governed* by one person, by several, or by all. These three forms of rule have always been differentiated; they correspond to the terms autocracy, aristocracy, and democracy, according to the number of persons involved. Kant does not repeat the classic distinction between good and bad governments according to whether the purpose of the leader (or leaders) is (or is not) the common good. He contrasts instead the forms of government in which the state—still founded in all cases on the general will—admits or does not admit the separation of legislative and executive powers, the government, strictly speaking, representing the executive function and the people, the legislative.

Even though there is no civil state separate from the general will, the form of government is despotic if the two functions are mixed. Peace cannot be guaranteed. When the same authority, whether residing in one, several, or all, both makes the laws and carries them out, what guarantee can there be against arbitrariness? The general will is absorbed into the particular will of the sovereign power. Therefore certain monarchies, certain aristocracies—and all democracies—are despotic forms of government. By contrast, in the monarchies or aristocracies organized as representative systems that conform to the notion of justice and in which the two powers are separated, the constitution is republican. The government executes what the general will has decided, not what its own will arbitrarily might want. There the particular is subordinate to the universal.

Granted all this, yet "given the depravity of human nature, which is revealed and can be glimpsed in the free relations among nations"[116] that are always in a state of nature vis-à-vis each other (as Kant reminds us), we understand why there is such frequent recourse to war to settle disputes: Human passions multiply the opportunities. What other rational solution but a "rightful" solution, analogous to the solution reigning in each nation and yet sui generis? For because each people has already a (rational) legal, internal constitution, it would be a contradiction to want to mix all peoples into a single state. Kant writes that one cannot "say of nations as regards their rights what one can say concerning the natural rights of men in a state of lawlessness, to wit, that 'they should abandon this state.' (For as nations they already have an internal, legal constitution and therefore have outgrown the compulsion to subject themselves to another legal constitution that is subject to someone else's concept of right.)"[117] Peace being a duty, the problem can have only one rightful solution—an alliance of nations that assures each member nation its freedom, except that it may have no recourse to war; for the laws of the "federation," backed by its power, would ever afterwards make war as impossible as the public power of the separate nations makes transgressions against their laws. "Reason can provide related nations with no other means for emerging from the state of lawlessness, which consists solely of war, than that they give up their savage (lawless) freedom, just as individual persons do, and, by accommodating themselves to the constraints of common law, establish a *nation of peoples* that (continually growing) will finally include all the people of the earth."[118]

There remains the third legal provision, "the right of an alien not to be treated as an enemy upon his arrival in another's country."[119] Kant is very cautious regarding not the *hospitality* accorded foreigners but their *behavior as visitors.* They must not act as if they are in a conquered country, for "a transgression of rights in *one* place in the world is felt *everywhere.*"[120] The idea of a cosmopolitan law, harmonizing with the natural right of every inhabitant of the planet, joins with public law and the law of nations in working toward the realization of "the public rights of men in general. Only such amendment allows us to flatter ourselves with the thought that we are making continual progress toward perpetual peace."[121]

If Kant had stopped here, we could admire the logic of his proposal but would class it unhesitantly among utopian inventions. Why would the human race become reasonable and accept rational solutions to problems it has always resolved by war? The supplementary articles try to *guarantee* not the work's coherence—for that is already assured—but the future realization of its ideas. We are familiar with Kant's postulate. Just as in 1784, 1786, 1790, and 1793, Kant continues to believe that nature seeks the flowering of reason and that it has the means for bringing it about: Nature uses war to constrain humanity finally to peace. "Perpetual peace is *ensured* (guaranteed) by nothing less than that great artist *nature*, whose mechanical process makes her purposiveness visibly manifest, permitting harmony to emerge among men through their discord, even against their wills."[122] This idea that reason has of the course of events is justified because "from the practical point of view (where, e.g., it is employed in relation to our concept of duty regarding *perpetual peace*), it is represented as a dogmatic idea and it is here that its reality is properly established."[123]

What, then, has nature done? It has scattered humans over the whole earth and taken care that they should be able to live there. It is war that has driven peoples into inhospitable regions that they would never have inhabited if they had not been fearful and defeated; it is war, too, that has forced them to initiate more or less just relations with each other. Humanity's industriousness owes much to war. War, it is true, "requires no particular motivation, but appears to be ingrained in human nature,"[124] and nature has used the human race, as it does any class of animal, to its own purposes.[125] In doing so, nature propels the human species toward perpetual peace, *as if* humans were obeying the law of reason.

> How does nature further this purpose that man's own reason sets out as a duty for him, i.e., how does she foster his *moral objective,* and how has it been guaranteed that what man ought to do through the laws of freedom, but does not, he shall, notwithstanding his freedom, do through nature's constraint? This question arises with respect to all three aspects of public right, *civil, international, and cosmopolitan right.*[126]

Kant tells us how, in the order of the three types of right.

Even more than internal conflicts, foreign wars impel a people to adopt a civil constitution, that is, to accept public laws that limit the individual's freedom; the individual becomes a good citizen without first being good morally. The republican constitution, the hardest to establish, can control a fiendish populace predisposed to lawlessness by its selfish instincts, because these same instincts also spur it to unite into a nation when confronted by a common enemy. The formulation of the original contract reminds us of Rousseau's, but Kant's differs from Rousseau's in that the details of the problem it is to resolve are not alike. For Rousseau, the challenge was to find a form of community that would safeguard "the person and goods of each associate" yet would keep him "as free as before."[127] In Kant's view, a person must above all be defined as a moral being. Not only is humanity's defining attribute at issue again in the problem posed by the nature of the human being, but this attribute causes peace to remain a duty over and above the civil society. As Kant frames the problem: We must "so order and organize a group of rational beings who require universal laws for their preservation—though each is secretly inclined to exempt himself from such laws—that, while their private attitudes conflict, these nonetheless so cancel one another that these beings behave publicly just as if they had no evil attitudes."[128] It is not, Kant tells us plainly, humanity's moral qualities that will be behind the good political constitution, but the inverse, even though it is the *duty* of every person to desire it. Yet duty is fragile among free beings. More reliable is nature, which "irresistibly wills that right should finally triumph."[129] And in order that peace may reign through right, nature has taken radical measures—war.

Sometimes it is the war of each against all, the war that goads us to establish the civil state. Sometimes it is the war between nations that nature has made neighbors and yet independent, hence inclined to want to prove their superiority over each other. (By this juxtaposition, moreover, nature does not encourage their fusion, but their federation, as differences of language and religion testify.) All are wars that will end, however, not only because of the disasters they entail but because human beings, who are enterprising, will have developed a "spirit of trade." What the notion of cosmopolitan right would not have accomplished mutual self-interest demands: Trade develops only in peacetime.

Kant added to all these reasons guaranteeing perpetual peace a "secret article." Philosophers do not have to be kings nor kings philosophers, but kings should let philosophers speak freely—and should listen to them. Only the philosopher is capable of knowing right.

Kant modestly said of the hope expressed in *Theory and Practice*, "Meanwhile, this is only opinion and mere hypothesis—as uncertain as all judgments claiming to set out the sole appropriate natural cause for an intended effect that is not entirely in our power."[130] Two years later we find that nature *guarantees* perpetual peace "by virtue of the mechanism of man's inclinations." Of course, it is not sufficient to "*prophesy* [peace] from a theoretical point of view, but we can so do from a practical one, which makes it our duty to work toward bringing about this goal (which is not a chimerical one)."[131]

In an appendix, however, Kant speaks of the practical man's "disconsolate rejection of our fond hope."[132] In his critique of prudent statesmen, he insists once more on the possibility of bringing morals and politics into agreement and of correcting the faults in a state's constitution by reforms. "It becomes a duty, particularly for the rulers of nations," he says, "to consider how [a fault] can be corrected as soon as possible and in such a way as to conform with natural right, which stands in our eyes as a model presented by an idea of reason; and this ought to be done even at the cost of self-sacrifice" on the part of those rulers.[133] We must not forget the importance that the concept of right and consequently—at least we hope as much—the concept of duty has in the eyes of even the most calloused. "Men can no more escape the concept of right in their private relations than in their public ones; nor can they openly risk basing their politics on the handiwork of prudence alone, and, consequently, they cannot altogether refuse obedience to the concept of public right."[134] The sentence could have been written by Machiavelli, though with a very different aim. Kant does not intend this observation as mere advice for rulers regarding political prudence. In right's ubiquity, he finds a reason to strengthen his hope that right is the final consequence of outward relations among people. Politics is not reduced to a "technical task"; it is faced with the "moral task" of bringing about perpetual peace.[135] "True politics cannot progress without paying homage to morality."[136] The best criterion that can be applied to any political action is that its author gave it "publicity" before carrying it out.[137]

So the "fond" hope gradually becomes a "serious" expectation. Progress toward perpetual peace by means of public right is a problem that must be resolved. First, however, the fundamental elements of the problem must be correctly formulated in order that, little by little, there may come to light the only solution suited to a race whose animal nature is coerced to work toward an end that freedom, because of *its* nature, prescribes as a duty. Nature and freedom are no longer in conflict; right has the universality and inevitability of rational law; universality and inevitability also characterize natural law, but humanity discovers them in its freedom because that freedom is identical with practical reason.

The *Philosophy of Law* will add some details worth noting. Kant reiterates that in the absence of any common system of laws, the nations are in a state of nature in respect to each other; they are, that is, in a state of war, perhaps "in order to establish some condition of society approaching the judicial state."[138] Yet the fact of war entails juridical problems. We can easily accept that citizens are the property of the ruling power because were it not for the national structure their lives would be endangered, their numbers few, and their nourishment spare. To accept this, however, would be to assign them the status of domestic animals, not of free people. Citizens are those who participate in making the laws; "they must give their free consent through their representatives, not only to the carrying on of war generally, but to every separate declaration of war."[139] Here, as in the earlier texts, we find that logic requires a state of right.

In the *Philosophy of Law,* Kant distinguishes right before going to war, right during war, and right after war. The "law of nations," as so divided, can have only one goal—the right after war, that is, "to constrain the nations mutually to pass from this state of war, and to found a common Constitution establishing Perpetual Peace."[140] In other words, in the disastrous natural state of war, the law of nations allows for the alliance of peoples but not a sovereign state over all the peoples, for its size would make any policing impossible. Kant therefore draws the conclusion that as rights obtained by a people at war are provisory because war can always challenge them again, only a true state of peace would make the rights of all peremptory. This would require a universal union of nations. But by 1797, the date of this work, Kant hardly believes any longer that it can be perfectly realized. *"Perpetual Peace,* which is the ultimate end of all the Rights of Nations, becomes in fact an impracticable idea."[141]

The importance of this work, the last concerned with war and peace, lies less, however, in these several details (which, after all, do not add very much that is new) than in how it connects to the two great works on morality and the *Critique of Judgment.* If peace is humanity's horizon, if the republican constitution and the federation of states are our duties, that we may end wars, it is because what is juridical—which is not the same thing as what is ethical—depends on peace. To institute right is, in Kant's view, to set politics on the road of rationality that history with all its ups and downs has so rarely taken. To institute right is also to show the real difference between moral and legal duty (both of which Kant has first proven to have a rational origin). By the logic of his system, this protects the republican constitution against the utopianism that would compromise its realization; for the constitution is not made for a perfectly reasonable being but for "reasonable finite beings," and even a "population of devils" can participate in such a constitution, based on morality instead of on dictatorship. It matters little that devilish people act from fear of the police more than from respect for law; what counts is that they obey the law *as if* they had willingly imposed it on themselves. Morality and legality prescribe the same duties, but they do so according to different modes of obligation.

———————

Kant's works are undoubtedly the most lucid and remarkable effort in the history of philosophy to release humanity from war. Kant tried to avoid the lure of utopia, as though the hope for perpetual peace seems more a dream than a realistic appraisal of the world. Did he nevertheless share the illusions of fantasy worlds? He constantly referred to the mediocrity and wickedness of humanity, whose vices inspire despair more than trust in those who are willing to face them. But despite this jumble of contradictions and atrocities we call human history, Kant never invented the idea of a constitution for human beings that would regiment them indistinguishably in communitarian systems and control every moment of their lives. We find in Kant none of the utopias' aberrations—centrally planned economies, denunciations, and the rest. On the contrary, he wanted to prove that freedom is the vocation of humankind, because unlike any other animal species, it has accepted freedom's risk since the beginning of time. Fragile freedom, forever in danger of directing itself to the attainment of senseless ends! It is true that reason has matured by creating terrible instruments of annihilation throughout all ages, but it still remains inseparable from its legislative function, both speculative and practical. Although freedom must be educated, it cannot be led or even aided, for then it would cease to be freedom. Even though it so often rejects its identity with reason, chooses evil, and enslaves human energies and inventions to evil's destructive power, freedom meets its opposite, nature, in a battle that began with humankind, its speculative successes, and its wars; and freedom finally comprehends the function that is its duty (not its necessity, because it can always refuse it)—to work for the coming of peace. Thus does nature thrust the human race toward peace by means of wars it would never have pursued had it not been free; thus does reason become capable of conceiving the intelligibility of history's course, a task it recognizes as its duty, once freedom unites with it.

But are we spared a utopia? To answer yes would be to accept Kant's *conjectures* as adequately supported, to admit that history progresses by means of wars toward the state of right, the states of right, the federation of states, and peace, the only resolution worthy of a reasonable being. We must still concede that peace is for the most distant generations, those so far removed from us that they are only a completely abstract *idea*. Flesh-and-blood creatures like ourselves, our loved ones, and our acquaintances struggle hopelessly in real-life situations that wars strip of all meaning. Is it reasonable to think that history has a meaning for the species when it is most often a nightmare for successive generations? To fall back on the concept of the life span of the human race in order to take it from the worse to the better amounts to dividing the race into a hierarchy of generations, the last being both the most warlike (because waging the most horrible wars) and at the same time the most reasonable (because able to imagine a federation of nations under law)? The unity of the human race has been broken into a multiplicity of eras of increasingly unbearable misery that yet work for ultimate happiness: Has the hope for perpetual peace not led to confusing technical progress with social progress? We are producing ways to make wars ever more deadly. Does it necessarily follow that some of us, at least, will one day give up hope of finally conquering the rest? The myth of the *last* war lives stubbornly on. Moreover, the earthly peace expected as the end of nature requires precisely the instrument—war—that we can never be sure will not, with *its* instruments, those of extermination, put an end to peace forever. Kant proclaims the human species immortal, but on what does he base such a belief? It is only one more *conjecture*. Why might humanity not fall victim to its own inventions and fail to adapt to the changes and destruction it has brought upon itself? The peace of cemeteries, with no one left to bury, would then be the final end. When it is "freedom for evil," it is in freedom's power to choose what is against reason. Given the right weapons, this choice could become the last. The evil choice that hurls us into war can devour the species, as it has so many of its members.

———————

Let us simply remember, in conclusion, that Kant's postulates and goals contributed to the revitalization of the utopian ideal among a large number of his contemporaries. Taken up by some of the post-Hegelians and rephrased in their own terms, Kant's postulates helped nourish not merely belief in peace but the confident proclamation of definitive peace, which they also promised as the end of history. Today our illusions about the meaning of history as Marx understood it have generally dissolved.[142] They probably also took with them Kant's dream, the beautiful hope of perpetual peace, for the philosopher's theory contained themes, perhaps faint as a watermark, that could be shown to be debatable in the light of how they were later put to use.

Although Marx often spoke of war, he did not analyze war per se. His works will not detain us long because they borrow the better part of their philosophical underpinnings from Kant and Hegel. Marx disagrees with Hegel, condemns him, yet makes use of his method of dialectic. In 1844 Marx wrote,

> The outstanding thing in Hegel's *Phenomenology* and its final outcome—that is, the dialectic of negativity as the moving and generating principle—is thus first that Hegel conceives the self-genesis of man as a process, conceives objectification as loss of the object, as alienation and as transcendence of this alienation; that he thus grasps the essence of *labour* and comprehends objective man—true, because real man—as the outcome of man's *own labour*.[143]

According to Marx, in effect, the human being is defined in his work, through the history of his own productivity. Starting from the relationship that the human animal, a creature of needs, has with nature, the human agent creates himself by his work from one generation to the next. But the Marxist dialectic does not operate on the same plane as the Hegelian; it declines the discipline of a proper exploration of the concept. Hegel found the true basis of his philosophy in that abstract necessity according to which reason is the structure of things. Marx again comments on Hegel in 1873 in the epilogue to the second German edition of *Capital*:

> My dialectical method is, in its foundations, not only different from the Hegelian, but exactly opposite to it. For Hegel, the process of thinking, which he even transforms into an independent subject, under the name of "the Idea," is the creator of the real world, and the real world is only the external appearance of the idea. With me the reverse is true: the ideal is nothing but the material world reflected in the mind of man, and translated into forms of thought.[144]

In the writings of Marx, his associates, or his successors, we can nevertheless find enough evidence to persuade us that the Marxist ideologies should be included among the utopias of peace. We could paraphrase (obviously, only summarily) that in place of wars, the scourge of the human race, there must be waged a *single* universal, radical, and definitive war, the proletarian revolution, in order to bring to a close the unhappy, though necessary, history of humanity. "Every revolutionary uprising, however remote from the class struggle its object might appear, must of necessity fail until the revolutionary working class shall have conquered. . . . Every social reform must remain a Utopia until the proletarian revolution and the feudalistic counter-revolution have been pitted against each other in a *world-wide war*."[145] Foreign wars and the great atrocities and increasingly great miseries they bring with them will at last bring humanity not to the realization of a "state of right" in which the "rights," as Marx sees it, will be merely formal, but to a war that, beginning as *civil* war, will—after total victory—inevitably bring about genuine freedom, equality, and peace.

The cause of wars, then, is found less in humanity's passions than in the economic contradictions burdening the various peoples and their political structures, of which the passions are only the result. History progresses through these contradictions, eventually dialectically transcended, that beget successive forms of defective—although necessary—civilizations and cultures, fated to a violent disappearance. The only scientific explanation of history is that these forms are momentary stages resulting from technological gains and economic changes. The latter are bound up with the means of production and with complex relationships of interdependence and conflict between those who do the actual work and those who claim its rewards. These relationships evolve over time because production techniques evolve. Although they have always alienated the workers (slaves, serfs, manual laborers, and so on), they are nevertheless necessary, for they shape the economic and cultural progress that bears the seeds of their destruction and the initiation of a higher stage:

> We thus see that the *social relations within which individuals produce, the social relations of production, are altered, transformed, with the change and development of the material means of production, of the forces of production. The relations of production in their totality constitute what is called the social relations, society, and moreover, a society at a definite stage of historic development,* a society with peculiar, distinctive characteristics. *Ancient* society, *feudal* society, *bourgeois* (or capitalist) society, are such totalities of relations of production, each of which denotes a particular stage of development in the history of mankind.[146]

Marx thinks that industrial society, at the point it has reached in the nineteenth century, marks the conclusion of this process, for it contains all the elements that will allow it to be transcended, this time by the final end of the workers' alienation. The last of the dialectical transformations is in fact possible, for economic conditions have led us to a clear consciousness of themselves that amounts to scientific understanding; and they have also set the stage for labor's genuine unity and successful struggle. The workers, the actual producers of economic goods, are not those who benefit from them; it is their employers—that is, their exploiters—who reap the rewards by appropriating the *increase in value* resulting from their labor.[147] In addition, the employers compete with each other. They must fight to acquire markets and even the raw materials they lack. The wars generally thought to be the consequence of their ambitions are the result, on a deeper level, of the inner logic of the relations involved in economic production. This has always been true. In the *German Ideology,* Marx wrote:

This whole conception of history appears to be contradicted by the fact of conquest. Up till now violence, war, pillage, murder and robbery, etc., have been accepted as the driving force of history. . . . With the conquering barbarian people war itself is still . . . a regular form of intercourse, which is the more eagerly exploited as the increase in population together with the traditional and, for it, the only possible crude mode of production gives rise to the need for new means of production.[148]

Henceforth, the bond between war and the economic state of affairs is clear. "The bourgeoisie," Marx writes, "finds itself involved in a constant battle. At first with the aristocracy; later on, with those portions of the bourgeoisie itself whose interests have become antagonistic to the progress of industry; at all times with the bourgeoisie of foreign countries."[149] It goes without saying that it is those who work and live in a condition close to destitution who are the intended victims of war, as "foreign policy [is] in pursuit of criminal designs, playing on national prejudices, squandering in piratical wars the people's blood and treasures."[150]

It is true that work is the essence of the human being and that the worker, in producing an object, also produces himself; nonetheless, in a capitalist society "the worker sinks to the level of . . . the most wretched of commodities . . . the wretchedness of the worker is in inverse proportion to the power and magnitude of his production. . . . [and] the whole of society must fall apart into the two classes—the property-*owners* and the propertyless *workers*."[151] If we grasp the whole, as Marx puts it, of the movement of humanity's history as in essence the history of human labor, we come to understand that the forms typical of nineteenth-century industrialism are "necessary, inevitable, and natural consequences" of the different previous economic forms.[152]

What he especially clarifies and explains is the logic of the contradiction that prevents the worker from becoming human through his necessarily alienated (*entfremdet*) work.

The object which labour produces—labour's product—confronts it as *something alien*, as a *power independent* of the producer. . . . In the conditions dealt with by political economy this realization of labour appears as *loss of reality* for the workers; objectification as *loss of the object* and *object-bondage*; appropriation as *estrangement* (*Entäusserung*), as *alienation* (*Entfremdung*).[153]

The laborer is alienated in the very essence of his work, because he is alienated in its object; he is alienated in the very act of production. His work is not spontaneous; it is "forced labor" that means nothing to him but a way to meet his animal needs. Finally, he is alienated in his "species being," for his conscious being no longer has any object of thought but its own wretched survival.

> An immediate consequence of the fact that man is estranged from the product of his labour, from his life-activity, from his species being is the *estrangement of man from man*. If a man is confronted by himself, he is confronted by the *other* man. What applies to a man's relation to his work, to the product of his labour and to himself, also holds of a man's relation to the other man, and to the other man's labour and object of labour.[154]

The characteristics of alienation, as Marx explains them, shape an anthropology born of "historical materialism." Society is "the product of man's interaction upon man," Marx writes to Annenkov in 1846.[155] But people do not choose the social form they live in:

> If you assume a given state of development of man's productive faculties, you will have a corresponding form of commerce and consumption. If you assume given stages of development in production, commerce or consumption, you will have a corresponding form of social constitution, a corresponding organization, whether of the family, or of the estates or of the classes— in a word, a corresponding civil society. . . . Man is not free to choose *his productive forces*—upon which his whole history is based—for every productive force is an acquired force, the product of previous activity. . . . The simple fact that every succeeding generation finds productive forces acquired by the preceding generation and which serve it as the raw material of further production, engenders a relatedness in the history of man, engenders a history of mankind, which is all the more a history of mankind as man's productive forces, and hence his social relations, have expanded.[156]

History has inevitably reached the time when consciousness of alienation becomes possible and a clear analysis of alienation can be made.

> The worker puts his life into the object; but now his life no longer belongs to him but to the object. Hence, the greater this activity, the greater is the worker's lack of objects. Whatever the product of his labour is, he is not. Therefore the greater this product, the less is he himself. The *alienation* of the worker in his product means not only that his labour becomes an object, an *external* existence, but that it exists *outside him*, independently, as something alien to him, and that it becomes a power on its own confronting him; it means that the life which he has conferred on the object confronts him as something hostile and alien.[157]

The Marxist solution consists in encouraging class consciousness among those whom Marx calls the proletarians. The term is not very clearly defined. Its meaning is not always the same—sometimes it is applied to those who sell their work energy in order to live, sometimes those forced into poverty, sometimes city laborers, and so on.[158] In any case, consciousness of belonging to an oppressed class hardly follows automatically from oppression. Who is more timid, who easier to keep in servitude, than a defenseless worker in dread of losing his livelihood in a situation where so many others want more than the chance to replace him? It is therefore initially incumbent on the few who have the ability to think about the proletarian condition, to evaluate it lucidly and then to draw up a battle plan responsive to the realities of the situation rather than to dreams of a more developed human nature or the building of a better society. For Marx is relentless in sniffing out utopias wherever they hide, whether in reform movements or in models proposed by revolutionary ideologies. History is a reality that follows ineluctable paths. In the nineteenth century, the conditions for the emancipation of workers "could be produced by the impending bourgeois epoch alone,"[159] just as that period had been produced by the preceding economic conditions. The right conditions do not come out of the blue, nor can they be invented—they simply are. Inventors of systems believe that "the gradual, spontaneous class organization of the proletariat" will yield "to an organization of society [that they have] specially contrived."[160]

However spontaneous it might be, the organization of the proletariat into a class capable of effective revolution nonetheless presents a problem. Marx constantly affirms, in accord with the logic of materialism, that "it is not the consciousness of men that determines their existence, but, on the contrary, their existence determines their consciousness."[161] The proletariat should therefore be in immediate possession of the consciousness created by its social position. Then we could picture the Communist party as the product of this consciousness rising in protest against the state, protector of bourgeois rights,[162] and against private property, "the final and most complete expression of the system of producing and appropriating products, that is based on class antagonisms, on the exploitation of the few by the many."[163] And so it is, for the most part; still, the notion of proletariat covers a variety of groups and is not applied solely to the working classes vis-à-vis the bourgeoisie. Marx, as we have seen, speaks both of a "proletariat which is itself a relic of the proletariat of feudal times" and of a "new proletariat, a modern proletariat."[164] Only the latter's situation is the kind that leads to revolution, and it is greatly helped in its struggle by the existence of the Communist party, which, though not "distinguished from the other working-class parties," is "practically the most advanced and resolute section of the working-class parties of every country, that section which pushes forward all others. . . . Theoretically, they have over the great mass of the proletariat the advantage of clearly understanding the line of march, the conditions, and the ultimate general results of the proletarian movement."[165]

There is, then, a group of those who are able to "express, in general terms, actual relations springing from an existing class struggle, from a historical movement going on under our very eyes."[166] Only one group from the mass of the proletarians comprehends the unstoppable flow of history. Acting as a yeast within the proletarian class, it makes it aware of itself and brings it to a conscious understanding of the "class struggle" that will end with the suppression of the propertied class.[167] Despite Marx's repeated explanations, we are left with the question of the party's *directive* role in dealing with the *spontaneous* actions of the masses, that is, of the role of the intellectual elite (for that is what it is) in respect to the working class as a whole. Advised by the party, but more often manipulated by it, the proletarian mass must ultimately wage *total war* as the way to *total peace*—definitive, of course, but distant, because it will not occur until after the complete destruction of the enemy of the class, clinging to its privileges and generally the less ready to give them up the more it believes in its *right*—its *unquestionable* right—to them.

The reason the final transformation of society must be violent and brought about by a bloody revolution is not solely the bourgeoisie's resistance to it. Marx never expected the peaceful reform of society because every reform is subject to the consent of the bourgeois establishment and is therefore no threat to its existence. The revolution, then, must destroy both private property, which is the bourgeois form of the appropriation of the laborer's work, and the state, which is the political face of appropriation, through its enforcement of bourgeois law. Marx very clearly showed the difference between past revolts of all kinds, which aimed only at being granted means of subsistence, and the total transformation implied by the term *revolution*. It is quite true that in a peasant revolt, for example, the rebels may be extremely violent, but their demands are far more likely to be for an improvement of their condition than for a radical overthrow of society. It was inevitable that the few attempts of this sort were pitilessly quelled, not, according to Marx, because they resulted from the work of isolated enlightened individuals but because the means of production were not such as to bring about either a transformation or an awareness of the needed struggle. The bourgeoisie, whose situation made them the revolutionary class in 1789,[168] acted the part and defeated their adversaries by destroying the old regime utterly. Marx believes that in the nineteenth century, barely a hundred years later, the "constant revolutionizing of production, the uninterrupted disturbance of all social conditions" linked to the presence of the bourgeoisie, has produced the conditions for revolution by producing an international class of proletarians.[169]

Wars throughout history have always had an economic origin; they are nothing but the consequences of the way production and commerce have developed. The invasion of Rome by the barbarians was thus only a "regular form of intercourse";[170] the struggles of industrial and commercial competition are "carried on and decided by wars";[171] in general, "all collisions in history have their origin . . . in the contradiction between the productive forces and the form of intercourse"[172]—including the decisive collision, the revolution. But it is the last collision, for the revolution can henceforth destroy anything hostile to each person's recovery of what Marx calls "human nature," by which he means the entire product of human labor.

Marx wrote, "History is nothing but the succession of the separate generations, each of which uses the materials, the capital funds, the productive forces handed down to it by all preceding generations, and thus, on the one hand, continues the traditional activity in completely changed circumstances and, on the other, modifies the old circumstances with a completely changed activity."[173] He believed that the moment had come when the development of productive forces in the midst of bourgeois society had created the means for resolving the antagonism between those forces and the structure of society. The history of succeeding eras of society's economic evolution ends with the bourgeoisie. "This social formation," he writes, "constitutes . . . the closing chapter of the prehistoric stage of human society."[174]

There must still come a time, however, when "the violent overthrow of the bourgeoisie lays the foundation for the sway of the proletariat."[175] No material condition is lacking. Fastidious research into the reasons for the failure of the Paris Commune in 1871, despite an apparently well-founded expectation of success, does not prove that this analysis of reality is self-contradictory. It remains true, according to Marx, that "things have now come to such a pass that individuals must appropriate the existing totality of productive forces, not only to achieve self-activity, but, also, merely to safeguard their very existence."[176] Bourgeois forms of industry and commerce have put the various parts of the world in relationship to such an extent that "this appropriation must have a universal character." This is not, Marx insists once more, an unrealistic dream. He believes that the materialist theory is scientific. He writes confidently that "the appropriation of these forces is itself nothing more than the development of the individual capacities corresponding to the material instruments of production. The appropriation of a totality of instruments of production is, for this very reason, the development of a totality of capacities in the individuals themselves."[177] And the appropriation will occur in only one way:

This appropriation is further determined by the manner in which it must be effected. It can only be effected through a union, which by the character of the proletariat itself can again only be a universal one, and through a revolution, in which, on the one hand, the power of the earlier mode of production and intercourse and social organization is overthrown, and, on the other hand, there develops the universal character and the energy of the proletariat, which are required to accomplish the appropriation, and the proletariat moreover rids itself of everything that still clings to it from its previous position in society.[178]

Marx adds that "the class *overthrowing* [society] can only in a revolution succeed in ridding itself of all the muck of ages and become fitted to found society anew."[179]

The vocabulary of the *German Ideology* suggests a transmutation by alchemy. After the bloodbath and the risking of life comes the rebirth, the new man, the real man, as Marx claims. In his circular letter of 1879, the idea that violence is imperative reappears. Here he employs the image of the red specter, representing the struggle to the death that terrifies a bourgeoisie destined to vanish.[180] He remained true to this belief, as have his successors. Initially, for strategic reasons, a national war, the revolution must spread worldwide. This is why the total peace introduced by total war is far in the future. Even after the (initially partial) victory, it will remain necessary to raise an impenetrable barrier against the still possible return of reactionary forces. It is imperative to destroy the bourgeois state, but to destroy every political form immediately would be to invite their resurgence. The "dictatorship of the proletariat" is the sole political form that can bring about all the needed changes. After triumphing in the struggle against the bourgeoisie, it can accomplish the goals of the revolution and at the same time prevent a renaissance of the old society by the systematic organization of the proletarian population, production norms, and norms of common and individual ownership. In the *Manifesto*, the communist revolution, "the most radical rupture with traditional property relations," is as a result marked by "the most radical rupture with traditional ideas"; it is "the first step" in the rise of the proletariat to the rank of "ruling class"; it is the way to "win the battle of democracy." The political supremacy of the proletariat is the weapon that enables it to "wrest, by degrees, all capital from the bourgeoisie, to centralize all instruments of production in the hands of the State, i.e. of the proletariat organized as the ruling class; and to increase the total of productive forces as rapidly as possible."[181] In 1875 in his critique of the program of the German Workers' party, Marx names this political power and indicates its place: "Between capitalist and communist society lies the period of the revolutionary transformation of the one into the other. There corresponds to this also a political transition period in which the state can be nothing but *the revolutionary dictatorship of the proletariat.*"[182]

In practice, who will exercise this dictatorship, if not those capable of discerning the historic moment when revolutionary action will have the best chance of succeeding? Because they have grasped the "historic destiny" of the proletariat, they are experts in it and know why it represents the crowning future of humanity. Even though this destiny is ineluctably unfolding, it is the leaders' role to hasten its arrival.

Such an analysis clearly identifies the enemy. The first enemy, before the enemy abroad, is the enemy within the nation. Civil war must therefore be the first war, fought with no holds barred. It must leave no institution in place that has ties to the former political regime or type of economic organization. Persons involved with these outmoded forms must be violently eliminated.[183] As soon as the new state is strong enough, its duty, if it wants to be consistent with its ideology, is to carry the war abroad by directly invading a neighboring country, actively aiding the revolution in another nation through its guidance, destabilizing resistant governments with terrorism, assisting like-minded political parties, supporting strikes, engaging in economic sabotage, even forging an opportunistic alliance with a nation that, though ideologically incompatible, is still the enemy of the targeted nation. It can, in short, use any means, from armed struggle to the most deceitful propaganda, not excluding diplomacy and its unkept promises. The goal is to seize key positions, strategic points from which the weakened "enemy of the class" can do no better than to withdraw. To reach total peace, we must use total revolution.

Marx gives scant description of the peace accompanying the disappearance of political power. It will result from the elimination of the inescapable contradictions that have shaped the course of history but that only the revolution and the dictatorship of the proletariat will be able to fully resolve. Human beings will thenceforth live *free*, that is, *freed* from the burden of their oppression; they will share equally in goods produced and owned in common, as through the transitory mediation of the socialist state their means of production will have become common property for all time. "Only at this stage does self-activity coincide with material life, which corresponds to the development of individuals into complete individuals and the casting-off of all natural limitations. The transformation of labour into self-activity corresponds to the transformation of the previously limited intercourse into the intercourse of individuals as such."[184]

In other words, the abstract human beings philosophers sought to know, mistaking them for human reality, have vanished; in their place are self-actualized individuals, products of their own work, in which they and others no longer meet as antagonists in a relationship of submission or domination. The *Manifesto*, too, proclaims the disappearance of class conflicts and the concentration of all production in the hands of individuals joined into one unit. Then "the public power will lose its political character. . . . The proletariat . . . will have swept away . . . classes generally, and will thereby have abolished its own supremacy as a class."[185] Is Marx more realistic in the *Critique of the Gotha Programme*? He does not conceal the problems of the first phase of communist society, which cannot yet do without the state. The future will be different, but its description does not relieve our skepticism:

> In a higher phase of communist society, after the enslaving subordination of individuals under division of labour, and therewith also the antithesis between mental and physical labour, has vanished; after labour, from a mere means of life, has itself become the prime necessity of life; after the productive forces have also increased with the all-around development of the individual, and all the springs of co-operative wealth flow more abundantly—only then can the narrow horizon of bourgeois right be fully left behind and society inscribe on its banners: from each according to his ability, to each according to his needs![186]

It is undoubtedly better to leave these future visions in the vagueness of a never-never land, a "uchronia," because for all the seeming rigor with which it proclaims effects linked to causes, this passage resembles utopian texts more than it does scientific proofs.

———————

There is no longer a need to expound the weakness of Marxist economic analysis, and it is pointless to cite the actual economic failure in Marxist countries, which led to their recent collapse. We are not yet ready to leave the theory, however. Marx's thinking was dependent on the existence of a mode of production and capital formation that was partly the same as that of the earliest capitalism. He did not predict that permanent growth in production would require more and more consumers and therefore a work force whose salaries would increase so rapidly that the richest capitalist countries would have to rely on foreign proletariats, which in turn would become educated and middle class. Nor did he take into account profound changes in capitalism itself, in respect to both corporate ownership and foreign trade. Wars obviously still occur, but have they no other causes than those Marx assigned them?

A second criticism bears on the utopianism of Marxist psychology. Very large groups of people can be mobilized and incited to revolt and destruction. Once past the euphoria associated with hatred and envy, though also with the hope of changing a constantly unsatisfactory state of affairs, energy wanes; for we cannot care about abstractions for long. People fight for them only so long as they have hopes of gaining what the abstractions are supposed to represent. When the hope of full ownership grows weary, boredom, disinterest, and laziness will replace energy and ambition. More significantly, we cherish only what we are sacrificing for, what we are not sure of getting; when we actually possess a thing, its value pales before the expectation of a new possession. The truth about the dynamics of human desire was much more profoundly understood by Hegel than by Marx. Socialist societies promised everything but were unable to fulfill the promise, for their very manner of giving killed the desire to get. Furthermore, what belongs to all belongs to no one. A possession is not a possession unless it is *someone's* possession. People agree to the idea of commonly owned goods and agree to respect them only when they have exclusive possession of their own goods.[187] We don't consider it worthwhile to maintain a public road unless it goes past our own houses. When of no use to us individually, common property falls into neglect.

Marx justifies equal ownership of the means of production by a postulate that is itself problematic—the actual, concrete equality of human beings. Since the appearance of Christianity, political philosophy has often made use of the concept of equality. The term is borrowed from a religious domain in which it is used in an ontological sense: All humans are equally creatures of God, degraded by original sin but equally redeemed and able to obtain salvation. Among the social contract philosophers, equality has a meaning of the same sort as Christianity's, namely, that in the state of nature, each individual's original situation is comparable to every other's. This equality of situation must be recovered in the civil state, where the equality of each citizen before the law will assure everyone the same juridical consideration, the same rights. Marx is not satisfied with this kind of equality. It is purely formal, he believes, and in its abstraction provides the concrete individual nothing but illusions. What does it matter to proletarians to be declared the equals of their employers before the law? The legal opportunity to obtain the same education, to have the same life-style if they acquire the same wealth—this could hardly affect proletarians. Proletarians are entirely lacking in means of bridging the gap between the possible and the real because of the concrete conditions of their place in life, which they cannot change in a capitalist economy unless they overthrow it by force. It is to the advantage of the system that made them proletarians to keep them in their condition of considerable inequality and wretchedness.

Even if we simply overlook the falsity of this assumption (what is to the advantage of the capitalist system has been proven otherwise), we must, if we would agree with Marx, admit that human beings are in fact born to be equal when in equal conditions, born to have equal abilities susceptible of equal development. What is true of no other living species would be true of humankind. To put it another way, the trait that defines humankind as radically different from all other species, reason, the human being's highest ability, would be concretely the same in every member of the human race. The differences that have always existed (excluding, of course, those due to physical afflictions) would be the result only of differences in economic status. Let us change conditions, and the generations born into genuine equality in all areas of life will be composed of equally gifted members.[188]

We see what self-contradiction such a postulate involves. It is no longer freedom, especially the freedom to oppose another human being, that enhances reason as it establishes differences; it is solely the freedom to oppose the conditions we are born to. But will reason, reduced to this secondary form of freedom, prove to be equal in everyone? Will we not more surely create equality by forcibly reducing the most gifted to the level of the dullest in the name of ideology, even if this should entail concealing, as happens in real socialist nations, the privileged status of those whose intelligence is useful to the state—while the state exists, to be sure?

Humans, of course, do not live by bread alone. Marx, too, was persuaded of this and tried to make the socialist economy the foundation on which *all* human values could be built. Yet albeit the economic situation determines the possibility of life, it is neither its cause nor its purpose. To make it the pivot of human life and, in particular, the ultimate explanation of war and peace is to make reason essentially technical. It is to see the whole of human history as a series of technical advances on which depend not only the sciences and their applications but social modes and, finally, the actualization and happiness of humanity that distant generations alone will experience when all the changes inaugurated by the revolution will have culminated in the perfect education of all peoples. The working class must reach the point of no longer needing leaders so that the political order may wither away and the social order suffice to manage the entire world.

It is true that Marx, unlike Engels, sketched these distant views with little detail; he simply referred to them as the logical outcome of progress. But we can raise the same objections to the ideas of Marx and his successors that we raise to every philosophy of history. In the first place, does history have a direction? If it does, is history progressing toward those "beautiful tomorrows" that have taken generations to prepare for those who will no longer have even a remembrance of the massacres required for their happiness? Above all, we may ask whether we are not trapping ourselves in an insurmountable contradiction if we follow Marx. If human reality is fundamentally economic, to what do we appeal in making value judgments about the production and distribution of goods? In other words, if consciousness and its values do not exist until produced by economic activity, how can we imagine anything, even economic activity itself? Either value judgment is based on something other than the economic order, in which case we can legitimately weigh the economic order according to criteria external to it; or else if every value judgment is a "superstructure," as Marx very neatly terms it, then the economy is, properly, "in-significant," without meaning. Marx's works attest to the problem. His tone is often that of a moralist, outraged—and rightfully so—by the extreme poverty of part of the nineteenth-century working class; but he is then the unconscious victim of an inadmissible superstructure, or else he speaks as a pure theoretician and hence obviously is unable to moralize to *homo economicus*.

Let us recall that in Hegelian philosophy, the transformation of self, the *Bildung*, that we achieve through our work has a meaning. Even if a slave has given up his freedom for the sake of his natural life, he once made the humanizing effort to rise above such a life by risking death. The original genesis of freedom was cut short in his case, but it allowed the establishment of a distinction between nature and nonnature. Freedom might yet be the fruit of a second genesis; the life of the mind still had the chance to become the horizon of human life. Marx did not preserve Hegel's legacy. Because wars have, in his view, a purely economic origin and are fought for economic purposes, each war throughout history raises again the question of how human values appear and change. The peace promised in a distant golden age distracts us from the absence of meaning in life when it is reduced to its economic dimension.

The fate inflicted on others during the class struggle poses another problem. Each of the two groups involved, employers and workers, is the unyielding enemy of the other solely as a function of its place in the economic structure. In the merciless war that they wage, the oppressed class can never see the other as human because it cannot legitimately act from any moral consideration. Every war has rules, whether much or little respected, that imply that the enemy is a person and that in certain cases we are even justified in sparing him. A war of revolution recognizes no rule except success. In such a war, the relation with the enemy is intrinsically what we might call "black otherness." For this reason, what "decent people" could not accept without a shudder takes on new meaning in revolutionary combat. Nothing matters but the goal of the war—the proletariat's rise to power, now become its only value. What would be intolerable in any other war becomes a "cost of success," certainly regrettable but not to be compared to the catastrophe that the revolution's defeat would be. If human beings *are* what they *do*, what do they become in a struggle where they permit themselves any measures in order to win?

Finally, why must the proletariat triumph in the end? Apparently not because of a lucid awareness of its own worth. One word says more than it seems to say: The "masses," a myriad, undifferentiated group, carries no weight except by its size. The rallying cry that ends the *Communist Party Manifesto* confirms it: "Workers of the world, unite." What can we say except that sheer size, lacking as such any value except strength, is assigned historical value solely because of its role in the economy? Now this role cannot be described except in terms of norms that it does not have, that are exterior to it, and that therefore depend on an ideology. If this is the case, then the role assigned to the party is also debatable. It is the party that sees the truth, that bestows value on the masses and on the struggle that must be carried on. But the members of the party are not necessarily laborers; they are those who understand the economy, direct it, exalt it. On what authority? Although Marx insists that a given idea is linked to a given economic activity, if a philosophy of the economy can arise outside the economy, we come once more upon a difficulty already noted and upon another as well: How can someone not be a producer within the economy and yet be a product *of* the economy? Marx thought that capitalism would die out because of its very contradictions. This is not an impossibility. But it has since become socialism, caught in its own contradictions, that could not be saved. This possibility apparently did not occur to Marx.

The whole theory rests on a materialism that is in no way well founded—far from it. Materialism is a convenient tool suitable for the exact sciences, which are—we often forget—the product of human thought using certain rigorous relations that hold under well-defined conditions. Can human beings, however, circumscribe their nature and the meaning of their lives by the boundaries of an explanation that constantly balks at questions it cannot resolve and transforms them to suit its own terms? Upon thorough examination of materialism, we can see that what satisfies our understanding—the aspect of materialism that our understanding needs and is confirmed by—turns, in the final analysis, against those wishing to experience reality in its full richness.[189] When we try to throw light on human life with scientific certainty, it crumbles and fades, for science cannot give it meaning. Revolutionaries realize this; they gather all their strength for the fight and always put off till later—much later— questions about the true value of the fratricidal combat. It goes without saying, however, that the incoherencies of human existence are no reason for doing nothing nor for giving any kind of answer we please, from the most fanciful to the most vacuous. It is urgent to combat poverty because it dehumanizes those who endure it and those, too, who selfishly take advantage of the scandalous conditions they force on others. We must also recognize the universality of moral values, which would obviously exclude certain types of means, revolution and dictatorship among them.

It is also apparent that Marx borrowed his moral categories from conventional morality, while at the same time criticizing such a procedure. We find in Marx traces of Kant's creative freedom. Kant conjectured that freedom was originally technical ability, a separation from nature instigated by the need for food. Next, freedom became capable, in respect to the sexual instinct, of postponing the satisfaction of a need—an early portent of moral behavior. But Kant took great pains to distinguish between what he called a history of the *development* of freedom and a history of the *progress* of freedom, the latter demanding not conjecture but evidence.[190] For Kant, freedom was above all the specific manifestation of human beings; it guaranteed them autonomy, alone among all living species; for freedom was the condition and even the raison d'être of moral law.[191] There is nothing like this in Marx. He emphasizes an equality among humans that will be owed to the equal and common ownership of the means of production, from which he expects the liberation of the mental powers of all. In fact, freedom has vanished, and the peace projected for the end of a history that never comes to an end can only remain a utopia.

Toward Peace

But where was I to look? Where could I begin? . . . You see, I had no touchstone. But the very fact that there are now two of us changes everything. The task doesn't become twice as easy: After having been impossible, it becomes possible. It's as if you first gave me, in order to measure the distance from a star to our planet, one known point on the surface of the globe. You can't make the calculation. Give me a second point, and it becomes possible, for then I can construct the triangle.

—René Daumal, *Mount Analogue*

C H A P T E R   8

The Ontological Rift

It is commonly said of utopias that though by definition they cannot be realized, they nonetheless encourage events to move toward what they describe. It is unfortunately on the basis of this sort of illusion that we commit and justify the wars and crimes that are supposed to lead to happy endings. The twentieth century has seen a new outbreak both of utopias and of the worst kinds of outrages perpetrated against human beings. Even a partial list of the latter should throw light on the function of at least some of the former. The utopias focusing on peace are among the most dangerous. They are fostered, we must acknowledge, by what wars and their technology have become today—by the nuclear arsenal and biological weapons, not to mention improved conventional arms. (Toward the middle of the century, the bombings of Dresden and Hamburg during the course of World War II caused as many deaths in each city as did the single bomb dropped on Hiroshima.) We understand the panic, the disorientation induced by the experience or expectation of catastrophe; a ravenous appetite for peace, however utopian, and a desire to stay alive at any price almost inevitably take hold of dismayed minds. Only later do the facts and calm reflection reveal to what extent the road to utopia is a dead end.

Must we therefore resign ourselves to war? Is it, as a number of philosophers have thought, humanity's ineluctable fate? It has been said to be inscribed in human nature; it has been seen as the paradoxical means to the degree of human development that is the most advanced, yet always threatened with disintegration into enslavement or apathy. Do these reasons suffice to persuade us that the truth of war is such as would defy aspirations to the peace that war would make use of only to regain its strength?

War, we remember, is the most persistent companion of human history. It has always been present, approaching, or simply interrupted by a truce we name peace. Will this always be true? Utopian mirages aside, the question has not received a single decisive answer. Wishing, hoping, conjecturing, and insisting are not the same as proving. We should probably begin by agreeing on what we mean by peace. Ought we to apply the term to periods when armed conflict has paused here or there for more or less time, considering war as either an essential human trait or else humanity's normal state? In that case, war and peace are not genuine opposites. They are not contrasting concepts, as they logically should be, because peace as so defined seems more like a component of war than a reality sui generis. We could divide war into beats, like music; a period of actual fighting would then be nothing but a strong beat following a preparatory beat and followed in turn by the beat of a truce that temporarily ends the war before blending into the next period of preparation. People are either waging war or are mobilized and actively preparing to wage war or else are recuperating from one, whether they benefit or suffer from its outcome.[1]

For war and peace to be truly opposite, neither of the two states should contaminate the other. We ordinarily think, as Saint Augustine did, that wars are made for the purpose of peace. We could reverse the terms: Peace is the time in which we make ready for war—despite our claimed (and frequently sincere) intentions. Under these conditions, war would have much more reality for us than peace, not only as a fact—as history proves—but also in the more abstract realm of definitions, where the contrast between the concepts war and peace would be far from absolute. It would then be legitimate to speak of peace only in reference to the war that includes peace as one of its stages. All other definitions would be due to error or illusion.

Still, it is necessary to make distinctions. In law-governed states, civil peace generally lasts for longer periods than international peace despite the inevitable repercussions of foreign wars on the internal stability of the warring nations. A sustained peace is also much more likely for the victorious party than for the vanquished—at least this has been true since the time of the French Revolution. (Before that event, political regimes were less often subject to disturbances.) The world's history has been and remains the history of one predominant reality, war; peace in all its fragility has been defined in relation to war. The tenacious illusion of peace as the opposite of war seems to increase the energy put into wars and the determination to win them, but in the final analysis, no one will be satisfied with winning a *single* war or with enduring a defeat. The victors turn peace into a time to plan other victories, in anticipation of attacking once more or merely of defending themselves against tomorrow's enemies, who will not necessarily be the same as yesterday's. Meanwhile, the vanquished endure the rule of the victors as they watch for the right moment to take their revenge—unless, like the inhabitants of Melos among others, they have been erased from history.[2]

Then we must, it seems, accept the conclusions of the philosophies of war: There is nothing *human* without conflict and violence, because of the feelings of insecurity and omnipotence that alternate or mingle within humankind. Once we admit that peace does not mean the eradication of war but is a mere, though needed, aspect of it, we can no longer delude ourselves about the limitations inherent to the whole human species as to each of its members. The serenity of Olympus is not for us. A longing for peace, for a way of living that would be truly the opposite of war, becomes confused with the dream—virtually a reflex, yet also both arrogant and laughable—of those who would transmute human nature into divine nature. A universal and unpredictable end of history replaces the visions of paradise after death promised by religion. It is also after death—the death of present and even of all imaginable generations—that the dream is supposed to come true. Hope may resort to *conjecture* or make claims of scientific justification; yet both are woven of the same illusions. Outside the historic eras (including those we like to call prehistoric), beyond the time, that is, of life as we know it, after such a time, peace shall replace war, because by necessity rather than by choice, humans will have become other than they are now. Or nature must have a plan. Or war, in the final analysis, must be only the struggle between classes on the way to their final disappearance. In fact, however, today as yesterday, the only reality available for our examination is war, both its periods of battle and its periods of nonbattle, the latter being called peace.

Those philosophers who saw in war either an inner tendency of human nature or a means for its emergence have given us significant grounds for abiding by this conclusion, however discouraging it seems. Their writings leave some questions unanswered, however. Machiavelli and Hobbes, for example, each in his own way made a profound analysis of the kind of fear that constitutes human nature, inclining humans to confrontation rather than flight. And the love of glory central to the anthropology of both philosophers (and to the thinking of all who have observed this trait in humans) is one of the most potent generators of war. These may be primitive qualities that are beyond argument. But if we probe more deeply, the distress we feel when we contemplate history and the titanic efforts of great thinkers to find meaning in it also suggest that there are unspoken questions that should be asked, even though there has never yet been anything but uncertainty or silence in response.

Why does human fear human? Is this really our original motivation? Has the self-confidence we might believe to have been our first sentiment melted away before fear, or has it always been unfounded? True, we are the only beings who realize we are mortal. We know our fragility, our limitations. Whatever we do, we cannot help but understand at once that we are not our own makers; we cannot escape what we *are*. We do not know where we came from and whether death has a meaning. We seek above all else to stay alive, yet at the same time we want to give our lives value by controlling others. We may well wonder what primordial contentment was taken from us, for we live lives so hollow that we would fill them, at the risk of death, by seizing others to make use of as mere means.

Does a "negative ontology" not show through Hobbes's impeccable mechanistic system? Can we not detect it, like a watermark, on all the pages of our race's history? In desire and in fear, the two deepest motives, this "ontological rift" is experienced. It determines—if not necessarily, at least usually—the warlike behavior that we engage in to *find our selves*. It is behavior that disappoints, behavior that the state of right restrains more or less well without being able to change it for the better, for war continues. Time and again, war bears the impossible responsibility of bringing complete affirmation of being to each of us as we seek the illusion of fulfillment through victory over another equally wounded being. The enemy, an opaque otherness, is never thought of as another *person*— unknowable, indeed, because other, but irreducibly a center of life and meaning. The enemy is condemned to obliteration simply for being the enemy. War kills the reality that is other, with no concern for the message it might carry.

We find this kind of idea implicit in Hegel's works, beginning with the origin of the human being (and continuing throughout history), when we notice that *Anerkennung* is always imposed on the other. The state, a realized form of self-conscious spirit, does not put an end to the imperialism of "recognition" because it is obliged to provide a police force and because war between nations goes on as before, for otherwise freedom would crumble. The self-conscious "I" uttered by the victor, the one who prefers to die rather than submit, is made possible not only by the tension that forces human beings to face their own greatest mystery but also by the other's defeat and submission. The conquered party will be forced to solve the material problems of the conqueror (whether person or state) and otherwise will be asked no questions nor provide any answers. And when nevertheless a vital contribution is made by conquered to conqueror—as happened when Greece, though politically a vassal, impregnated Rome with its civilization—such events occur only obliquely, so to speak, without being genuinely realized. Language is unilateral and, with the risk of impersonal death typical of modern warfare, genuine speech is no longer uttered, although there is the clamor of speeches, proclamations, analyses of the situation, and so on.

The power of Hegelian philosophy lies largely in the fascination of the *negation* in it. To act is to negate an object; to be free is to negate nature (even life); to say "I" is to negate the other, to negate the "I" of the other. Because the "thou" knows nothing of reciprocity, any hope of using the pronoun *we* is vain. But whereas laws and the police restrain the life-and-death struggle inside the state that establishes mutual recognition as an *institution*, that struggle continues to foster freedom in wars abroad. Is Hegelian man not born of a failed human relationship, one based on war and starting war upon war as repetitive means of preserving and developing himself? His genesis, as endless as the succession of wars, involves no exchange or reciprocity that is not short-lived. The desire that initiates it is a lack, a vacuum, a nonbeing. He cannot help but bring this emptiness into his relationships, stamping them with his deficiencies. Though war may be the necessary and unending means of arousing what is human in us, is it not at the same time an impoverishment? It is all the more tragic for persisting as the unconscious recourse of beings who are amputated of something they feel to be part of themselves. The emptiness in us is surely the place for the other; but the other has been reduced to an object to be destroyed in our defense against possible attack, to be humbled in the triumph of glory, and to be exploited in the demand for acknowledgment. Experienced in this kind of incorporation, the other is indeed part of everyone's reality. But even by risking life, that reality cannot be made to surpass the quality of being allowed the other in so partial a relationship. For all the euphoria of victories, the hope of wholeness is vanity. War inescapably begins again.

If we come up against hard facts, and there is nothing to understand except the relations among causes and effects, then not only is the expectation of peace a pipe dream, but war itself may not be a proper object for philosophical thought. It is of interest to the historian, the sociologist, the strategist, the politician, but it has so little intrinsic significance that its data, its reversals of fortune, even the upheavals it forces on human history are unimportant.

Before abandoning peace to utopian dreams or to the realism of those who classify it as part of war, let us try to detect in the origins of human life the most tangible signs of this fissure in being that we have emphasized. One of the most direct signs involves the condition in which we each arrive in the world. Despite the triteness of the observation, Descartes repeats several times that "we have all been children before being men."[3] Such an obvious point is not made without a purpose. But whereas the philosopher was lamenting how feebly and slowly judgment is formed, we may also wonder to what extent the unavoidable state of infancy and childhood represents an intractable component of the universal propensity for war.

It has become very hard to speak about childhood. It is the territory of educators, psychoanalysts, demographers, and the like. It is not, it seems, a topic that a philosopher can approach from any perspective other than that of the social sciences, especially a philosopher who intends to include it in a study of war. The child's education is a theme that has always aroused interest, of course—and passions—which would tend to prove just how vital it is. With the exception of Epicureanism, the great philosophies have contained a *paideía* [philosophy of education]. Every generation since World War II has been the guinea pig for a great many pedagogical experiments. Behind avowed intentions, there have too often been political concerns, bringing educators into conflict in the name of what is in children's best interests. Thus the child becomes both alibi and victim of ideological conflicts. Our contemporaries did not invent such conflicts. In the battle among Sophists, moralists, democrats, and conformists, Socrates was killed "because he was corrupting the youth" . . . and Athens nonetheless lost the Peloponnesian War and, with it, its political hegemony.

I will take up the state of childhood with a specific intention—to show its condition of being, to investigate to what degree this condition can be changed, and to ask whether the causes of war are not irremediably bound up in it. We are in the habit (a recent one, admittedly, dating only from the period of romantic literature) of making the child an object of wonder or compassion. We forget what childhood *is*, distracted by the emotions it recalls or arouses in us. The fashion of starry-eyed or heartrending books of "childhood memories" began in the last century. Centuries of indifference had preceded these attitudes. We recall that in Greece and Rome the newborn was as a matter of course exposed to the elements—invariably if the infant was defective, less often if it was healthy. Its life did not come under the protection of the law, moreover, until it had been ritually acknowledged by the head of the household. Despite contemporary sympathies, in our era we have partly reclaimed the right to consider the fetus, and perhaps soon the child born handicapped, as something we can get rid of. What concerns us here, however, is the general status of childhood as it is, as it has always been. Whatever our attitude toward the child, it is a *thing* under the control of what is not itself. Even without considering what possible ability the child has to control its own life, it is beyond doubt that those around it determine its idea of what suits it and the child itself has few means of expressing a desire or opinion. Leaving aside extreme cases marked by crying, digestive upsets, sickness, even death, as children we were all cared for and educated according to the *idea* of childhood entertained by adults.

It cannot be otherwise. The child is an organism without power, controlled by the necessary omnipotence of those who take care of it and of statutes it has not made. It is perhaps more this than it is a potential adult. It is a *product*; and if its caretakers get the idea that they do not want to influence it, then it is the product of *not* being told what is good for it—which in most cases is worse than the reverse. Contemporary indifference to opinion is the fruit of that unfortunate experience. Because the child cannot take responsibility for itself, for a time at least it must be subject without its consent to the will of another, like—let us dare to say it—a slave[4] (which in no way implies that its parents should behave like prison guards). Whether absolutely necessary or not, the impression on the child is more or less indelible. We can say that the child is in a state of *alienation* that cannot be helped because its very being depends on another who by definition is *foreign* to what it is.

In saying *child*, we designate a being that is, so to speak, the headwaters of the being it is not; and perhaps this status, experienced by all humans without exception, is the first sign of that ontological rift that philosophers show us in their descriptions of the race and its development. Descartes frequently reminds us of the feebleness of our judgment, marked from birth by the tyranny of our needs, by "foolish nurses," and by the "authority" of tutors.[5] Eudoxus' question, he writes, could be paraphrased, "Can it be . . . that there is in nature any evil so universal that there is no remedy to be applied to it?"[6] In respect to childhood, the answer is not certain. Can we recover from this disease that is its distinguishing trait? Can we say of people that they ever become adults other than biologically? Can we say without self-contradiction that we are not free to determine what we become and at the same time that we become adult? An adult human would surely be more an ideal being, a dream being, than a reality; for we are inevitably prisoners of this fracturing of our selves that occurred prior to what we are now and that was the beginning of what we are now. Descartes proposed a method for guaranteeing the correctness of thought processes burdened by distorting habits, but his hope of providing a firm basis for rational behavior fell short of its goal.

It is noteworthy that the fecundity of psychoanalytic literature rests entirely on the study of childhood and the impressions that children receive from occurrences they take in without comprehension. Psychoanalysis believes it can find in individual history and even in the history of peoples reasons exterior to the patient for the malaise of the adult. The efforts of psychoanalysis are clearly valuable, but perhaps they do not go back far enough. It is true that the adult is a *consequence*; the adult is a result because he or she was already a result as a child. But from the grotesque wail of Molière's *bourgeois gentilhomme*, "Oh! My parents, what harm I wish you!" and the subtle anathema of Nathanael, "Families, I hate you," to the political scheme that would remove children from their parents so that only the state might put its stamp on them, or to the Swedish legislation that gives the child the right to "divorce" its parents— everything bespeaks the alienation of the status of childhood, the impossibility of doing anything about it, and the determination, in consequence, of the status of humankind. To have been a child before being an adult is to be destined not to be oneself.

The age-old indifference to the charms of childhood and the rather silly admiration that it excites today undoubtedly express a more or less unacknowledged discomfort—even a latent rejection—in respect to a state that no human being has avoided and the aftereffects of which may be irreversible. (Self-satisfaction can restrict those who indulge in it to unawareness of these early beginnings.) Psychoanalytic therapy tries, certainly, to help heal its clients of the traumas that take root in childhood, but it does not try to touch the malaise inherent in our *being*, and it is too often content with denying it. Moreover, if the state of childhood is an unyielding barrier standing before being, it goes without saying that being is not healed by any course of treatment.

So to grow up is not necessarily to recover from this illness that seems very like a curse. This is what Plato was telling us through the myth in the *Statesman*. He barely hides his view of childhood as a disease. "Of all wild young things," he has the Athenian say in the *Laws*, "a boy is the most difficult to handle. Just because he more than any other has a fount of intelligence in him which has not yet 'run clear,' he is the craftiest, most mischievous, and unruliest of brutes."[7] Will the scrupulous care taken with all the details of education make a man of the little brute, or will the educator be satisfied when enough impression has been made on him to control him?

In the myth that the Stranger develops at such length in the *Statesman*[8] and that the Athenian recalls in the *Laws*,[9] the human creatures who live in the reign of Cronus do not have to be children before they are adults. Although they cannot have the perfection of gods, they are nonetheless free from domination by other human creatures from the moment they come into the world. The earth that brings them forth is of a different nature than theirs. She, the oldest of the divinities, has no influence over her children. At their birth, they possess the wisdom of age, and as their life advances toward the state of infancy that portends their death, they pass through the age of passions endowed with a knowledge that lets them more wisely weigh their desires—if they should have any. Tutored by Cronus himself in face-to-face lessons that forgetfulness never dims, they know neither wars nor quarrels. Peace, then, requires both divine instruction, immediate and transparent, and the abundance that makes the struggle to survive, makes even work, superfluous; but it also requires an adulthood unaffected by prior helplessness. If human beings did not have to be children, they would behave reasonably and peacefully, in concord from the start with a world that is divinely ordered.

It is not thus in Zeus's world—our world—the world of history and its wars, where we start out as defenseless children. The myth's lesson is never out of date: Humans are prey to illusions, to every kind of misconception, to passions. Adults forget earliest beginnings not owed to a life-giving earth; but they retain the marks of their contacts with other humans and know well that though not born from the earth, to it they must inexorably return. Between their births and their deaths, humans must learn everything and fear everything. They have no instructors but other humans. They can obscure the fissure that affects their being; they cannot heal it. Their reason grows as their bodies grow. They excel in progressively more extraordinary feats. They increase in size and in intelligence. One day they will be factory workers, technicians, mathematicians, engineers, doctors, politicians. Even when their aptitudes and education make them capable of the subtlest thought, some part within will remain small, forever wounded by its original inadequacy, by having been a child. The mental faculties can recover from childhood, but not the being, deprived at the outset of a part of itself. This is why there is usually such an obvious disparity between the great accomplishments of thought and the mediocrity of deeds. In this gap grow dread of nonbeing, fear of our own weakness, fear of the strength that we cannot keep from attributing to others, fear of death, and here also grow the insatiable need for self-affirmation, for besting others, for subjugating them and forcing them to show us deference. Once more we find all the causes of war, the ones that bring us to negate the other because the other frightens us—or because we refuse to give way to fear ourselves, so closely are the two passions, fear and glory, linked to the irretrievable absence of being. The child whose fragility invites such care is the crucible in which the wars of the adult are seething.

Perhaps because they have sensed the irremediable ontological rift within the human heart, some philosophers have asked history to force into growth what atrophied in it at its beginning. By means of wars that are the consequence of the original illness, nature, they say, will inevitably drive both individuals and nations to make peace with each other. Or perhaps the productive energies, thanks to their continual progress, will bring about an era beyond class struggles, when the political state will have withered away. History would be the history of the species that matures without aging and becoming corrupt. Once past the interminable routines of childhood, the being would at last be cured of it. We construct the greatest illusions; because the child grows and our way of life is transformed by technological accomplishments, there is a great temptation to believe in a healing of our being that could be brought about by these changes. To live in a fully adult world at the end of history! Does not the hope reveal the fissure in childhood all the more, the better it thinks to have concealed it?

———————

We must, however, go back even farther. Childhood seems to be the first state of each individual, but no child comes into the world without the help of those who conceived it; and although heredity mingles the contributions of the one *and* the other sex, the human being produced by the act of conception belongs definitively to one *or* the other. The child is born male or female. Whatever its luck, its rebellions, its habits, its life will be played out as one or the other. We are so used to knowing that there are both men and women[10] that we seldom seek to find what that might mean in the realm of being. We speak of the battle of the sexes as of a commonplace or of a reality that has had various forms over time. Except in matriarchal civilizations (of which we know very little anyway), the human male has sought to think of himself and experience himself as a complete being. He has tried to persuade himself of the fact and virtually everywhere has written codes of law embodying this belief. As for woman, she has had to make do with a defective, less well formed nature than does he who thinks he can proclaim himself whole from the start. Or she has had to reject the characteristics (usually taken to be negative) of a difference that she risks denying, despite all evidence of its reality. The origin of these age-old attitudes usually goes unnoticed. It lies in the fact that man and woman, the one as much as the other, are fundamentally deficient beings. It is the single real equality that they can claim. Each of the two is faced with an *other* who resembles him or her and at the same time differs absolutely. Neither alone is a whole; neither can claim to be a representative member of the human species, because the other, similar and different at once, brings each one face to face with the original lack, the fissure inherent in being, whether male-being or female-being. How does a man live in accord with his own being in the presence of the being of another who is so nearly the same and yet so strange? His awareness of irreducible duality is also evidence that the individual, man or woman, is not a perfect unity. Man is only part of a race, deprived forever of one who seems a mystery—a mystery that is all the more unfathomable because she is the same, almost, as he. Philosophies of the isolation of the individual veil the problem; they do not resolve it.

Fear of the other, fear of what is unknown in the other, incomprehensible in the other, indeed seems linked, since the origin of the human condition, to our dual embodiment. Once again, we must acknowledge that all have suffered the amputation from their being of what is *not* their being.

Freud initiated investigations that stress the importance of what he called the castration complex. According to classic psychoanalytic theory, a young girl experiences her body as lacking what a little boy fears he will lose as his mother and sisters have. The distress of the two sexes and their fear of each other are considered to have originated in this childhood experience of having and not having, of fear of not having and fear of no longer having. Freud's successors had serious reservations about this kind of reasoning, but the debate remained focused on *having*; it took scant interest in *being*.

Be that as it may, it seems that the passion that thrusts us into war must be sought prior to sexuality, in an ontological reality that indeed has psychological implications, though they are not its primary ones. Bisexuality in fact plays two roles. It constitutes a fissure cutting across each person's very being, and at the same time it is the unquestionably necessary condition for the creation of other beings, who will be marked in turn by their sexual status and by the state of infancy into which they are born. Can a human being, man or woman, recover from the original cleavage of the race of which each is only an incomplete member? Is not every person's being condemned to the passion of fear? There is assuredly some vague reminiscence of this sort in the myth, attributed by Plato to Aristophanes, of the cutting in two of the first men.[11] Will we ever know whether nostalgia for a basic androgyny, present at the origins of an undamaged being, turned into the distress, fear, and aggressiveness that predispose each of us, *defective* beings that we now are, to warfare? Philosophy, it is true, has more often spoken of man in general than it has troubled itself over a status that the "reasoning animal" seems to share with every other organism (protozoans, microbes, and such excepted). But that status has a significance for those who practice "the love of wisdom" that ought to have been more often investigated. The concept human loses meaning when we forget that there are both male humans and female and that their coexistence is harmed by the fear of *not being* that is inscribed in the heart of the *being* of both, whether they like it or not.

The most primitive fear, the fear each sex has of the other, would result in mutual hostility, leading to actual war to the death, were this fear not so intimately intertwined with the nearly irresistible attraction each feels for the other. The sexual instinct is so powerful that it usually eclipses the ontological tragedy of our differentness. The primordial need for healing of being impels each sex toward the other. Their union is the hope for recovered unity, and it is not by chance that the pursuit of the bliss it grants involves so profoundly even the physical sources of life.

Yet is it not reckless to trust the sporadic action of an instinct with the task of healing a wound to our being? Desire flames up and goes out, returns only to disappear again, requires new objects. Despite its illusions when it rushes toward what it wants, in the end it is unsatisfied, and its disappointment gives rise to exasperation. All of us have feelings that we realize dimly or distinctly to be mixed with hostility: Is it not the other who is responsible for our mortification? Can we ever be secure enough in ourselves, because by ourselves we are not whole? Fear was only sleeping; now it awakes. Being seeks its completeness in other ways— love of glory is a rampart against fear; what frightens us or what we frighten must be combatted and brought down. The analysis applies to both sexes. We are familiar with the countless ups and downs of what we now call *machismo* and *feminism*. These ridiculous weapons have struck none but those who were already wounded. They have mended nothing. On the contrary, they have done, and continue to do, much harm. The one has been naively at work since the beginning of Western civilization. The second has, as well, but it has had a name and explicit methods only since the end of the last century. The depths of terror men feel toward women, to which their manifold subjugation by men bears witness; the fear involved in women's submission to the orders of a "lord and master"; women's ways of evading orders by seduction; their defiance through rejection, rebellion, and denial—these defeat imagination. On both sides are the same isolation, the same imprisonment in the impossibility of recognizing a common misfortune: Each, on the ontological plane, lacks the other and will forever.

It is also worth noting that the most recent attempts to obscure reality have settled nothing. At the end of the twentieth century, men have learned that women have the same capacity for intellectual exploits as they. Women know that they possess as much mental ability as men. As a result, fear and the desire for glory have become more obvious on both sides, to such an extent does every avatar of a civilization bear the same stamp. What difference does it make that positions of power are reversed if they are still in confrontation? In response to women's educational achievements, to the new roles they have taken, we find the spiteful clannishness of groups of men who feel their prerogatives threatened, or their hurt and impotent retreat into being "buddies" with other men in relations without genuine fellowship and intimacy. And women, mean- while, risk their identity in crude self-affirmations that will never turn them into anything but imitation men, not into beings in their own right. For a fairly significant number of both sexes, recognized or latent homo- sexuality may permanently seal off the question of being that must be faced before we can claim that human life has meaning.

Perhaps because his Jewish background gave him an inclination to metaphysics (an inclination he later renounced completely), the young Marx had glimpsed the importance of the role of bisexuality when he wrote in one of his *Manuscripts of 1844*, "The direct, natural, and necessary relation of person to person is the *relation of man to woman*."[12] By contrast, we can cite the words Nietzsche puts into the mouth of Zarathustra a few years later: "Man should be educated for war, and woman for the recreation of the warrior; all else is folly."[13] It goes without saying that the two ways of thinking are mutually exclusive. Marx has an inkling that the relation of the similar and the different, of "same" and "other," symbolized by the relation of man and woman, is at the origin of the relations of all human beings with each other—relations of domination and servitude, power and submission. Nietzsche ratifies the standard view of the relations usually considered acceptable between the sexes. Marx, however, despite his intuitive statement, does not give the corollary of his own proposition, namely, that we must not consider only the relation of man to woman but also the stance woman takes toward man if we are to genuinely understand the relations linking human beings in general—relations of violence and domination; relations of fear, hate, defeats, victories; and, more broadly, relations of war. By this omission, Marx subtly identifies with Nietzsche's point of view, and though it is beyond debate that history throws more light on the relation in the direction these two authors speak of, this is no reason to continue neglecting the other direction, the one that is over-shadowed. If we do, we will have to admit the vileness and stupidity of one sex and the innocence of the other, which would hardly reflect the reality of the status of either.

Marx, it is true, saw in woman one of the emblems—and in 1844 probably the foremost emblem—of the victims of economic oppression. He conceives of the relation of man and woman only from the perspective of the man's *need*, which does not describe the full relationship, though correctly enunciating one of the aspects and one of the directions of the primary human relation. "In the approach to *woman* as the spoil and handmaid of communal lust," he writes, "is expressed the infinite degra- dation in which man exists for himself, for the secret of this approach has its *unambiguous*, decisive, *plain* and undisguised expression in the relation of *man* to *woman* and in the manner in which the *direct* and *natural* procreative relationship is conceived."[14]

Marx is not among the apostles of women's "liberation." Far from it. As his successors understood very well, an implication similar to the following can be drawn from his works: If woman is alienated from economic power, her liberation will result from the disalienation of the economy. Would she then, however, have found her being as a *woman*, or less significantly, as an oppressed human being? History has remembered, furthermore, women who were perfectly capable of oppressing those of both sexes. To refuse to limit oneself to the question of being is not the same as silencing it. It keeps arising, because the existence of bisexuality is, despite our ideologies, the sign of an original laceration of being within all the members of the human species.

Whether fear, glory, or forced deference, any source of the passions and proclivities that lead to war is ready at our birth because we are human, male or female. Is not the cry for peace only the united wail of two beings, each broken by the inescapable presence of the other?

Although the two sexes are prone to conflict to the degree that the other represents for each of them what it is not, still it would be incorrect—and futile, besides—to forget that at least until very recent times, history has taken the apparent inferiority of women for granted. Men, it is true, can make direct use of their physical strength against creatures generally less strong of arm, and they can easily attribute to their whole being what they take to be a natural advantage. For their part, women can let themselves be convinced that men are worth more than they, regardless of frequent evidence to the contrary, the absence of convincing reasons, and the discomfort this belief inspires. A natural gift like strength has, however, no value in itself. It is obvious and impressive when put to use, without proving anything whatsoever. Reason and intelligence are not involved except in choosing ends to which strength is sometimes the means; in themselves, they have nothing to do with animal self-assertion.

It would be impossible to tell all the endless and disgraceful history of the degradations that men, on grounds of strength or superiority, have inflicted on women; the number of victims would exceed imagination. The most frightful abuses, including humiliations of every kind, from the denial of their person and their individuality to amused or arrogant scorn—the full gamut of manifestations of the fear that women provoke in men can be a disheartening study. Few are the girls who, in order to reach womanhood, have not had to suppress memories that would have stripped them of the courage to grow up. Few are the women who have never had to ask themselves why the fact of being male authorizes men's stupidity, cowardice, and the appropriation as their personal property of good qualities that are just as apparent in women. Myths have even illustrated the theme of female responsibility for the evils humanity endures, war among others. Although their traditions are independent of each other, both of the wellsprings of occidental culture, the Greek and the Jewish, encouraged men's distrust of women. We remember Pandora, whose curiosity could not resist a closed chest. When it was opened, there escaped from it the blessings and evils that gratify and afflict humankind. Epimetheus was surely imprudent, but it was not he who turned misfortune loose on the world.[15] So goes the story that Hesiod tells. It does not fully exculpate the man, but it most surely heaps blame on the woman, though it was Zeus who created her as an instrument of his vengeance.

It is the same in the biblical narrative. The prohibition was given the man before the woman's birth. Who told her of it? God does not speak to her before the sin. The first words she pronounces are in answer to the snake's questions. "The man who was with her" does not intervene.[16] He is perfectly happy to let her eat some of the fruit, then to eat some himself when she offers it to him. Yet he knew what they were doing, as did the woman, who was able to repeat the divine command word for word. But *she* is the temptress, *she* the one who corrupts one whose only wrong is to have yielded to temptation. Men's immemorial distrust of woman bears witness indeed to the assumption that she bears the primary guilt for original sin.

Should we draw the conclusion from the status to which man has confined woman that her hostility is a *reaction* to his, in the sense that Nietzsche uses the term when he speaks of "reactive wars"? The explanation contains an element of truth, but it leaves the enigma of male behavior untouched: Why are men so afraid of women that they hold women responsible for mistakes and wrongs committed by both? Why do they consider women so different that what they think of as "serious" pursuits become less so when women engage in them? Is it only because of men's arrogance that women, in turn, are afraid of men?

We must go back to the rift affecting the being of both, to what makes men and women alike but also immutably different; we must explore how their lack manifests itself and whether it in fact begets the passions that lead to war.

We can induce from the obvious similarity of man and woman that there is a natural *liking* between them, apart from sexual desire, that inclines them to seek, rather than flee, each other's company. This is true, but only in part. Aristotle, speaking solely of men, reminds us that like seeks like, but he also states that in order to associate harmoniously, it is not enough to belong to the same species. Affinities of another sort are also needed.[17] The *philia* that almost universally draws one human being toward another is not long-lived and does not truly ripen unless each finds in the other the same attraction to what he himself values to the highest degree. Can what is true of men in their relations with each other be said of relations between man and woman? Let us note first of all that not *all* men, of course, are inclined to get along well. Kant described the "unsociable sociability" that he believed inherent in humankind. But is this a primary reality, or is it, as Marx thought, a consequence of the relation between man and woman?[18] In different terms, is it perturbing for man and woman to discover they are alike, and does their anxiety shape relations among members of the human species in general?

Resemblance draws each to the other these two beings who, each *with* the other, manifest the species. But at the same time it troubles us. Why must we be of two kinds? Why are we not *one*, a sufficient representative of a whole race? Duality is the beginning of multiplicity. Although the number of men and the number of women there are is not necessary to the definition of the human being, it is indispensable that there be one man *and* one woman. Because they resemble each other, are almost identical to each other, the mystery of the original rending of their unity is all the deeper. We understand, then, that *others*, men or women, who could have been nothing but mirrors infinitely repeating the same unity, need not have been frightening. Despite their multiplicity, had human beings been of one sex, no break would have occurred in the unity that each would have adequately embodied. But such is not the case. Even before having to reproduce a man or a woman, in order that we be human, we must be two—man *and* woman. We must not be alone, we must have being in the other, through the other, we must depend from the moment of self-identity on what resembles one's self but is not one's self, in order to possess at last an identity more shared than separate.

We understand now the impulses that the ontological break stirs even in the midst of similarity—essential self-doubt, a tendency to retreat to others of the same sex, but also the discovery that they are not "safe" either. For both men and women, the others of their sex are no more than mirrors that reflect not wholeness but the same fissure. Both the harmony and disharmony between man and woman testify to their resemblance, and because they are two inseparable segments of the human being, the ambivalence of their relation determines the texture of all human relations.

What may we say of difference? It, too, attracts and repels, seduces and terrifies. Except in myths, there is no human male who is not born of a woman. Who is he, coming from what he is not? And who is she, who must bring forth what she is not? Literature has plumbed the theme of the son's love for his mother but also its obverse, the theme of the jealous love of a mother for her son, a love sometimes deadly even when not actually bent on murder. We know that girls feel an attraction toward their fathers that may conceal mistrust, and that fathers love their daughters so much that they sometimes do not allow them to live their own lives. Psychoanalysis has explained all these dynamics by desire. Oedipus, Jocasta, Antigone, and the rest have been stripped of their tragic truth to serve as prooftexts.[19] Is it so evident that sexual desire is primarily the issue and that the tragedy of *being* is not the source of the tragedy of human relations? Is it not rather the original fear of what the one is to the other, in his or her being, in his or her "sexation"[20] that is deprived of the other's being and deprives the other in turn—is it not this fear that opens the door to bafflement, suspicion, sometimes rejection, until *sexuality* comes to hide the mystery of being, which it nonetheless reveals in spite of itself? A richer psychology could result from an ontology attentive to humanity's dual nature. We may ask why philosophical thought has so often abandoned sexation, an axis of ontology, to psychology. The behavioral sciences are hardly worthless, but they are not philosophically sound. At the very heart of being are born the passions that no education has ever succeeded in overcoming. The sexual instinct in particular owes to the fracture in being its ecstasies and its deliriums alike.

CHAPTER 9

A Neglected Ontology

The bafflement and fear that glory's victories and coerced deference try to overcome have taken the most varied forms in the course of humanity's history, from concealed hostility to open aversion in personal relations, from simmering conflicts to those that erupt into civil and foreign wars. This gamut of confrontations has manifold causes. Famine drives one people to invade another; the desire for conquest leads some to roam the world, brandishing their weapons; a buildup of defenses against some future invader precipitates his attack. . . . All these reasons are "good" reasons, but why should an incalculable number of ambitions and problems find but one way—war—to a temporary resolution? And because human beings want peace, too, why does diplomacy so rarely halt reliance on arms, even in those cases where hope of military success depends largely on luck? Why does it, on the contrary, often encourage war? Zeus, says the tragic poet, blinds those he wishes to destroy, and humans, it must be admitted, are not good at remembering that it takes a sharp eye to see catastrophes coming.

In Plato's myth, peace is the natural state of humans who live in direct contact with Cronus. Original oneness and principle of harmony, the god embodies the world order where all have a place. What difference does one person's lot make to another, because each is all that one should be in the blessedness of contemplation? The question of *healing* does not arise. No one has need of an *other* in order to be in perfect relationship with the fullness of being. That the human being is not a god, that other human beings exist, that both men and women exist—this state of affairs does not destroy the serenity and meaning humanity is born to and knows at first hand. Sexuation seems to be of no consequence. Peace is therefore humanity's essential state, which existence manifests without hindrance. But "ever to be the same, steadfast, and abiding, is the prerogative of the divinest of things only. The nature of the bodily does not entitle it to this rank."[1] Our own world is no longer the world of Cronus, in which there were "no political constitutions and no taking of wives and begetting of children"—and consequently no unanswered questions about the being of the other. The world of history is one where memory of our essence

213

has vanished, where existence leaves essence farther and farther behind, for "time goes on and forgetfulness of God arises in it."[2] We are not *guilty* because we are fearful and look to glory to distract ourselves from the anguish of being; it is the movement of time that, in separating us from knowledge of our beginning, also separates us from God, from the order of the world, and from our own being.

Man and woman can, however, regain at least inner peace and live in the peace of the City. It will not be done, though, by arguing the question of bisexual being, but on the contrary by seeing that both sexes are the same in their essence, by defining a single human essence in respect to which, except that they bear children, women do not differ from male human beings. They, too, *are* human beings.[3] Plato does not take up the question of the relation of male and female human beings as it is affected by their difference. He may sometimes approach it but only in repeating commonplaces that ascribe to women unimportance, bad temper, vanity, complaints—the comparison of the male character with the female is always to the latter's disadvantage. Plato goes so far as to allow woman the same intelligence and access to the intelligible as man, on condition that her female humanness be ignored. We are reminded of Socrates' asking whether war is an evil or a good. The postponed inquiry was never undertaken. Women who are equally entitled with men to the study of philosophy are, like them, warriors fit to defend the City.

According to Plato, the human being can recover his essence and abide by it in his existence, that is, he can return to his peaceful being, if he submits to the long, difficult discipline demanded by the road to knowledge. Because he masters his passions and engages in dialectic, the philosopher is "habituated to . . . the contemplation of all time and all existence"[4] in a serene vision of their first unity. Peace would blossom from contemplation if each accepted his *responsibility* to discover the intelligible definition of humankind, for each possesses "this indwelling power in the soul and the instrument whereby each of us apprehends."[5] But most individuals pay no heed to this; their petty interests bring about the disappearance of their being in the tumult of excessive or ridiculous passions. A few—their sex does not matter, and they are very rare, it is true—a few are enough to give proof that despite the most bloody wars ceaselessly devastating the cities, humanity's true vocation is of another kind. We must also realize that if a "divine grace," a *theía moîra*, does not sustain even the most gifted nature, (as was true for Socrates), then the way to attain knowledge necessarily lies in the relationship of teacher and pupil. The return to our forgotten essence cannot grow elsewhere than in this relationship, this asymmetrical pairing. The talented pupil will become in turn a teacher. The pupil will then be the equal of the teacher, identical in having also found true being, and will take on the obligation of helping those in whom he recognizes the ability to become like himself.

Plato brought humankind as far as he could in the process of self-healing to which all are summoned. At the cost of making man and woman identical by characterizing them in a way that excludes the disturbing dimension of similarity and dissimilarity, he points the way to the soul's peace for a very restricted number of the "best," the *áristoi*, men or women. Christianity will rediscover this path in the lives of the men and women saints, but with the difference that the way no longer lies exclusively through knowledge but through faith and charity above all else. This way returns us to the essence of the human being as God's creation, born for love and for peace. In the course of the history of Western civilization, however, was a teaching perhaps lost that would have thrown a brighter light on war and peace, if humankind had not so often obscured it?

And yet, besides its usual interpretation through the centuries, how many commentaries the book of Genesis has inspired! It is true, as Kant's essay, for example, testifies, that more of these commentaries have been based on the second chapter than have begun with the first. I begin a study of the latter by highlighting among its philosophical implications those that bear on war and peace. Does this betray the holy writing? We might say that any interpretation is generally a betrayal when the richness and meaning of the narrative are owed to divine revelation. When standing before the Word of God, philosophers are human creatures like any others; it is not within their right to give an authorized opinion. But all of us can try to understand a text and probably have a duty to do so when it concerns our being. On condition that we do not take ourselves for theologians, our undertaking is proper and our interpretation is unrestricted. In addition, of course, we must not abuse the plain meaning of the text in order to enlist it in proving what we want it to. To question a text is not to take hold of it to force it to say what it does not say. And never is it to insist that we have given it a definitive interpretation.

When dealing with Scripture, the obstacles are many. Translation raises a barrier that study of the original language fails to remove. Contemporary exegetes have proved this.[6] The texts of the Bible, nonetheless, and especially Genesis, have permeated the Western world, whether faithfully translated or not. From a purely philosophical perspective, we will apply ourselves to the "creation myth" as written and as most usually understood. In this endeavor, we are not concerned with faith any more than with the findings of modern linguistics.

We know that the first chapter of Genesis describes the creation of the world and of the human being. God establishes time and imposes a rhythm on all life by creating light, the symbol of knowledge. With the separation of the waters, a space for living things takes form. The four elements of all traditions—fire, air, water, and earth—are given their place; animals are created, each suited to the nurturing element where it can grow and multiply without need to attack others in order to survive. The diversity and numberless multiplicity of God's work are the sign of an infinite creative power, an unlimited organizing spirit. God contemplates his work and sees that "it was very good."

Yet the creature that is the most perfect is missing. It will not be the most complete, as are the plants or animals that do not transform themselves. It will be the creature that, mirroring God, will itself also be capable of creation, because, made in the image of God who creates through the word, it will have the ability to speak. Here is the reason that all other creatures will submit to it, not as things to be used as it wishes but rather because this creature—the human being made in God's image and likeness, but not itself God—is the intermediary bringing all creation to God. Angelus Silesius has admirably expressed it in these lines:

> Man, creatures love you so, it's you they are pressing toward;
> Hastening to come to you, thus to attain their God. . . .
> If you possess your God, all else will follow suit,
> Man, angel, sun and moon, air, fire, earth, and brook.[7]

What is the "man" that God created and then, looking at all he had made, "saw that it was very good"?[8] Created in the image and likeness of God, he is not God, he cannot *be* God. God creating God would be an absurdity. Oneness does not divide nor multiply itself. And yet, if man is other, absolute other, how could he resemble his Creator? The image nearest unity, though not unity, is duality created in a relationship in which union becomes unity. "God created man in his own image, in the image of God he created *him*; male and female he created *them*."[9] And of these two together it is said, "Let them have dominion over the fish of the sea, and over the birds of the air, and over the cattle, and over all the earth, and over every creeping thing that creeps upon the earth."[10] These are the two whom God blesses, the two to whom he says, "Be fruitful and multiply, and fill the earth and subdue it; and have dominion over the fish of the sea and over the birds of the air and over every living thing that moves upon the earth."[11]

The command to be fruitful and multiply within the overflowing abundance of creation is given to both animal and human creatures. The command to subdue the earth and have dominion over the living things around them applies only to man and woman. The bisexuality that the human species shares with the other species and that does not differentiate it from them in respect to the natural act of procreation has, in the creation myth, central importance for the human species: Before being a means of procreation, the existence of two sexes is the ontological foundation for resemblance to God of a being who is not and, by definition, cannot be God. This is why duality in the human being is "dyad": It cannot be eliminated, yet at the same time it cannot be dissolved. Each of the two human realities is not itself and is not a human being, except in combination with the other in an original bond that alone grants it access to humanity, the image of divinity.

The presence of the other—natural, immediate, ordained—includes no fear of either conflict or loss. No evil surprise awaits the image because the dissimilarity of its two parts corresponds to the logic of the description of oneness. Because oneness cannot reproduce itself, the creation of either a single man *or* a single woman would have been meaningless, and the creation of *two* men or *two* women would have been pointless repetition of a parcel of being. Because they resemble each other yet are different, only the creation of man *and* woman could allow a union representing oneness. The human being, made of both "same" and "other," is partnership and harmony, unsevered image of the originating Oneness. The human being enters the world an adult, man and woman complete in the perfection of their being—adult being, companioned being, representing the double presence necessary to the oneness we call harmony.

The metaphysical import of the text is easily recognized. In the view represented by the first chapter, the partners are not separated from their being because—far from being androgynous—the human being whose model is God is immediately born into the union of man and woman. There is nothing unknown; there is no risk of being mistaken. Neither of the two can wish ill to the other because they are united with each other as with the source of their being. Neither feels a lack; on the contrary, each is fulfilled by the other in harmonized likeness and unlikeness. When it bestows oneness, otherness is life itself.

Such is the human being's essence in accord with the divine plan that rules human existence—to make one another fruitful by reciprocally giving the gift of being, to multiply through children who resemble one or the other, to subdue the earth *together* by calling forth its every treasure. Whatever the vagaries of historical existence, the original peace that emanated from the human dyad to every kind of being will continue to be our deepest longing. It is symbolized by the day of rest for God and human creatures, the seventh day. God rests "from all his work which he had done in creation."[12] Newly born, the man and the woman peacefully contemplate Creator and creation before beginning their own work according to divine direction. The eternity of God, the youth of the world, the youth of humanity in harmony with its being—the texts tells us no more.

Men and women, however, fear each other, they desire each other, and they battle each other like born enemies. Wars mark off the periods of history, armies deploy with their train of miseries, and conquerors spurred on by lust for glory think themselves gods, free to decide the fate of the conquered—all this that we live as daily reality has smothered our original calling. The disunion of man and woman has blurred the image of the human being's oneness. War has driven peace into the fog of utopian dreams; humanity blindly gropes for peace yet strains to invent ways to keep it at a distance, as if war were its fate or proof of its freedom.

For following this first narrative of the origin of the human being is another that might have had the same implications as the first but instead contains the seed of the "accident" that obscured essence and filled existence with catastrophes. Whether the story is from the Elohist or Yahwist tradition is not of consequence here. Western civilization inherited both legends, but it seems to have remembered the second far better than the first in the history it has lived and that has determined relations between persons.

In the second narrative of Genesis, God creates man immediately after the heavens and the earth. Space and time, represented as a sequence of divine acts, are the minimal conditions for the appearance of life. Somewhat as in the myth in the *Statesman*, man comes from the earth already adult. He could not be expected to increase the race, as this human male is alone. It is worth taking note that when he creates woman, God intends her as a help to man, and no reference is made to future generations. Differently than in the Greek myth, here man's soul is breathed into him by a divine breath. This tells us that he is part of the world's order and capable of knowing what it is. But he is born solitary, and although in having a soul he shares the nature of his Maker, he cannot be in his image and likeness. Nothing in the text suggests it; in fact it implies just the opposite. He is a male human being, an incomplete being; for God himself states that "it is not good that the man should be alone."[13] After the birth of the first living creature, God plants a garden in Eden that becomes the man's home, a place in which he finds plentiful means of sustaining his life and that he must tend and watch over.[14] Man's task is to preserve and reproduce God's handiwork, though without being God's image. Is this one of the reasons that he is forbidden, at the risk of his life, to eat of the tree of the knowledge of good and evil?[15] There is no longer any question of exercising mastery over the earth but simply of taking care of it as it is.

Whom does this man resemble? God wants him to have a helper similar to himself,[16] and he first creates all the animals, which he forms, like man, out of earth, but into which he does not breathe his breath. God shows man the different species and asks him to give them names. In this encounter with what resembles him and is not he, there appears a fundamental difference. Because God has given him a living soul, man can form concepts. An animal cannot. Man assigns the animals names without escaping his solitude, for not one word comes from them in reply. His being is vague, without identity. The creation of the male human being is imperfect, unfinished. It must be reconsidered and improved. The beasts are not helpers similar to man and certainly a second man would be too similar, would be no more than a reflection, responding with mimicry void of meaning. A man confronted with another man would gain only repetition, not the utterance that consists of question and response, not, that is, meaning. The lesson will be almost completely forgotten for centuries. Most of the time men will be content to speak only among themselves and to make war on each other.

Next, in order to repair his creation, the one into whom he has breathed his own breath, God puts him to sleep (as if he had returned to nonexistence), takes a rib from him, and makes from it another being, woman. Now the man is awake and in the presence of what God has brought him. Notice how long it takes for the human couple to appear in this Yahwist version—God's mistake in fashioning a creature he is dissatisfied with, and then other creatures, and finally from the first creature he fashions the last, one who is given to be a helper similar to him. In what way is she different from earlier creations, she who, through her origin in man, also comes from the earth? Although the text does not say so, it is evident that she shares the divine breath present in man. The man does not mediate the divine breath, otherwise the female body would have only a secondary reality; it would be without speech, like the beasts. This is the reason that her role, the help that she must give and that cannot be expected from any kind of animal,[17] is precisely to furnish humankind with language, true language, language that does not stop at using words to distinguish objects but that creates its meaning through exchanged speech.

The man understands this immediately, but his helper has been long in arriving. In a fine burst of youthful joy, he exclaims, "This is bone of my bones and flesh of my flesh; she shall be called Woman, because she was taken out of Man. Therefore a man leaves his father and his mother and cleaves to his wife, and they become one flesh."[18] With these words a future can be envisioned—father and mother left behind by the couple who go off together to their own life. Unfortunately, it is not *to* woman that man speaks. He speaks *about* her, in front of her, without eliciting an answer or awaiting one.[19] We must acknowledge that he is stating, literally, a truth. But he is only stating it, not sharing it. Before the birth of woman,

man was alone and as good as mute, as no animal involved him in anything more than its naming. With woman present, he is no longer alone, and he speaks; but he is not aware that he is speaking as if alone. She does not answer. Even if we attribute an enthusiastic tone to the man's words, the woman, a witness to the truth of the statement, is not invited to speak. There is an "I," but it is childish because there is no "thou." How could there be a "we"? This is the lesson the Occident understood.

A *couple* has been created but without a *dyad* whose union would be the image of oneness having been genuinely formed. For the truth stated by only one of the two members required to form a human being can be but partial. In his utterance, the man hymns the joy of finding himself in one like himself, reunited with him in the flesh: She is "bone of my bones, flesh of my flesh," she is "taken out of Man," they will "become one flesh." Indeed. But that is not enough, for the helper who is like man, even taken out of man, is *not* man. She is other. Man speaks at once of union, of likeness, *before* becoming conscious of the difference that only woman can speak of. Even though she is of man's flesh and bone—of earth—like him, she is *not* man; she is *she.* The similarity and difference of bodies made for uniting are symbols of another similarity and another difference, that of their being deep within them, being that can come into its fullness only through the harmony of speech flowing between them, expressing the divine breath, giving the physical union of the sexes its deepest joy. Human beings do not couple as beasts do. In the fine biblical expression, the man "knows" the woman, the woman "knows" the man, for if they come to the point of each speaking his or her truth, their union becomes primarily an ontological joining, a return to the creative oneness, resembling it as only its image could. The outward expression of their oneness is the union of bodies, but though inseparable from it, this union is not its foundation. In contrast, the bodily union owes to that oneness its sense of infinity and the blissful loss of each one's individuality in its accomplishment. "Animal triste post coïtum," the saying goes. The *animal,* certainly, when the human being acts as such. When human beings bring the animal into the harmony of human reality, there is only bliss.

Nonetheless, as we grow up we still must leave childhood behind, part from father and mother, as the text says, and recover from an injury to being. Though it may be possible, we do not yet know how. The young adult satisfied with his solitary expression of delight was still a child. Between the partial truth of the words uttered by the man and the manifestation of the truth we quicken in each other through shared speech, there is, from the start, a gap that history will widen. It is the first sign of the still unnoticed status of each one's being.[20] The resemblance and difference of man and woman are not yet recognized as a rift of being; in the third chapter, they will deepen the chasm that later generations know. Because of them, the tumult of history that sets men fighting will be the sad outcome of fruitless dialogues, of the fear lurking in each person's solitude, of the desire for glory that is, at bottom, only the challenge hurled by one who believes himself absolutely alone.

From the very start, we have no hope that the first human couple, despite their state of primitive innocence, will manifest in words and deeds the world order, the divine order, of which they are part. For man and woman have not attained awareness of their common being through attuned speech. On the contrary, the distance between them is evident from the narrative of the temptation. The first living thing to speak directly to the woman, to her who was not yet born when the divine prohibition was uttered, is not the man but the serpent. His words lie somewhere between truth and falsehood: God has not forbidden *all* the trees in the garden. The woman knows the truth and corrects the statement. "We may eat of the fruit of the trees of the garden; but God said, 'You shall not eat of the fruit of the tree which is in the midst of the garden, neither shall you touch it, lest you die.'"[21] Why this tree and why is it forbidden? The rest of the text seems to indicate that this is not done to test man but for some very different purpose. It is absurd to imagine God himself creating a being that he considers unsatisfactory, providing him with a helper, and after an inadequate trial, placing him—his own creation—in the way of the most crass temptation, thereby setting in motion the inhuman history played out by all generations since the beginning of time, with an ending that can only be imagined as universal cataclysm leading to either extinction or utopia. It would be pointless to dwell on the impoverishment of these explanations.

The serpent utters lying words that are to be taken in the precisely opposite sense. "You will not die," it says, "for God knows that when you eat of it, your eyes will be opened and you will be like God, knowing good and evil."[22] In order to live, all members of the human species must enter, with their differences and similarities, into the dyadic union that is the image of divine Oneness. Death, in contrast, follows from the solitary and illusory self-elevation of both (or of either of the two) who wrongly take themselves for complete wholes. "You shall be like God": Both eat of the fruit of the tree of knowledge, both believe, foolishly, that having good and evil revealed to them will fulfill a being whose essential completeness cannot be found except in another being.

We see to what extent the second chapter both resembles and differs from the first. The ontological message is the same: Only in harmonious union are man and woman the image of Oneness. Alone, no one is whole. In the first chapter, the essence of the human being is intact from the start, the plan of existence is clearly laid out for him. The two beings have been able to glimpse something of God's Oneness and bounteous might, something, too, of the fruitful relation that they in their dyadic being have with God. In the second chapter, the lesson is more clouded. Man, a lone creature, knows himself first as a divided being, cut off from himself, for all that he has received the divine breath. The man and the woman must each succeed in reaching the other, and this is not easy. It requires repeated intervention by the One of Being, the source of a creature that resembles him but is not he, the One who has created both man and woman in manifest separation from each other.

To find themselves, both must know themselves in the wholeness of their being. They have stopped part way there. The exchange of speech is the condition for step-by-step creation of dyadic being. One word has been spoken. It expresses a truth, but it is neither completed nor answered. The first *dialogue* will be initiated by a liar. The serpent proclaims nonbeing, nothingness, echoed in the divine pronouncement, "You are dust, and to dust you shall return."[23] Because she has not been spoken to, the woman eats the fruit. Because she has not spoken to him, the man agrees to eat the fruit she offers him. It is striking, moreover, that they still do not speak to each other. It does not even occur to them to consider the serpent's words together. Each unthinkingly capitulates to the material part of his or her being—in this case, an enticing fruit symbolizing worthless autonomy. As they have never heard a word in *reply*, each turns to what both in their ignorance take for fulfillment of their being—whereupon the would-be gods discover they are naked: "And they knew that they were naked."[24] Then they hide from each other—they who did not see one another because they did not hear one another, who yet had eyes for seeing and ears for hearing. They are henceforth isolated, in the awareness of their incomplete being. The wrong they commit, the original sin, is not this puerile transgression; the sin is that both of them interpret sexation as an exclusive *possession* of the other and a deprivation of the self, instead of understanding it as residing in their common being. For two separated and truncated beings (for as we have seen, man and woman are in the same condition), desire acquires a different meaning. Experienced as an essential lack, it becomes panicked by the emptiness and alights on an obvious part of being but one disconnected from the whole. Desire covets its object so keenly, so painfully, that it must hide it like a shameful secret. Man and woman are now prisoners of the sexual difference that obscures the bisexual completeness of being. In itself, sexual desire is innocent. It exists from the very moment of the creation of two human creatures, man and woman. Its purpose is to make of them one flesh. But when it grips a man or woman who has not reached harmony of being through another, no erotic relation, whatever its pleasures, can call itself a union. Sexual desire is subordinate to being that is restored to its wholeness through the marriage that is speech, exchanged between two human creatures, alike and, at the same time, of different sexes.

Beings diminished by the ambition of each to become a god ("you"— *both* of you—"will be like God"), the man and woman hide from each other behind their fig leaves[25] because they are afraid of the mystery of an otherness that cannot warn against mistakes. And they hide from God because they are afraid of the Being whose divinity they wished to seize, without having succeeding in being truly his image. The consequences flow from the logic of the initial failure: Each one answers God's question by trying to claim innocence. The one says, "It was the woman you gave me," and the other, "It was the serpent." There was still time to accept the blame *together*. No. The barely perceptible dissociation of their first meeting is now consummated. God is obliged to curse the serpent and the earth, but he curses neither the man nor the woman. He simply unites them in the same fall from grace. It is not in accord with the order of the world that woman should suffer in childbirth and that her desire should make her submit to man, that man should toil to live and must return to nothingness. Neither is it a punishment. God only states consequences, he does not make laws.[26] The consequences fall upon the human species, all of whose members, both men and women, are incapable of union; but consequences are not blame, nor are they barriers to reconciliation through speech. Human societies will invent punishments to prevent lawbreakers from doing harm. They have no other choice, unless they would let evil spread, even to the point of decimating or annihilating the species. When punishment turns into revenge, it then becomes an evil itself. It should only serve to set things right and to be a warning that every action has consequences and that the one who would prefer to avoid them must accept them all the same so that he may try to become a human again, even at the risk of his physical life. God does not need to invent penalties. He has only to tell what follows logically from what men have done. The corrections humans inflict on other humans are always incommensurable with the offenses for which they are sanctions. The consequence is not intrinsic in the deed; there is no necessary relation between a transgression and the length of a prison term. But if the correction did not exist, the deed would persist unmitigated. There could be no remission for the one who committed it. Punishment does not erase a misdeed; if it is understood, punishment removes from it the evil effects of its actions. Because every offense is to another's detriment, it is an amputation not only from the other's being but also of the offender's. A double healing, and this only, is the purpose of corrective suffering.

How strange is the story of humanity's origins! We are the children of this couple who were made to unite as a perfectly whole being but who have only been able to unite through the flesh. Men know, because they have known from the start, that no animal can respond to them. They need those who alone can perfect their incomplete being and of whom they can say that they are flesh of their flesh. They must, however, say it *to* them, as something other than an expression of their own happiness or a way to seduce them, and they must listen to their life-giving answer. Women, too, have their own knowledge; they know that the sweetness of the tribute paid them by those who speak *about* them is not what they require. They let themselves be fascinated by it, but they do not find themselves through it. When man speaks of woman, he exalts her resemblance and preempts it: Here is flesh of my flesh and bone of my bones. He has forgotten that there is the deeper resemblance as well as the difference, and that although woman came into existence through him, she is also the one, irreducibly herself, through whom he exists. The woman accepted her disappearance from the words the man spoke. Resemblance imprisons both in the tragic error of judgment. In their imperfect being, both believe that they will become like a god, thus making of their resemblance a rift in the heart of being. And their difference from each other, so disturbing that even in the Garden of Eden neither speaks of it, will take on the most varied disguises. Men will mistake themselves for women and women for men; some will try to withdraw but will end in confrontation or die all alone; all will have to struggle to discover what they are.

The most usual way of interpreting the story of the temptation is to see in it the first manifestation of freedom. God created humans free to go against the world order, which is a benign order, and to replace it with their own, which is a transgression of the divine order. This explains why the earth has become the vale of tears of which the prophet speaks, why the history of nature begins, as Kant tells us, with good, for it is God's handiwork, whereas the history of freedom begins with evil, for it is the work of man; or again, it explains why the penitent will be saved; or why future generations will reach peace, both by choice and under compulsion, after the most horrible wars; for though history is inescapable, it is still the history of freedom.

It is quite true, according to the narrative, that God did not create man in the same way he made lifeless things and animals. And although God made man subject to natural law, with the first words he addressed to man, God was obliged, even as he lavished the gifts of creation upon him, to forbid him their full use. God had, in effect, given humankind *freedom*, the freedom to obey or to rebel. Against what? In the story as we have it, the object of the prohibition is a food, a fruit that is not for nourishing the body, as are other fruits. To do good or evil means to live in accord with the true character of the human being's essence or to live in defiance of it. Immediately after he forbids the fruit, God proclaims that it is not good for man to be alone. In other words, despite the divine breath within him, man in solitude is not a human being; in order that he may be genuinely human, there must be another living creature similar to him. It is in respect to this creature, and hence in respect to the divine plan, that man is free to accept or reject difference and similarity. The woman is also endowed with *the same freedom*—freedom to live in accord with the order of the world or to want to be what she is not, denying her own nature and man's as well—to want to be God and not a human being. Such is the choice that each is free to make.

To think, to develop one's reason is natural: The human creature is a rational animal. Reason is in principle less contrary to nature than we have been willing to admit since the seventeenth and, especially, the eighteenth century. To have dominion over the earth, to till the garden— these mean of course to transform what is given. They are not the same as to create something and obviously not the same as to "render ourselves masters and possessors" of it, as Descartes hoped.[27] For however original the products of humanity, they depend on an order that man has not made. Among human works, there are some that have moral implications, depending on the use they are put to. Others are evil from the start. None is good in itself; the purest intentions can result in disasters. (Let us, however, except the masterpieces of art, for they put those capable of sounding their depths in direct contact with the essential reality of the human being, the world, and their intelligible principle.) The *value* inher- ing in the products of human activity—the simplest as well as the most sophisticated—derives from anything in their conception, realization, and use that lets us consciously or unconsciously renew our being that the first choice committed to insufficiency. Unless this were true, we would not understand why there is such a gulf between humans' brilliant feats of intellect and technology and the pitiful way they manage their lives. We are often fooled about this, it is true. Vanity exalts those who succeed and ignores the rest or degrades them. The excitement over human achieve- ments as such is sufficient proof of how important it is to us to conceal the universal rift in being that no invention, no technology has ever succeeded in filling.

The first man and the first woman (and the generations after them) forgot that *sameness* and *otherness* must be faced in order to become oneself. We must accept similarity and difference in order to *be*, and we must accept them together. The first couple begot Cain, who killed his brother Abel. History was beginning. We recognize it. We make war, we dread war, we acquiesce to it, and we do not know how to end it. Yet we also want peace. Humans rarely eat others to survive, but in anger and victory they grow drunk on another's blood. When rage subsides, when wounds are too deep for licking, or when the fantasies spawned by their vanity and glory crumble, humans long for peace; they want it as they want their being, the being of which they feel continually bereft.

Do humans have any chance of recovering their truth, of finding beneath the tangle of war engines they themselves have built the lost road that leads to peace?

God, says the tale, drove the human creature out of the Garden of Eden "lest he put forth his hand and take also of the tree of life, and eat, and live forever," because he had become "like one of us, knowing good and evil."[28] Are we to understand that no return to peace is possible, that in barring the way to the tree of life, the cherubim and the whirling flame of the sword bar forever the pathways of peace?

An interpretation something like a hope can also be based on these verses. The human being, blameless, was ignorant of his dual essence. He could have been satisfied to follow it without knowing its barriers and snares but also without learning its possibilities. Knowledge of good and evil revealed to man and woman their maimed being when it revealed their sexation, a state that immediately became unbearable except in fleeting moments of gratified desire, because neither alone could be a whole, could be unique, could be God. But each one grasps that it is possible to play at being God. He has become *like* one of us, God says. All it takes is to reject the other, to refuse to acknowledge the essential similarity and difference of a member of the human species. To eat from the tree of life would have been, symbolically, to petrify their mistake, to make it irreversible, to live forever like the gods they were not (for they were man and woman), to be forever unable to live as humans. This would mean living eternally in a state of nonbeing—and we are led into absurdity. God did not want this, but he could not do otherwise than abandon the human creatures to history, their own history—the history of their wars, though they were born for peace. Where does the path start that would let the human species draw nearer to peace?

CHAPTER 10

Authentic Speech
and Peace

The children of Cain, the men and women who increased and multiplied on the earth, have been making war since the dawn of history. They inherited from their progenitors the ontological rift that prevents the existence of the human dyad and that repeats itself in their helpless offspring, so inept at recognizing its own true nature—the child.

Myths, we must grant, are *not* history. Additionally, to believers, the Holy Scripture is a mystery, the word revealed to *faith*. Even less are myths scientific knowledge, in the sense that we have understood this term for three or four centuries. They embody teachings, and their symbols, rich in meaning, open new paths of inquiry when all routes attempted have reached impasse. This is the function Plato attributed to them. After thought has toiled vainly to increase its understanding of an issue by tested methods, it turns to myth, which revitalizes it through the multiple directions suggested by the meaning of symbols and helps it return to its quest with a new plan. "We have to bring in some pleasant stories," says the Stranger from Elius, for "there is a mass of ancient legend a large part of which we must now use for our purposes; after that we must go on as before . . . until we arrive at the summit of our climb and the object of our journey."[1] Myth guides our steps toward knowledge, fills reason with an energy that it thought to find no more and that in fact it could not find in the ground it had been working. But it is obviously reason that must examine the new contributions in order to assure them of rigorous analysis or to recognize that all that is fertile in the realm of thought cannot necessarily be reduced to mathematical proofs without becoming ridiculous or being forced into self-contradiction.

In spite of their wishes, at times their most ardent wishes, human beings do not live in peace. They even go so far as to believe that war is vital to the health of nations, that if we were to taste peace and become fond of it, we would come to resemble the dead bodies in a graveyard or, at best, those old men who incessantly recount the deeds of their distant youth. Peoples can fall into dotage as individuals do and can slowly fade from having lost their will to fight. Or we may justify cowardice and laziness by claiming that we hate wars, that even slavery is better, and we baptize our dishonorable pacifism with the name of peace. But if peace were only the morbid withdrawal of those who have lost both youth and courage, it would mean that only death inflicted by or upon another has the power to give life its fullest meaning, which would be absurd by definition, not to say monstrous.

Why are people chronically at war; why can they not attain peace? Another examination of these questions gives us the chance to seek not an answer but a different approach to war and peace in the meanings symbolized by myths. Myths have taught us that though we cannot avoid childhood, in order to live in peace we must at least not live like overgrown children who, despite their age, never reach adulthood.[2] They have also taught us that despite the illusion of appearances, the human being is not, cannot be individual. The human being is either dyadic or does not exist at all. If we succeed in the dyad, we also succeed at attaining the peace that is our original status.

Each of us, however, begins life as a child, as a male or female individual. And now history proves to us that to make peace the constant state of political societies either at home or abroad, it is not enough either to grow by adding years or to marry (with or without rites). We would be wrong to blame the succession of generations, believing the youngest more eager for war than their elders. It is not our youth who declare war, however fiery their passions. When the young seem intoxicated by the smell of gunpowder, they are usually under a legal obligation or tricked by ambitions they believe to be their own though they are not. We must return to the myths to understand why it is false to believe that relations between humans must be essentially warlike and how we can hope to bring peace nearer. We begin by questioning an overly mechanistic view that leaves us mired in war.

Only *human* beings enact what we call war. These same beings aspire to peace and are impaled on the most deadly contradiction: By increasing their disastrous consequences, wars will finally be replaced by peace. Now, human beings are men and women whose *ontological* relation determines the historical relation among all individuals. The symbolic significance of the biblical narrative enables us to see that history and its conflicts spring from the rift separating man from woman, cleaving the being of each because *a common being* has not been undertaken.

Morality has always tried to combat the results of the break; it has never succeeded. Precepts, directives, prohibitions encourage guilt and rebellion; they restrain only timid souls. No morality is persuasive unless the evil that necessitates it is clearly obvious. When a moral system insists on its autonomy, it assures its own ineffectiveness; it is worthless, it speaks

Westview Press/Promotion Department

5500 Central Avenue • Boulder, Colorado 80301-2847
(303) 444-3541 • FAX (303) 449-3356

Here is your complimentary review copy:

FROM WAR TO PEACE

JANINE CHANTEUR

PUBDATE: August 11, 1992   (hc) $ 52.50
                                             (pb)   17.95

Please send us copies of any reviews or listings.

to an abstraction, not a human being, and it becomes normal to conclude that there has probably never been a human capable of authentically moral conduct. Only the biblical myth has provided an absolute basis for norms of human behavior, because in the simple style of a nursery tale, it starts with the portrayal of a realistic ontology: The human being is man and woman; we can speak only of a living relation of each to each, not of man alone nor of an asexual entity representing nothing.

The Greeks indeed saw the need inherent in morality for a definition of humankind, but they did not provide a definition that did justice to all human dimensions. By closing their eyes to reality, by limiting it to the abstract person or to the male alone, they were unable to speak of the peaceful nature of relations between people, though they sensed such relations as well as anyone could when they made *philía*, "affection," the trait defining man as *zôon politikón*, a "political animal." But the human's inclination toward other humans does not reach its fullest meaning except when founded upon the first real relation, that of the man and the woman. Plato assimilating woman to man and Aristotle, even more, making the couple the kernel from which the City grew came close to an essential ontological reality, but they did not linger over it. It fell to the Jews to define it in all its richness and dangers.

Reviewing the story told in Genesis, we have seen man announce a partial truth, whereas woman shared in the word only as a third party, as the one spoken *about*, not as a genuine partner in dialogue. The couple's innocent child, the shepherd whose offerings were pleasing to God, owed the pureness of his soul to the truth of what his father had said and his mother did not contradict, at the beginning of time. But the truth was incomplete and was not shared—and the child could not survive. He died a violent death at the hand of his own brother, whose passions of anger and jealousy caused the first murder.[3] Cain is conceived immediately after the loss of Eden. He inherits the split that his parents had produced in their being, the terrors that had assailed them, the intensity of the desire they felt when they sought refuge there, trying to forget their distress in its promises. The character of Abel, the second son, represents the enduring truth in man and woman. It is fragile, endangered, and though not destined to vanish, yet continually beaten down. Of the unachieved relation between man and woman, the fratricidal struggle is born, the war that pits one human creature against another.

The first man and woman both broke the law in order that each might become the equal of the divinity. Their wrong is less that they gave in to that illusory desire than that they did not jointly accept responsibility for having done so. By shifting the blame to another (the serpent, the woman), they prepared the way for that tragic utterance implied by the actions of every man in history who has gone off to fight—"Am I my brother's keeper?"[4] The consequences of their actions were diabolical, in the original sense, for they not only separated humans from each other but truth from itself. It is beyond debate that to be truly responsible for our brothers, we must sometimes rely on war. Between killing a brother and letting him be killed by others lie all the forms of war—and the dissolution of the hope of peace.

In our passion to destroy the other, moreover, or in the passion we feel when threatened with destruction, the other, whether our prey or our predator, appears in his radical otherness. He is *other than myself,* beyond comprehension. Any concern I may have for him has grown silent within me, as any concern for me has become silent in him. As inscrutable as a flake of obsidian, the individuality of one and the other is restricted to a style of attack or defense. Nothing of what is not myself matters to me except as an object of subjugation or death. Nothing of what is not himself matters to him except in its death or defeat. The *other-than-self* will not cease to be other unless negated, destroyed as other, and assimilated as *another self,* its otherness torn from it. Whether spoken by a single person or by a people, in the dialectic of the other-than-self and the other self, the individual "I" is always the negator of another individual "I" that threatens its life or glory, that tries to wound its fragile identity.

Unless we glimpse a different way. Each of us considers our primary reality to be the affirmation of our being, which we define as our unique self. We forget that we cannot say "I" except in the presence of another whom we fear, yet whose absence we feel as a void in the core of our being. In solitude we can say nothing, not even "I think," for there is no thought without language and no language without an other. Thought does not prove existence unless it is itself founded in human relationship. For this reason, each one's being is, by nature, incomplete in itself.

How can individuals overcome their fear, they for whom the presence of the other is simultaneously the sign of their own wound and the necessary condition for their humanity?

Plato did not ask the question, but he started us on the road to an answer. With the exception of the *Letters,* his writings take the form of dialogue.[5] Whether there are two speakers or several, whether or not some in the scene merely listen, whether the dialogue plunges immediately into the topic or is preceded by an introduction (often written itself as a little dialogue setting forth the circumstances of the discussion), it is through questions, answers, shared consideration, and study that thought advances or acknowledges obstacles to its further progress. What is most important for humans—to understand who we are, where we come from, where we are going, what can be known, what our conduct must be within the human community—is never the object of a speech or an explanation but of a common search. This tasks leads partners who are often very dissimilar, not always possessed of good faith, never sure to be inclined to get along, down the road to the accord indispensable to the search for truth. Plato did not choose the genre of dialogue for mere aesthetic reasons; it was inescapable because it was, according to him, the only form appropriate to the human being's ontological situation.

Obviously there can be pseudodialogues. Most of our daily conversations are among them. Diplomatic negotiations are practically nothing else. Plato knows this, and Socrates points it out. "It is obvious from what Polos has said," he tells us, "that he is much better versed in what is called rhetoric than in dialogue."[6] What Plato asks of dialogue is agreement among those who are partners in inquiry—growing agreement, then definitive agreement, for then they have been able to shed light on a topic worth arguing about; then uncertainties, fears, hasty or dogmatic assertions have been overcome—everything that clings to the personality of beings who cannot escape their own limitations, to the detriment of what they are trying to understand. "If I cannot produce in you yourself a single witness in agreement with my views," Socrates says, again speaking to Polos, "I consider that I have accomplished nothing worth speaking of in the matter under debate."[7] Socrates is the leader in appearance only, for it is true, as he so often repeats, that he knows nothing when he and others do not know a thing in common.

Is it simply a question of our acting as a check on each other, of going forward on the path of knowledge only when reassured by another's approval? When Socrates' companions are youths inclined by their lively temperaments more to giddiness and prejudice than to thoughtfulness, how can they provide a guarantee that is of any value? There is no question moreover, of arousing their interest by dazzling them with elegant speech, as the rhetoricians do, nor of fooling them into thinking they are engaged in genuine inquiry when in fact the principal speaker knows in advance the reasoning and the outcome. The dialogue derives its pedagogical power from being something quite different from this. As the discussion moves back and forth, it runs up against the *subjectivity* of the interlocutors, just as it initially arose from it. Socrates is especially watchful lest any *individuality* be satisfied merely to best another, not only by pointing out possible contradictions but also by using those contradictions to awaken in himself and the others the intuition that truth is on a different plane than individual facts. To call truth *universal* is to discover that apart from the rushes and tides of passions that make up each person's life, rendering it unknowable to others, incapable of seeing others, heedless of every truth, there exists a center capable of saying "I." It will not be an individual "I," submerged in its moments of fear, pettiness, and vanity, but an "I" that we may call *impersonal*, at once the intimate essence of each and an indestructible accord with all others, a union evidencing an underlying unity. (It does not matter whether or not the other has attained impersonal speech, for a human being is *always of more value* than what he has painfully achieved.) "The river of speech, which flows out of a man and ministers to the intelligence, is the fairest and noblest of all streams."[8] It gushes forth only in the presence of the other. We do not speak in isolation any more, of course, than we think in isolation.

Those who journey from the individual "I" to the language of the impersonal "I" have surmounted boundless diversity, in which the true nature of what we seek is engulfed and mired. They have not eliminated multiplicity; they have discovered what unites same to same, other to other. They have learned that same *and* other have their place and role in the manifestation of the intelligible. Thinking, according to Plato, is not speaking *about* the other, but *to* and *with* the other of the ground of being of both. In the *Phaedrus,* Socrates makes an important criticism of "written words" in contrast to speech. "They seem to talk to you as though they were intelligent, but if you ask them anything about what they say, from a desire to be instructed, they go on telling you just the same thing forever."[9]

How could there be *communion* when there is no *communication*? Words that are exchanged must combine into truthful speech, not into a mere artful persuasion that is the way of the Sophists. From one dialogue to the next, the endeavor proceeds to this end. After having honed our under-standing of dialectic, we must work at it for a long time. This method of *órthos lógos,* "true discourse," allows us to join forces instead of confront-ing each other in sterile argument. To monopolize speech is to reject the other, to prefer the affirmation of our own subjectivity to the common search for truth. When all may speak as they struggle with what seems, on first analysis, to be a jumble, a faint pathway appears, leading each as far as it can toward the serenity of shared knowledge. Although in Aristotle and Saint Thomas, dialectic does not make use of dialogue and has different characteristics than Platonic dialectic, it nonetheless compares and scrutinizes what a group of speakers might be able to say together.[10]

In this way does each discover in himself or herself both what is most genuinely the self and what, though not the self, is yet attuned to it. It is clear that fear dissolves and glory disappears from our consciousness.

Such is the voice of peace—harmonized speech that, in moving from the particular "I" to the impersonal "I," forms the strands binding humans in authentic relations of *philía*, because affection is the feeling that ex-presses the completeness of their reconciled being. This is the human being's truth, so profound that diplomacy—whose usual language consists in lies intended far less to create accord among individuals than to divide them by imposing the intentions of one on the other, diplomacy that is bent on the victory of self-seeking goals—even diplomacy employs phrases and manners that though a comic parody deceiving no one, pay ideal human speech the pitiful respect of those who are not even aware of their own wrongdoing. Whether in business meetings, academic meetings, councils of war, or councils of the church, the ego game is played. Woe to those who refuse to play it; they are cast out from the pretended unity behind which opposing interests battle—as was Socrates, and Christ, too. They accepted it. They had found the paths of peace; their deaths bore witness to the fact.

Yet as Plato says again and again, though all are called to the common self-denial that would lead their being to itself, few ever reach the goal. Why is the mass of humankind in the thrall of war when, by nature, the deepest human truth is peace? Marx clearly sensed the problem, but he deprived humankind of its solution. The masses will live at peace because peace is an attribute of humans as a species, but they will be only an instrument. Indeed, they are more *predestined* to peace than *agents* of peace, because class awareness is itself only the product of the appropriate economic conditions. The Greek words denoting the masses are instructive. *Tò pléthos* means "the crowd," a large group; *ho óchlos* is "the throng," an undifferentiated multitude. The implication is that in the masses individuals are all alike. The individual "I," the starting point for moving beyond passions and opening the way to the impersonal "I," is practically nonexistent. The mass does not know what it is or what it wants. It clamors, it does not speak, it does not think, it cannot think.[11] To designate a *people* (or any group) by the word *mass* is to reduce it, deliberately or not, to the state of a thing. It is an insult to the human beings it comprises, for the mass is an assembly whose strength is manipulated from without; all those in political life know this. So do generals, who sometimes need to make their armies into masses that are heedless of the actual individuals who happen to be thrown together in them. We need only recall the attacks, bayonets fixed, by the infantry of both sides during World War I or, to take a recent example, the charges of battling *masses* in some episodes of the war between Iraq and Iran. Were there any human beings there?

We cannot believe, any more than did Plato himself, in the reign of the philosopher who would guide not only the lives of true human beings but the lives of those incapable of authentic speech and so of life as humans—through laws that would reflect, as faithfully as possible, the order of the world. We refer to his teachings for their value as reminders of what was, for him, the only path to the authentic exchange of speech and to truth. The parties to the dialogue are first of all individuals gradually rising above the individuality that artificially cut them off from one another and from the source of knowledge, as their accession to the impersonal "I" attests. The word is born in the silence slowly won from all that entraps us in the imperfection of our being—from the shouting of desire, the uproar of the passions, the buzzing, babbling clamor of our amusements. In the first stage, as the intellect withdraws from the pounding din of the sensible world's wonders and scandals, it gains the ability to reach agreement on the definition of things that do not engage the senses, as, for example, mathematical theorems. The formulation is worked out in common; its meaning belongs to all, no single person considering laying claim to the discovery. Each of us knows, beyond all dispute, that we share with all the understanding of what we or some other articulates.

When, moreover, the training of the dialogue's participants is properly guided, this sharing of truth leads all to the realization that what is said— and cannot be said differently—is of more importance than to know which person is saying it. There resides in each of us, then, an urging of truth. Common to all, it is more real than the displays of the individual "I"; it is independent of it yet able to calm it, to teach it—with its many adornments, its dazzling pronouncements—what it did not know it was seeking, what it finds only when it withdraws.

But mathematical truths would be but poor nourishment for the soul, if the confidence they give it did not rouse it to ponder itself and to seek, in the same communality and the same shared peace, knowledge of its nature. *Dialogue* turns into *dialectic*; it keeps the individual sensitivity in bounds, forbidding it to disturb a quest that is closing on its most vital goal. In the order brought about by meticulous language, all will discover they are manifesting what their desire clamored for with all its might but what, in its neediness, it utterly hid from them when it was seeking gratification in the multitudinous objects of the world. The completeness of the underlying unity transcends every being. Each is only its partial manifestation, even when he or she reaches the perfect ordering of the ideas accessible to a correctly trained mind. Then the heterogeneity of words, even of true words, vanishes; speech is stilled. In the silence of the deepest contemplation, those who attain absolute abstraction from their individual "I" understand that they are beyond being one *and* the other. They are united one *with* the other within that which animates their being. Humans can find their nature only in what transcends the intelligible. They do not *prove* it by reasoning but discover it, unalterable, in its perfection. Truthful speech will not have a role until the moment of ineffable union has passed. Its mission was to lead human beings to knowledge. Its next will be to pass knowledge on through words that express it as closely as possible but that will never be able to represent its perfection, for the most adequate word always falls short.

When the individual "I" becomes capable of elevation to the impersonal "I," its adventure helps us understand humankind. So long as we cling to our individuality as though it fully expressed our being, we are unwittingly at the mercy of mistakes, lies, and illusions. We rush into war because conflict within is tearing us apart. The impersonal "I" does not strip us of personal identity except in moments of deep contemplation. Now become our self-aware center, it enables us to know what we are and how to behave among others and with others. Individuals who bear the word of truth continue to do so, more especially as they discover the same-as-self in the presence of the other-than-self, sharing words for the sake of reaching accord. Neither is any longer bereft by the other of what he or she is not. Without repeating the sterile act of appropriating another individuality, without attempting to subjugate it, they attend to its voice, absorb its message, send it back, and, if they can, enrich it. Thus is the other revealed, accepted, become being's ally—threats vanished—when its profound kinship in the depths of being has been discovered in the peace of the One that is the Good. The philosopher contemplates "all time and all existence."[12]

Have they attained peace, those true lovers of the intelligible who, through the reconcilement of shared speech, might bring integrity to their being, wounded by childhood and the presence of so many others? This would be proof that humanity has not been handed over without hope to the conflicts that divide both persons and their Cities. But this would not be the end of wars, for those with the talent for the dialectical ascent are rare. Can we go farther in the search for peace?

First, is man the other who is the most "other" to man? Is it not woman, just as for her it is man who is the most other? Must we not once again return to their dialogue, the one that did not take place, to all those that lie and insult, that wound, that reject, that can go so far as to kill, and, finally, to the person who perhaps is just visible, despite the unhappy failures of the past?[13] If man and woman became aware of the dyadic union that is the human condition, if they recovered it, would they not be establishing the pathways of peace on earth?

It is—almost—as utopian to expect this as to have faith in international law or beautiful tomorrows. Not quite, however, for utopias are based on a yearning that knows nothing of its own source. This is because the dyad is human and therefore different from a pair of animals, but it has been wrenched apart, and the human species alone among all that live has been engaging since its appearance on earth in what we call war. Can humankind hope to unite its members or at least draw them closer to each other? The chance of peace is tied to the chance that being may be restored.

The presence of one or the other element of the human species can seem to be an immediate stimulus to conflict, as we have seen. The ontological threat of the most "other" other, sexual desire's ambivalence toward the other's otherness, confusion in the face of the other's mysteriousness, for the other represents the ineluctable unknown—all this because neither can ever be the other, a man will never understand a woman perfectly, nor a woman a man. The denial of couples who claim to be fully transparent to each other covers an unconscious fear that the miracle of their present happiness may somehow disintegrate or that the peaceful comfort of habit may grow dull to one or the other. Few are the men, few the women who are prepared to confess, especially when they value it, that their "shared" life is usually a battle contained by defeat or weariness. The dyad is in our nature, but it cannot be taken for granted. Perhaps we should begin by accepting this fact: It is impossible to understand another absolutely. The doubts, resentments, uncertainties, confusions that one inspires in the other are mutual. Truths indeed rain down from heaven, but amazingly enough we have no aprons strong enough to catch and hold them while we examine them differently than do those observers who are not so much involved as merely curious, like most psychologists, sociologists, and even novelists.

If we confess the radical otherness of the other, consent to the notion that *nothing* can eliminate it, we can—perhaps—quiet in ourselves (and probably in the other) one of the springs of insecurity in a being who needs the other being precisely *because* it is impenetrable. Let us make no mistake—we no more *resign* ourselves to what creates the human condition than we resign ourselves to the definition of a planet or a vertebrate. Resignation is fraught with passivity; it waits for death. Man and woman have life before them; they can also give life. To accept what is *given* is, on the contrary, to become sure of it, to stop asking of it more than it could possibly *give*; it is to leave daydreams behind, to part from utopias, to enter reality. The other is not the whole that we are not. The other is not a god; it is not his or her fault, and there is no wrong in not being one. The other does not possess and improperly deprive us of what we want to be, any more than the other is what we are not. At the same time, neither of us is the other; our difference is irreducible. And that is the way things are. This is not grounds for bearing grudges, for attempting enslavement or seduction, scorn, worship, or negation. On this foundation, built of an initial common acceptance of being's opacity and deprivation, the structure of healing speech can rise as the very first manifestation of being, which will take on meaning only when founded on the shared word.

Before analyzing this language, we should recall that moralists have sought in the desire that drives man and woman together (at least for the duration of an embrace) the source of the evils besetting humanity. Its consuming flame has been compared to madness. It is an "imperious need and fiercest passion," says the Athenian of Plato's *Laws*, that "fires men to all manner of frenzies . . . with its blaze of wanton appetite."[14] "It is a disease of the soul," Socrates says in the *Timaeus*.[15] We recall the frightening universality Plato attributes to it: "There exists in every one of us, even in some reputed most respectable, a terrible, fierce, and lawless brood of desires."[16] Nietzsche also notes this universality and for once not disagreeing with Socrates, speaks of sexual desire as the most jealous desire for possessing, for having. "One comes to feel genuine amazement that this wild avarice and injustice of sexual love has been glorified and deified so much in all ages—indeed, that this love has furnished the concept of love as the opposite of egoism while it actually may be the most ingenuous expression of egoism."[17]

Wars may be born of the impetuosity of love or of the violence of love repressed. According to Freud, all energies flow from a single source—the sex drive, kin to the death instinct.[18]

The works of the Marquis de Sade constitute an exemplary warning against this instinct's aggressiveness when, forgetting its origin and betraying the life it carries, the sex drive despotically announces its superior rights and makes use of the most brilliant human talents to set man against woman, woman against man, men against each other, women against each other, and adults of both sexes against children. Recall, for example, the frightening plan of the *One Hundred Twenty Days of Sodom*. Those who are the most innocent, most pure, most beautiful, most beloved will be pitilessly seized, corrupted, tortured, and massacred with the complicity of men and women temporarily united, but united in evil. The visceral hatred that each sex feels toward the other, and at bottom toward itself, seems to be based entirely on the violence of an instinct that, according to nature, should have moved them to mutual desire. De Sade pushes to extremes his demonstration of the consequences of rejecting the dyad and its origin. He goes so far as to turn the château where the crimes are committed into a caricature of a sanctuary—latrines replace the chapel—reached after difficulties that are meticulously described in all their gradations. It is situated in the total isolation suited to an ascetic ascent of the soul toward its transcendent principle. The discipline ruling the life that is lived there is an *orderly* subversion of the *order* of the universe, and the spiritual exercises are replaced by those named incest, sodomy, onanism, adultery, rape, coprophilia, parricide, infanticide, torture, assassination. These are the actions commanded by the "categorical imperative" articulated by one of the characters:

"But must the one criterion for judging everything be our feelings?" asked the Bishop.

"The only one, my friend," said Durcet; "our senses, nothing else, must guide all our actions in life, because only their voice is truly imperious."[19]

The *One Hundred Twenty Days* was written in the Bastille in 1785, the year that the *Foundation for the Metaphysic of Ethic* was published in Königsberg, though Kant and de Sade did not know each other's writings, did not meet, and probably never heard of each other.[20]

Is it the sexual instinct, strictly speaking, that is at work in the deliriums described by de Sade, even though the senses determine the norm? All his novels insist on the power of imagination, the seat of the specifically human ability to invent and organize criminal acts by stimulating the ardor of the *passions*, which instinct could not do by itself. "There is no conceiving the degree to which man varies them when his imagination grows inflamed."[21] In work after work, the same idea is expounded. "The imagination," Dolmancé instructs, "is the spur of delights; in those of this order, all depends upon it, it is the mainspring of everything; now, is it not by means of the imagination that one knows joy? is it not of the imagination that there come the most piquant delights?"[22] Juliette's cruel tutor asks her: "Do you not know that the effects of an imagination as depraved as mine are like the impetuous currents of a river in flood? Nature wants it to wreak devastation, and it does it any way that it can."[23]

For nature is in reality the great arranger of human conduct and makes all moral concerns superfluous. Both nurturer and destroyer, nature ordains the violence of the sexual instinct, whetting it with murders and with wars. "Destruction being one of the chief laws of Nature, nothing that destroys can be criminal."[24] Man is part of the natural system; he is only one of its components, and he can disappear like any other. "Totally to extinguish the human race would be nothing but to render Nature a service. . . . Wars, plagues, famines, murders would no longer be but accidents, necessary to Nature's laws, and man, whether instrumental to or the object of these effects, would hence no longer be more a criminal in the one case than he would be a victim in the other."[25] Nature inspires no sentiments other than those dictated by unalloyed self-interest. Humans are *individuals* who form relations with each other only in order to use each other as necessary instruments for the satisfaction of their passions. "Are we not all born solitary, isolated? I say more: are we not come into the world all enemies, the one of the other, all in a state of perpetual and reciprocal warfare?"[26]

This state of nature is barely tempered by a summary utilitarianism: "Train [your children] to cherish the virtues . . . which, without your religious fables, are sufficient for their individual happiness. . . . If you make them sense the necessity of virtue, uniquely because their happiness depends upon it, egoism will turn them into honest people, and this law which dictates their behavior to men will always be the surest, the soundest of all."[27] Utilitarianism was in style, but this forerunner of the "arithmetic of pleasures," as conceived by de Sade, is far from resembling the ordinary morality of Jeremy Bentham's calculus. Murder in particular remains acceptable, for "man received his impressions from Nature, who is able to forgive him this act; the law, on the contrary, always opposed as it is to Nature and receiving nothing from her, cannot be authorized to permit itself the same extravagances: not having the same motives, the law cannot have the same rights."[28] Well-made laws should respect nature, not run counter to it:

> Nature, mother to us all, never speaks to us save of ourselves; nothing has more of the egoistic than her message, and what we recognize most clearly therein is the immutable and sacred counsel: prefer thyself, love thyself, no matter at whose expense. . . . There it is, the primitive state of perpetual strife and destruction for which Nature's hand created us, and within which alone it is of advantage to her that we remain.[29]

Nature wills war, but peace is not the far-off goal of nature's scheme. In language that recalls Kant's, skirts his thought, yet totally contradicts it, de Sade offers his volume to his readers and urges them to draw sustenance from its principles, for they are on the side of the passions, "and these passions, whereof coldly insipid moralists put you in fear, are naught but the means Nature employs to bring man to the ends she prescribes for him; harken only to those delicious promptings, for no voice save that of the passions can conduct you to happiness."[30] It is the happiness of the senses and the imagination, the happiness of an individual destined for personal combat, for civil war, for war between nations, an individual deprived of peace except in death. We read, however, that the commander of the pike bearers was against the death penalty. There was no contradiction—law, not nature, had initiated it.

The sexual instinct, war, death—this is nature's "plan"[31] for a species that matters no more than any other and that is faced with no questions concerning the human *being*. It is coherent with an individualism untempered by any friendly inclinations or common undertakings, that no attachments develop aside from those desire briefly inspires. And desire rushes to attach itself to external objects only in anticipation of turning inward to savor its satisfaction. "Your body is your own, yours alone; in all the world there is but yourself who has the right to enjoy it as you see fit," Madame de Saint-Ange lectures the young Eugénie.[32] The characters in all the novels will, however, agree—this universal prescription is absolutely subordinate to the wishes of the strongest. In the battle for pleasure, there is necessarily a victor and a vanquished.

If the sexual instinct, by nature an instrument of life, can so easily turn against life that we can mistake war and death for its ultimate purposes, it is because it usurps a role that does not belong to it. The sexual instinct becomes tyrannical only when it claims to be the single and eternal truth of a being who has no self-knowledge and refuses to acquire it. It is evident in these writings that misogyny is never far off. Whether wildly aggressive or barely appearing, it is a major theme of the argument even when women play the role of executioner. The androphobia that parallels it is perhaps less directed against *men* than against any human creature once it has ceased to serve desire. For the normal union of the sexes is, according to de Sade, what nature values least. In a speech to women, "feeble, enfettered creatures destined solely for our pleasure,"[33] the Duc de Blangis recommends that they expect nothing but "humiliation and obedience." He reminds them that "contempt almost always followed by hatred instantly assumes the preeminence hitherto occupied by our imagination. . . . If yet you breathe," he says, "'tis by our pleasure. . . . The lives of all the women who dwell on the face of the earth, are as insignificant as the crushing of a fly. . . . The most fortunate thing that can befall a woman is to die young. . . . It is not at all as human beings we behold you, but exclusively as animals one feeds in return for their services, and which one withers with blows when they refuse to be put to use."[34] When instructing an adolescent girl, Dolmancé teaches her that "woman's destiny is to be wanton, like the bitch, the she-wolf; she must belong to all who claim her."[35]

Man's profound aversion to woman is matched by woman's aversion to man and leads to indifference, sometimes to hatred, among members of the same sex. Against this background of radical individualism, the human dyad has not even suspected that it could be the central human reality. Should we blame instinct for this, should we identify it with a death wish that is involved in murder and war? Can we join Dolmancé, calling to witness "philosophy's sacred flame," when he asks, "What other than Nature's voice suggests to us personal hatreds, revenges, wars, in a word, all those causes of perpetual murder?"[36] It would be futile to try to deny that there is an element of profound truth expressed by the words and deeds of the actors de Sade sets before us. The readers' curt rejection, their denial of the agitation that comes over them, their cries of offended condemnation—are these not proofs that our hearts are less pristine than we would like to think? To repress hallucinations does not get rid of them. Does the indestructible reality of war and war's abominations not confirm the correctness of de Sade's analyses?[37] The evil humans are capable of visiting on each other is the fruit of an imagination never at a loss for means to "sadistic" ends; the ingenuity invested in instruments of torture and destruction attest to it. But in contrast with the rich variety in technique is the monotony of its use. Whatever the profusion of humiliations and wounds we can inflict on a man or woman, the body has limits that satiety or death confirm. The most subtle inventions are condemned to repeat themselves.

We can learn from this. In writing upon writing, the same actions, the same amusements, the same justifications disguise a tragedy that the executioners and their victims (except perhaps Justine) enact without wanting, or without being able, to intend to do so. In the solitude of being of the one dispossessed of the other's being, instinct is swayed by an imagination ignorant of the reason for its delusions; it yields to delirium in the hope of charming away at any price the bitterness or fear of the man (or woman) trapped in solitude for dread of the throng of *others*. The most cruel conflict of all is that of man and woman, because they were born—together—for peace and not for war. This is the truth strikingly thrown into relief by the contrasting example of the interminable repetition of afflictions that are the same, whether called wars or crimes.

We should not blame desire. Despite appearances, it does not bear the responsibility for war. Its energy can flow in every possible direction. It may be party to the foulest murder, or on the contrary, it may direct its vitality—through objects of the most diverse forms—to studying and seeking the source of being. Desire is a priceless tool. Although not a guide, it is the sign of the urgency of the pursuit fueled by its power. This is why it is true that to have no desire is to die. But it is also true that sexual desire's tyranny, whether expressed through different types of eroticism, through the violence humans do each other, or even through escape into some universally approved social activity, is nothing but the multiform expression of the distress of *being* and perhaps of its death.[38]

The *healing* of human being is not found in desire's adventures. It is not entrusted to the sexual union, which can only bear witness to it. Desire, her own and that of the men she served, was changed by a woman called Mary from Magdala into something perfectly meaningless when she used it no matter how, aroused it in no matter which man, out of a love of money and seduction. Yet she was the woman whom Jesus loved with a different sort of love; spreading on his feet the perfumed oil that she had earned in the battle of desires and wiping it off with her flowing hair, she came to understand her woman's being in its relation to man's being. To her, the son of man was intrinsically the son of God, whose daughter she became once more. She was also the first to look on Jesus in his glory, as the beloved son of the Transfiguration. *Noli me tangere*, do not touch me, he says. These words have elicited many a commentary on the gulf separating a body in glory from a body of flesh, divine nature from human nature, and so on. Can we not understand that *being*, which in this life is indissolubly melded for the human being with the body of flesh, is not absorbed into it? Body and being together make up *a* whole, but the body is not *the* whole of being, although it is the most immediate manifestation of it that we can grasp. Mary Magdalene no longer needs to kneel bodily at the feet of Jesus. She has united with the divine element in her own being, perfect beyond the evidence of the senses.

For us, men and women, the body is included in the definition of being, its joys, and its sorrows so long as we live, but the truth of being transcends the body. The disjuncture of being in everyone originates before we have a body. Perhaps it only appears to be the basis of individuation. Bisexuality reveals our duality. But the unity or the separation of male and female goes deeper. Let a man or woman forget or refuse the exchange of words, then each settles into his or her insularity and drags all others into the insane adventure of those who confront and kill instead of uniting.

What sort of speech, you will ask, and what words? For neither could ever have uttered them to the other, as their history is one of wars sparing not even a generation here or there.

Does it involve, as Plato taught, overcoming the inevitable heterogeneity of each one's individual "I" in order to realize the universality of the impersonal "I"? Not exactly. It is not necessarily on the intellectual plane that man and woman must draw closer to each other. Rarely does either attain the serenity of intelligible truths. And truths of ordinary understanding are clearly inadequate. Generally, in fact, things that belong strictly to understanding eliminate all our differences while we are engaged in pursuing them. Plato asked his pupils to cling to the union created in this way in order to seek its source and go beyond it, with no concern for the difference between men and women—in fact quite the contrary. Things have become more complicated in our day. When women are educated "like men," they indeed succeed just as well as men at scientific work. But does this mean that the two sexes are identical, that male and female have the same reality? Our era answers readily in the affirmative, so true is it that time-honored habits had withheld the skills of the intellect from women. When we speak of equality, however, has it a meaning other than mere quantitative comparison? Outside the quantitative domain, we fall into absurdities, as contemporary politics is proving. As soon as we leave the mathematical sciences, the word takes on a "magical" connotation likely to addle the wisest heads. It goes without saying that using the terms *more* and *less* to quantify the being of humans is also a distortion. This mistake, ages old, has multiplied the confusion and hostility that keep man and woman apart. These reactions have in turn generated both the chasm between humans and the wars they justify or endure, because they have failed to remember that man's being and woman's being do not exist except through the other. The mutilation is equal, if we absolutely insist on using an inappropriate term. It will only be healed jointly, because each, mutilated as much as the other, though differently, is generally ignorant of the nature of what he or she lacks and can never know with absolute certainty what the other lacks.

If, considering their being, we attempt to grant both man and woman what belongs to each beyond the purely biological domain, without freezing it from the outset into rigid hierarchical roles, passions may break loose. And yet we must venture such an attempt if we want to advance toward peace in some other way than by simply dividing the world into masters and slaves whose functions may be filled by either sex, even if filled differently by each. To say a man and a woman have the same reality (childbearing excepted) because they possess minds capable of equal brilliance and the same achievements is surely as wrong as to affirm—as is still often done—the superiority of the former. At this time, we could say, the world has doubled its intellectual and technical potential, and women contribute the same quantity of *products* as men. If we take into account only this kind of result, there is no chance of discovering what might typify language capable of finding the harmoniously united being of the dyad; for homogeneity has no place for the exchanged word other than for discovering and confirming quantitative relations. The quality of the relationships that men will be able to have with each other, women with each other, and the one group with the other depends on the primary relation that can be created between a man and a woman. Between man and man, woman and woman, and, more generally, human being and human being, the whole range of language that expresses the individual-ity—instead of stimulating the hostility—of partners in search of a mutual understanding is founded on the primary reconciliation of man and woman, on their harmonized word.

To preserve original peace, to give historical peace some chance of ending wars, it is not enough, as myth and history teach us, to speak *about* the other, even when we speak the truth. Human beings are not geometric shapes of which we can say, for example, "These figures are composed of three connecting straight lines; their three angles are equal to two right angles." Geometric shapes do not reply, acquiesce, refuse; they have nothing to *say*, these forms that human thought has defined. Everything a man can say *to* a woman, everything a woman can say *to* a man—affirmations, questions, answers—exemplifies human language, be-cause speech is born from what is the most unknown and yet nearly the same. Face to face, when strangeness and mirror are confounded, each person is free to accept the dialogue or to decline it, to adjust being to being or to break it. To be other is to experience the need to join again the two severed pieces of the pattern in order to be truly one's self. The pieces are dissimilar yet of the same nature and, when combined, will show us what the broken object really is. Between man and woman, we are concerned with something quite different from the mere intellectual cooperation that any reasonable mind could accept. This kind of accord had to be reinstituted, as men had thought they could deny it to women, but human speech is not based upon it.

Recall that Plato directed the apprentice philosopher to look beyond this ordinary stage of knowledge. In the *Republic*, he described the steps necessary to recognize the true nature of humans, which became intelligible once its principle had been attained. In the *Symposium*, Socrates shows that the ascent is not possible, that what the *Republic* describes will not become a reality, unless the one in search of himself and his essential truth is guided by an elder who has traveled the same path, met with the same obstacles, and been himself aided by an elder in the same way. The road to knowledge stretches unobstructed before the master and his disciple because love empowers the two to undertake "beautiful discourses," the exchanged word, until they reach the ecstasy of contemplation. But the lover and the beloved also need the courage to resist the fleshly desire that had drawn them together. This desire was merely the sign of another, for after one "has been initiated so far in the mysteries of Love and has viewed all these aspects of the beautiful . . . there bursts upon him that wondrous vision which is the very soul of the beauty he has toiled so long for. It is an everlasting loveliness. . . . And if, my dear Socrates," the priestess of Mantinea concludes, "man's life is ever worth living, it is when he has attained this vision of the very soul of beauty."[39]

For the man and woman born together, as they are in the first chapter of Genesis (and even in the second, as they were already both present in a sense), there is no human master. Neither can be a disciple. They must share in finding the word that is the one thing able to lead them to their being and the source of their being. In the course of history—*their* history—the memory of their origin faded. It became so blurred that forgetfulness tried remedies that sometimes proved worse than the disease. Panicked by their solitude, men have mistaken themselves for the masters, and they have made war without respite. Although women had every right to wish this ancient, wholly unjustified claim abolished, in trying to escape it, they unfortunately denied the difference that would have allowed each one's being to unite with the other's. Henceforth, they, too, serve in the military; now they, too, are ready to wage war. "You shall be as gods," the serpent promised—an empty promise, resulting in the fear that has so thoroughly contaminated our being. Humanity is full of mortal gods whom it has itself created, to its misfortune. In its eagerness to become *what it cannot be*, humanity has assented to the idea of deifying some men (and some women), has invented supermen and their glorious departures for war (cheered by women), their triumphal returns (crowned by women), and all the woes it staggers under. Humanity has yet to become once more its true self, male and female, and to retrieve its speech in order to remake its being.

The peace the Platonic philosopher experiences at the end of his quest does not exclude the possibility that wars will be waged in mankind's Cities. The philosopher will take part in them to defend his own City. In Plato's works, the other is not the most other of all others, is not woman. The way to primordial Unity is clear. Love gives the travelers the will to begin and to persevere. But the return of being to itself does not give rise to peace, the mediator (*metaxù*) having mistaken its object: Love for Plato is homosexual, though it is never to be consummated by a sexual act. Plato, who gave the fullest meaning possible within Greek philosophy to what humans do on earth between birth and death, failed to consider the primal human rupture and its need of healing so that the term *human being* could be truthfully spoken. The sickness of being that we call homosexuality is the decisive sign of the ontological rift. To say this is not to condemn. Neither law nor morality matter much here. They serve as no more than guardrails.

What word, then, could spring from human lips that has not already been spoken but that, despite the distance placed between man and woman by all of history's wars, it is again time to utter? "Another self," says resemblance; "other-than-myself," says difference at the same moment—each as indispensable, each as precious as the other, for neither one can be negated without casting the human being into the woes and failures of history. "Do you want to come to me, you whom I know and do not know, you who know me and know me not, you without whom I am incapable of learning of myself, you who allow me to speak and to be, because at the same moment and with the same act and impulse you utter with me response and question, O Same-as-Myself who causes me to be, O Other-than-Myself who comes into being through me, even though I am not the absolute object of your search and you cannot be the absolute object of mine?" Here is the foundation of the impulse that begets genuinely human speech.

The dialectic of "same" and "other," of man and woman, is abolished in a common being and yet renewed as long as there are humans. It has nothing to do with rationality except in respect to the little spark within each of us that flames up gloriously in the sciences and technologies but that wavers and risks losing itself in shadows as soon as we would experience *being* and not *doing;* and so it corrupts the *doing* of generations by its deadly acts—we call them war—on behalf of *being*.

No sooner do we consider the "other-than-myself" than we hesitate between respect for the worth of this other-me-apart-from-me and the temptation to annex it, to deny it its reality, however similar to our own, in order to enhance our own nature by means of the power a possession gives us. The speech of the master to what he has subjugated knows no other mode than affirmation and command, solitary pronouncements, barren of any question directed to the other and of the infinite treasure of the other's responses. And the "other-than-myself" fascinates and frightens, promises and provokes, and hides and reveals the danger that flight or capture were meant to save us from.

Speech has no chance to *heal* being unless speech is aware that it is born from a lack that must be met by the other *as* other, as one not yet defined, classified, subjected, or taken to be harmless. We must accept the risk of rejection, even of attack, in order to dare the silence that encourages response. For authentic speech must know how to await and even elicit the other's speech. Authentic speech is both speech and silence because it is query and not certitude. The most fertile answer comes from someone who is most other, provided that his or her difference is yet so similar that it bars each one from exercising an immediate self-affirmation (which affirms nothing but a failed being) or an avoidance (which merely gives permanence to that failed being).

Will men and women of today agree to give up the naive complacency that makes them call themselves "individuals" and abandon themselves to the anguish of existence while waiting to thrust themselves into the tumult of war?

It is risky to give the other the fearsome power of enabling me to reach my own being through its bond with another while believing I am stripping myself of the same power. It is a power less apparent, and yet much greater, than that of parents over the child they begot. Even in the Garden of Eden the first man did not chance such an adventure, and the first woman thought she could keep prudently silent.

In this mystery where neither I nor the other is what we are, unassisted reason, up against the uncircumventable fact of sexation, can only put forth arguments. It defends "man as idea," for example, implicitly denying the existence of concrete men and women, or it simply ignores women. Reason moves in a world of knowledge where *being* has nothing to do. With every page of history shrieking out the endless suffering of humanity, reason can only invent *systems* by which it offers abstract and hypothetical solutions.

We must not leave everything to reason alone, even though we are justified in trying to understand how it functions. As Plato considered the mediation of love necessary to those in search of the absolute principle, for without that love they would not have suspected that there was something to seek, so is love also the necessary intermediary between man and woman. It weaves the strands that draw us back from our misunderstanding of self and other to the wholeness of being that was lost through the empty utterance of individual "I's" unable to join together in an authentic "we."

Can this "we" be identified with the impersonal "I's" that Plato's lovers were to attain? Yes, in the sense that each "I" that believed it could determine itself in its solitude can now stop imposing those false claims on itself and the other. But man and woman are not present to each other as two scientists, however much they may be in love. Their mutual presence is fundamental, it is a foundation. Although not the *first* principle, it is the principle of the *humanization* of the species; that is, it is the principle of meaning, because sexation, despite its avatars, is the origin and being of thought. Language is born between man and woman, the similar and the different, because they are the primary human reality, begetting what is human.

If man and woman recover their vocation as joint creators of being through adjusted speech, they will be able to escape a double temptation: first, the temptation to take the world and the humans in it for an illusion that has no other value than teaching them to escape into an "elsewhere," a domain beyond the present, making them forget that all reality and value are created *hic et nunc*. The other, inverse temptation consists in taking this world for an end in itself, in which science will finally permit the human race to reach the Eden it has longed for in vain, as if the material progress of humankind—abundant, inexhaustible, and rational— implied an equal progress toward the satisfaction of its hunger for happiness and for the absolute.

Whether hostile or cautiously neutral, once man and woman have passed successfully through the trials of dissociation and solipsistic speech, they are capable of forming the dyad, restoring its resemblance to unity. The dyad would then once more be unity's faithful image in that cosmic union upon which, as told by the myth of creation, God looked and said, "it was very good."

Still, no immediate response is possible to the question one asks the other. No one can promise to be what he or she knows nothing of. We can only undertake to search together—with a single certainty: The common effort of those attempting openness is necessary for the coherence of their lives and for the future of their relations with others as well as relations between themselves. To approach peace we must travel the route that itself attests to the unity of our being's origin as it moves from brokenness to reconciliation. Love is necessary to that journey, the love of the heart and love of the body. The ecstasy of physical love is the sign of the unity of being. But by itself, this love cannot achieve that unity. It is not the same for humans as it is for animals. Among animals, the sexual act is performed in ignorance of its consequences and in equal ignorance of its significance. For human beings, the sexual act is a trace in a matrix of meanings. To separate it from the whole is to condemn being to chaos. This is why, in spite of what ignorance, headstrong instincts, or ideologies try to teach, our tender sentiments are also uniquely human. They distinguish humans from animals as much as reason does. We must not confuse them with the various kinds of mawkishness and sentimentality that are nothing but their degraded forms. Just as sophisms proclaim themselves true reasoning, so sentiments obviously can turn into their opposites. Hatred is as distant from love as war from peace. Our sentiments are far from being absolutely reliable, but we cannot be human without them.

To be satisfied with emotional harmony is nevertheless inadequate. We easily fall into the mistake of Pausanias or Aristophanes, even in respect to heterosexual love. The world is closed to happy lovers because they have forgotten that love is only a means. Moralists will readily speak of selfishness; they will help no one. Language fails, and love is undone because it has mistaken itself for an end. We must renew our inquiry in order to become aware that a human never reaches completion, even through another. To return to one another is ultimately no more than a necessary means. It affects human history, but the origin of harmonious being is beyond the dyad. Human beings cooperate in their own creation, but they are not their own ground. Language comes as close as it is possible to come to the truth of being, but by its very nature it is still a kind of distance. The Platonic lovers, we recall, did not directly sense the unity of their being except in silence, when its source was revealed.

The most intense experience can both guide us and lead us astray, depending on whether we focus on the experience itself or read it as a sign. We know the multiplicity of forms and meanings sexual union can take, the purposes it devises, the violence that intensifies it, its terrible griefs, and its unparalleled joys. We have been living for a century as if we had discovered a general truth—that human existence was to be interpreted only on the basis of a sexual hunger that most books, films, and lectures insisted had to be satisfied. We have inquired too little, however, into what lies behind the exaltation of bodies and the imagination. We concede that it is tempting to be absorbed by sensations and fantasies, without wondering what underlying need they might suggest. Although the transports that seize the living are almost unquenchable (repression aside), does not an equally irresistible summons call them to the deepest ecstasy, that of finding, of being driven to find, an *absolute* without which they are nothing. The beasts never know it and human beings but rarely. The sexual instinct involves the sources of life, is the bearer of life; for all its unawareness and violence, it testifies to the infinite and perfect life that it is not, that it can never be. For it is nothing but the consequence of that life. Neither is the union of bodies the absolute. It is only its sign. It evokes by its ardor the transcendence of the absolute. Surely this is the reason that there is neither speech nor fantasy in the most nearly perfect unions.

Thus are man and woman called to find their being, through each other and beyond each other. They are able to judge the snares and dangers that commonly mark the path of their history, along which the din of warfare and the stillness of death replace the exchange of speech and the silence where their origin appears.

Are we at last nearer peace? But what about childhood? someone will ask. It cannot change what it is. When we are born, we are not ourselves. The chances of becoming itself doubtless increase for the child if the father and mother, by trying to find their own being, pass on to it (along with the lack that is inevitable for a human being) the hope that it can do so. Too often women "drop" their young like animals, although their calling is to "bring into the world" the children of the self-renewing dyad. We must realize that even intensely desired children are never responsible for healing the wound that is as inherent in them as it is in their parents. To ask this of them is to weigh them down with a load they cannot carry. The child, too, is evidence of the multiplicity that, by its presence in each of us, shows the failure of our own unity. Philosophers have demonstrated how the very passions that grow in and around the child lead to war. The children of a restored dyad would not, for all that, be sure of peace; there is no life insurance for the essence of being. They would simply be born into a world more competent at helping them discover what they are. By consciously accepting the rift in being, they could come to grips more wisely with the uncertainty of the future. In spite of childhood, they would have more chance of becoming adults. I tremble at the idea that some women—whose mothers, it is true, have been the victims of unjustifiable moralizing for generations—intentionally inflict on children the wound of being born without a father. Though the pendulum's swing is reversing, its stereotypes remain; it does not come into balance, nor can it move on a different plane.

The way is narrow that leads to peace through the healing brought by common being. It is like a road on a ridge between two abysses. It requires, we will grant, each one's inner *conversion* more than any scientifically reached certainty. We do not prove being; we try to experience it. Humanity, aware of its bisexuality, acts as if it had forgotten it. It has taken it for granted yet at the same time distrusted it. Humanity has preferred to speak of "man" or "mankind" in the abstract, concealing from itself the reality of its men and women. How much talk *about* mankind, instead of the exchanged word that brings life to the one and to the other! How much open hatred, suppressed despair! Let us not have too many illusions. Peace is the human being's most difficult undertaking precisely because life and death are at stake in it. His—or her—being is at stake. Between wars and utopias, a hope lies nonetheless. It depends on how women will speak and how men will receive their words and reply to them. At present we have almost no cause for rejoicing except in some groups too limited in number. Contemporary Amazons have not truly helped men, and men are no longer confident of their identity. This would not by any means be an irreparable evil if men's ancient fear had not been increased by seeing women become seriously threatening. Men are paying a high price for their facile self-affirmation. And women, whatever justification they may have, are in danger of committing exactly the same mistake as men. What use is it then that they have experienced misfortune if they are driven to re-create a similar misfortune for others? Let either part of the human being believe it is possible to triumph at the other's expense and that is the end of being; war goes on—between the sexes, between generations, within nations, among nations.

War is now waged with the technology of the nuclear age. Will the threat of annihilation give pause to those who have never escaped Hamlet's question? Perhaps—if we finally realize that though sexation is our shadow, it can become our light.

NOTES

INTRODUCTION

1. Augustine, *The City of God,* trans. William Chase Greene (Cambridge, Mass.: Harvard University Press, 1960), vol. 7, pp. 163, 165.

2. Carl Schmitt, *Der Begriff des Politischen,* 4th ed. (Berlin: Duncker und Humblot, 1963). The subject of the presuppositions of politics is discussed by Julien Freund in his work *L'essence du politique* (Paris: Sirey, 1965).

3. One of my grandfathers, who was of pure Corsican ancestry, claimed that a family without a *bandito* was a family without honor.

4. Dino Buzzati, "Douce nuit," *Le K,* trans. J. Remillet (Paris: Laffont, 1967). [The work, originally in Italian, has not been translated into English. Cited passage translated by S. W.]

5. See *La paix indésirable,* 3d ed. (Paris: Calmann-Lévy, 1984).

CHAPTER 1

1. Plato, *Republic* 373e, trans. Paul Shorey, in Bollingen Series 71, *The Collected Dialogues of Plato,* eds. Edith Hamilton and Huntington Cairns (Princeton, N.J.: Princeton University Press, 1987).

2. In the *Republic,* trans. Paul Shorey, and the *Laws,* trans. A. E. Taylor, both in *The Collected Dialogues of Plato,* especially bk. 1.

3. Plato, *Republic* 462a-b.

4. Homer, *Iliad* 4.225, trans. Richmond Lattimore (Chicago: University of Chicago Press, 1951).

5. *Iliad* 4.124.

6. *Iliad* 6.125–126.

7. *Iliad* 6.444–446.

8. *Iliad* 6.476–481. See René-Antoin Gauthier and Jean-Yves Jolif's analysis of *areté* in which they refer to this passage in the Commentaire in *Ethique à Nicomaque* (Nauwelaerts: Louvain, 1970), vol. 1, p. 102.

9. *Republic* 430c.

10. *Republic* 429b.

11. *Republic* 429b.

12. *Republic* 430b.

13. See Aristotle, *Nichomachean Ethics* 2.1155b. See also *Eudemian Ethics* 1235a.25.

14. Heraclitus frag. 21, in *The Art and Thought of Heraclitus,* trans. and ed. Charles H. Kahn (Cambridge: Cambridge University Press, 1979).

15. Herac. frag. 75.

16. *Iliad* 18.98.

17. *Iliad* 18.107.

18. *Iliad* 18.120–125.

19. Herac. frag. 124.

20. Herac. frag. 82.

21. Herac. frag. 83.

22. See Théodor Gomperz's analysis in *Les penseurs de la Grèce* (Paris: Payot, 1982), vol. 1, p. 95.

23. Herac. frag. 100.

24. Herac. frag. 77.

25. *Nichom. Eth.* 2.1155b.

26. Herac. frag. 75.

27. Empedocles frag. 22, in *The Fragments of Empedocles*, trans. William Ellery Leonard (La Salle, Ill.: Open Court Publishing, 1908).

28. Herac. frag. 21.

29. Herac. frag. 16.

30. Herac. frag. 17.

31. Ibid.

32. Aristotle, *Physics* 4.187a.20–26.

33. Emped. frag. 17.

34. Emped. frag. 20.

35. Aetius 1.26.

36. Emped. frag. 22.

37. Emped. frag. 124.

38. Emped. frag. 17.

39. Plato, *Politics* 272d.

40. Emped. frag. 273d.

41. Exod. 22:13. (All biblical citations are from the Revised Standard Version.)

42. Lev. 19:18.

43. Matt. 5:17.

44. Matt. 5:9.

45. Matt. 5:21–22.

46. Luke 2:14.

47. John 14:27.

48. Matt. 26:52.

49. Catechism of the Council of Trent.

50. Matt. 10:34–35.

51. Augustine, *City of God* 1.19.

52. Thomas Aquinas, *Summa theologica* Q.40.2a, 2ae, in *Basic Writings of Saint Thomas Aquinas*, ed. Anton C. Pegis (New York: Random House, 1945).

53. Matt. 26:52.

54. Matt. 5:39.

55. Rom. 12:19.

56. *Nichom. Eth.* 1.1

57. See Michel Villey, *Questions de saint Thomas sur le droit et la politique* (Paris: PUF, 1987), p. 57.

58. Augustine, Letter 138, *De puero centurionis.*

59. Augustine, *Reply to Faustus the Manichaean,* trans. Richard Stothert, in *Select Library of the Nicene and Post-Nicene Fathers of the Christian Church* (Grand Rapids, Mich.: Eerdmans, 1956), vol. 4, p. 301.

CHAPTER 2

1. Konrad Lorenz, *On Aggression,* trans. Marjorie Kerr Wilson (New York: Harcourt, Brace & World), 1966.

2. Benedict de Spinoza, *A Theologico-Political Treatise,* in *The Chief Works of Benedict de Spinoza,* trans. R.H.M. Elwes (New York: Dover Publications, 1951), p. 200.

3. Marcus Tullius Cicero, *De finibus bonorum et malorum* 3.5, trans. H. Rackham (New York: Macmillan, 1914).

4. Plato, *Gorgias* 491e, trans. W. D. Woodhead, in Bollingen Series 71, *The Collected Dialogues of Plato,* ed. Edith Hamilton and Huntington Cairns (Princeton, N.J.: Princeton University Press, 1987).

5. See *Gorgias* 491e and 494b.

6. Plato, *Republic* 2.360c, trans. Paul Shorey, in *The Collected Dialogues of Plato.*

7. Niccolò Machiavelli, *Discourses on the First Ten Books of Titus Livius,* in *The Prince and the Discourses* (New York: Modern Library, 1950), p. 302.

8. Ibid., p. 304.

9. Ibid., p. 305.

10. Ibid., p. 305.

11. Ibid., p. 305.

12. Ibid., pp. 302–303.

13. Jean Raspail's novel, *Le camp des Saints* (Paris: Robert Laffont, 1973), shows how the modern "transhumance" is primarily peaceful but still retains some of the warlike characteristics typical of this sort of migration.

14. Machiavelli, *Discourses,* p. 302.

15. Niccolò Machiavelli, *Tercets on Ambition,* in *Machiavelli: The Chief Works and Others,* trans. Allan Gilbert (Durham, N.C.: Duke University Press, 1965), vol. 2, pp. 735–737.

16. Machiavelli, *Discourses,* p. 274.

17. See Alexis Philonenko, "Machiavel et la signification de la guerre," in *Essais sur la philosophie de la guerre* (Paris: Vrin, 1976).

18. Machiavelli, *Discourses,* p. 124.

19. Machiavelli, *Ambition,* vol. 2, 737.

20. Ibid.

21. Niccolò Machiavelli, *The Art of War,* in *Machiavelli: The Chief Works and Others,* vol. 2, pp. 592, 593.

22. Machiavelli, *Discourses,* p. 117.

23. Niccolò Machiavelli, *The Prince*, trans. and intro. Harvey C. Mansfield, Jr. (Chicago: University of Chicago Press, 1985), pp. 14–15.

24. Machiavelli, *Discourses*, p. 358.

25. Machiavelli, *The Prince*, p. 98.

26. Ibid., p. 23.

27. Ibid., p. 78.

28. Ibid., p. 79.

29. Ibid., p. 69.

30. Machiavelli, *Art of War*, 1:576.

31. Ibid., 1:592.

32. Niccolò Machiavelli, *History of Florence and the Affairs of Italy* (New York: Harper and Row, 1960), p. 158.

33. Ibid., p. 159.

34. Machiavelli, *The Prince*, p. 69.

35. Machiavelli, *Art of War*, 1:566.

36. Machiavelli, *The Prince*, p. 22.

37. Ibid., 1:102.

38. Machiavelli, *Discourses*, p. 138.

39. Ibid., pp. 138–139.

40. Machiavelli, *The Prince*, p. 70.

41. Ibid., pp. 29–30.

42. Ibid., p. 70.

43. Machiavelli, *Discourses*, p. 500.

44. Machiavelli, *The Prince*, p. 23.

45. Ibid., p. 24.

46. Ibid., p. 61.

47. Ibid., p. 58.

48. Ibid., p. 77.

49. Ibid., p. 71.

50. Ibid., p. 13.

51. Machiavelli, *The History of Florence*, p. 204.

52. Ibid.

53. Ibid.

54. Machiavelli, *The Prince*, pp. 12–13.

55. Ibid., p. 103.

CHAPTER 3

1. Niccolò Machiavelli, *Discourses on the First Ten Books of Titus Livius*, in *The Prince and the Discourses* (New York: Modern Library, 1950), p. 474.

2. Ibid.

3. Jean-Jacques Rousseau, *A Discourse on Inequality*, trans. and intro. Maurice Cranston (New York: Penguin Books, 1984), p. 114.

4. John Locke, *The Second Treatise of Government*, in *Two Treatises of Government*, ed. Peter Laslett (Cambridge: Cambridge University Press, 1967), pp. 26–30.

5. Thomas Aquinas *Summa theologica*, Q.91.2., in *Basic Writings of Saint Thomas Aquinas*, ed. Anton C. Pegis (New York: Random House, 1945), vol. 2, p. 750.

6. Thomas Hobbes, *Leviathan: Parts I and II* (Indianapolis: Bobbs-Merrill, 1958), p. 109.

7. Ibid., p. 46.

8. Ibid., p. 42.

9. Ibid., pp. 47–48.

10. Ibid., p. 132.

11. Ibid., p. 109.

12. Ibid., p. 52.

13. Ibid., p. 53.

14. Ibid.

15. Ibid., p. 52.

16. Ibid., p. 59.

17. Ibid., pp. 59–60.

18. Ibid., p. 110.

19. Ibid., p. 130.

20. Ibid., p. 90.

21. Raymond Polin, "Vie de Thomas Hobbes," preface to Thomas Hobbes, *De Cive* (Paris: Sirey-Publications de la Sorbonne, 1981), pp. 5, 17, 14. [Citation translated by S. W.]

22. Hobbes, *Leviathan*, p. 55.

23. Ibid., p. 86.

24. See Raymond Polin, *Politique et philosophie chez Thomas Hobbes* (Paris: PUF, 1952), p. 131f.

25. Hobbes, *Leviathan*, p. 86.

26. Ibid.

27. Thomas Hobbes, *The Elements of Law, Natural and Politic* (hereafter cited as *Elements*), ed. Ferdinand Tonnies (London: Simpkin, Marshall, and Co., 1889), part 1, chap. 14, sect. 2.

28. Thomas Hobbes, *De Cive; or, The Citizen*, ed. Sterling Power Lamprecht (New York: Appleton-Century-Crofts, 1949), p. 25.

29. Hobbes, *Leviathan*, pp. 104–105.

30. Hobbes, *Elements*, part 1, chap. 14, sect. 2.

31. Hobbes, *De Cive*, p. 25.

32. Ibid., p. 26.

33. Ibid.

34. Hobbes, *Leviathan*, p. 105.

35. Hobbes, *De Cive*, p. 26

36. Hobbes, *Leviathan*, p. 106.

37. Ibid., p. 105.

38. Hobbes, *De Cive*, p. 24.

39. Hobbes, *Elements*, part 1, chap. 14, sect. 3.

40. Hobbes, *De Cive*, p. 24.

41. Ibid.

42. Ibid., p. 26.

43. Hobbes, *Leviathan*, p. 59.

44. Hobbes, *De Cive*, pp. 65–66.

45. Polin, *Politique et philosophie*, p. 70. [Citation translated by S. W.]

46. Hobbes, *De Cive*, p. 25.

47. Ibid.

48. Ibid., p. 26.

49. Ibid., p. 29.

50. Jean-Jacques Rousseau, *On the Social Contract, Discourse of the Origin of Inequality, Discourse on Political Economy* trans. and ed. Donald A. Cress (Indianapolis: Hackett Publishing, 1983), p. 39.

51. Hobbes defines liberty for both persons and things as "the absence of external impediments" (*Leviathan*, p. 109). His definition has no possible relationship to free will nor to any type of metaphysical capacity, even a sense of morality.

52. Hobbes, *Elements*, part 1, chap. 14, sect. 10.

53. Hobbes, *De Cive*, p. 28.

54. Hobbes, *Elements*, part 1, chap. 14, sect. 10.

55. Ibid., sect. 11.

56. Hobbes, *De Cive*, p. 29.

57. Hobbes, *Leviathan*, p. 110.

58. Hobbes, *Elements*, part 1, chap. 14, sect. 11.

59. Hobbes, *De Cive*, p. 29.

60. Hobbes, *Leviathan*, pp. 106–107.

61. Hobbes, *Elements*, part 1, chap. 14, sect. 12.

62. Hobbes, *De Cive*, p. 30.

63. Hobbes, *Leviathan*, p. 107.

64. Hobbes, *De Cive*, preface and chap. 1, sect. 2, Note; and Hobbes, *Leviathan*, chap. 13.

65. Hobbes, *Elements*, part 2, chap. 8; Hobbes, *De Cive*, chap. 12; and Hobbes, *Leviathan*, chap. 29.

66. Dedicatory letter to the Count of Devonshire in the Latin edition of the *De Cive*.

CHAPTER 4

1. Georg Wilhelm Friedrich Hegel, *Hegel's Philosophy of Nature*, ed. and trans. M. J. Petry (London: Allen & Unwin; New York: Humanities Press, 1970), vol. 3, p. 102.

2. Ibid., p. 104.

3. "The need is specific, and its determinateness is a moment of its universal Notion, although it is particularized in an infinite variety of ways. The drive is the activity of overcoming the deficiency of such a determinateness, i.e. of overcoming its form, which is initially merely subjective. . . . The drive constitutes purpose, and confined solely to living existence, instinct." Ibid., p. 145.

4. Ibid., p. 146.

5. Georg Wilhelm Friedrich Hegel, *Phenomenology of Spirit* (hereafter cited as *Phenomenology*), trans. A. V. Miller, with analysis of the text and foreword by J. N. Findlay (Oxford: Clarendon Press, 1977), p. 157.

6. Hegel, *Philosophy of Nature*, p. 151.

7. Hegel, *Phenomenology*, pp. 113–114.

8. See Alexandre Kojève, *Introduction à la lecture de Hegel* (Paris: Gallimard, 1947), p. 16ff.

9. Aristotle, *Politics* 1.3.1253b ff.

10. "In the battle for recognition and the subjugation under a master, we see, on their phenomenal side, the emergence of man's social life and the commencement of political union. *Force*, which is the basis of this phenomenon, is not on that account a basis of right, but only the necessary and legitimate factor in the passage from the state of self-consciousness sunk in appetite and selfish isolation into the state of universal self-consciousness. Force, then, is the external or phenomenal commencement of states, not their underlying and essential principle." *Hegel's Philosophy of Mind, Being Part Three of the Encyclopaedia of the Philosophical Sciences*, trans. William Wallace (Oxford: Clarendon Press, 1971), pp. 173–174.

11. See Kojève's analyses in *Introduction à la lecture de Hegel*, p. 529ff.

12. Hegel, *Phenomenology*, p. 115.

13. Ibid., p. 116.

14. Ibid.

15. Ibid.

16. Ibid., p. 117.

17. Ibid.

18. Ibid., p. 118.

19. Ibid.

20. "In the Dialectical stage these finite characterisations or formulae supersede themselves, and pass into their opposites. . . . But in its true and proper character, Dialectic is the very nature and essence of everything predicated by mere understanding,—the law of things and of the finite as a whole. . . . By Dialectic is meant the in-dwelling tendency outwards by which the one-sidedness and limitation of the predicates of understanding [are] seen in [their] true light, and shown to be the negation of them. For anything to be finite is just to suppress itself and put itself aside. Thus understood the Dialectical principle constitutes the life and soul of scientific progress, the dynamic which alone gives immanent connexion and necessity to the body of science; and, in a word, is seen to constitute the real and true, as opposed to the external, exaltation above the finite." In this paragraph on logic, what Hegel says of the dialectic in its relationship to understanding is also true for history, in which the action of freedom becomes intelligible in terms of necessity, as we look back on it. *The Logic of Hegel*, trans. William Wallace (Oxford: Oxford University Press, 1959), pp. 147–148.

21. Hegel, *Phenomenology*, pp. 356–357.

22. Georg Wilhelm Friedrich Hegel, *Philosophy of History*, trans. J. Sibree (New York: Willey Book, 1944), p. 442.

23. Ibid., p. 443.

24. Hegel, *Phenomenology*, p. 357.

25. Ibid., p. 359.

26. Ibid.

27. Ibid., p. 360.

28. Hegel, *Philosophy of History*, pp. 450–451.

29. Malet et Isaac, *La Révolution et l'Empire*, (Paris: Hachette, 1929), p. 156. [Citation translated by S. W.]

30. "This tyranny could not last; for all inclinations, all interests, reason itself revolted against this terribly consistent Liberty, which in its concentrated intensity exhibited so fanatical a shape." Hegel, *Phenomenology*, p. 360.

31. Ibid., p. 361.

32. He obviously means the leaders of the Convention.

33. Georg Wilhelm Friedrich Hegel, *Hegel's Philosophy of Right*, trans. T. M. Knox (Oxford: Clarendon Press, 1967), p. 258.

34. William Shakespeare, *Macbeth*, act 5, sc. 5.

35. "The *goal*, Absolute Knowing, or Spirit that knows itself as Spirit, has for its path the recollection of the Spirits as they are in themselves and as they accomplish the organization of their realm." Hegel, *Phenomenology*, p. 493.

36. Hegel, *Philosophy of Right*, p. 160.

37. Ibid., p. 161. See also para. 537 of Hegel's *Encyclopaedia* and the note to para. 260 in the *Philosophy of Right*.

38. Hegel, *Philosophy of Right*, p. 161.

39. Ibid., p. 162.

40. Ibid., p. 164.

41. Ibid., p. 189.

42. Ibid.

43. Ibid.

44. Ibid., p. 145ff.

45. Hegel, *Philosophy of Mind*, p. 263. (The state as such is exterior to civil society.)

46. Hegel, *Philosophy of Right*, p. 152.

47. Ibid., p. 146.

48. This is Kojève's interpretation. See his *Introduction à la lecture de Hegel*, p. 145. Jean Hyppolite gives a different interpretation. See *Phénoménologie de l'esprit* (Paris: Aubier-Montaigne, 1939), p. 311.

49. Napoleon abdicated 22 June 1815, the surrender was signed 3 July 1815, and Napoleon died 5 May 1821. The preface to the *Philosophy of Right*, which appeared in 1821, is dated 25 June 1820.

50. Hegel, *Philosophy of Mind*, p. 279.

51. Hegel, *Philosophy of Right*, p. 13.

52. Ibid., p. 174.

53. Hegel, *Philosophy of History*, p. 72.

54. Ibid., pp. 72–73.

55. Ibid., p. 74.

56. Ibid., p. 75.

57. Ibid., p. 78.

58. Ibid.

59. On this subject, see Eric Weil's analysis of the sentence from the preface of the *Philosophy of Right*, "What is rational is actual and what is actual is rational." *Hegel et l'Etat* (Paris: Vrin, 1950), p. 25.

60. Hegel, *Philosophy of Right*, pp. 155–156.

61. Ibid.

62. Georg Wilhelm Friedrich Hegel, *Natural Law: The Scientific Ways of Treating Natural Law, Its Place in Moral Philosophy, and Its Relation to the Positive Sciences of Law* (hereafter cited as *Natural Law*), trans. T. M. Knox (Philadelphia: University of Pennsylvania Press, 1975), p. 93. Heraclitus (frag. 77) used an analogous image when he wrote, "Even a potion separates if we do not stir it" [Citation translated by S. W.]

63. Hegel, *Phenomenology* pp. 272–273.

64. Hegel, *Philosophy of Right*, p. 210.

65. Hegel, *Natural Law*, p. 91.

66. Hegel, *Philosophy of Right*, p. 210.

67. Ibid., p. 208.

68. Ibid., p. 209.

69. Ibid.

70. Ibid.

71. Ibid., pp. 210–211.

72. Ibid., p. 211.

73. Ibid.

74. Ibid., p. 212.

75. Ibid.

76. Ibid., p. 295.

77. Ibid., p. 212.

78. Ibid., p. 213.

79. Ibid.

80. Ibid., note to para. 278, p. 181, and para. 328, p. 212.

81. Ibid., pp. 180–181.

82. Ibid., p. 181.

83. Ibid., p. 210.

84. Ibid., p. 215.

85. Friedrich Nietzsche, *Thus Spoke Zarathustra*, trans. Walter Kaufmann, in *The Portable Nietzsche* (New York: Viking Press, 1968.), p. 160.

86. Ibid., pp. 160, 162–163.

87. Friedrich Nietzsche, *The Gay Science*, trans. Walter Kaufmann (New York: Random House, 1974.), p. 336.

88. Though he calls him a "puny pedant" in *Unmodern Observations*.

89. Friedrich Nietzsche, *Human, All Too Human*, trans. Marion Faber (Lincoln: University of Nebraska Press, 1984), p. 230.

90. Today we could say the same of Western civilization.

91. Nietzsche, *Human, All Too Human*, pp. 230–231.

92. Ibid., p. 230.

93. Nietzsche, *The Gay Science*, pp. 291–292.

94. Ibid., p. 96.

95. Nietzsche, *Human, All Too Human*, pp. 232–233.

96. Nietzsche, *The Gay Science*, p. 161.

97. Nietzsche, *Human, All Too Human*, p. 46.

98. Friedrich Nietzsche, *On the Genealogy of Morals*, trans. Walter Kaufmann and R. J. Hollingdale, in *On the Genealogy of Morals and Ecce Homo* (New York: Vintage Books, 1967), pp. 40–41.

99. Nietzsche, *The Gay Science*, p. 235.

100. "I see many soldiers; would that I saw many warriors!" Nietzsche, *Thus Spoke Zarathustra*, p. 159.

101. Ibid., p. 394.

102. Friedrich Nietzsche, *David Strauss: Writer and Confessor*, trans. Herbert Golder, p. 103.

103. Nietzsche, *Human, All Too Human*, p. 97.

104. Friedrich Nietzsche, "Philosophy During the Tragic Age of the Greeks," in *Early Greek Philosophy and Other Essays*, trans. Maximilian A. Mügge (New York: Macmillan, 1924), p. 125.

105. See *Aurore* and Philippe Reynaud's preface to the edition in the Pluriel series (Paris: Hachette, 1987).

106. Friedrich Nietzsche, *Werke. Kritische Gesamtausgabe*, ed. G. Colli and M. Montinari (Berlin: de Gruyter, 1978), sect. 5, vol. 1, p. 500. [Where—as here—the author cites French versions of texts that have not appeared in English, they are translated from the original German by Professor Hugo Schmidt of the University of Colorado at Boulder.]

107. Friedrich Nietzsche, "Das griechische Musikdrama," in *Werke*, sect 2, vol. 3, p. 11.

108. Nietzsche, *Thus Spoke Zarathustra*, p. 308.

109. Nietzsche, *Genealogy of Morals*, pp. 25–26.

110. Ibid., p. 31.

111. Ibid., p. 33.

112. Ibid., p. 40.

113. Ibid., p. 41.

114. Ibid., p. 37.

115. Ibid., p. 39.

116. Nietzsche, *Thus Spoke Zarathustra*, p. 168.

117. Friedrich Nietzsche, *Beyond Good and Evil*, trans. Walter Kaufmann (New York: Vintage Books, 1966), p. 118.

118. *Will to Power*, p. 489.

119. Ibid., p. 129.

120. Ibid., p. 228.

121. Nietzsche, *Genealogy of Morals*, p. 37.

122. Ibid., p. 38.

123. Ibid., p. 33.

124. Ibid., p. 44.

125. Ibid., p. 43.

126. Nietzsche, *The Gay Science*, p. 279.

127. Nietzsche, *Will to Power,* p. 37.

128. Nietzsche, *Werke,* sect. 3, vol. 4, pp. 48–49.

129. Ibid., p. 48.

130. Ibid., pp. 25–26.

131. Ibid., p. 386.

132. Ibid., pp. 462–463.

133. Nietzsche, *Werke,* sect. 3, vol. 4, p. 18.

134. Nietzsche, *Will to Power,* p. 256.

135. Ibid., p. 217.

136. Nietzsche, *Werke,* sect. 7, vol. 1, p. 264.

137. Nietzsche, *Will to Power,* p. 466.

138. Ibid., p. 137.

139. Ibid., p. 466.

140. "And who knows how to laugh anyway and live well if he does not first know a good deal about war and victory?" Nietzsche, *The Gay Science,* p. 255.

141. Nietzsche, *Thus Spoke Zarathustra,* p. 126.

142. Ibid., p. 169.

143. Ibid., p. 149.

144. Nietzsche, *Genealogy of Morals.*

145. Nietzsche, *Will to Power,* pp. 487–488.

146. Nietzsche, *Thus Spoke Zarathustra,* p. 401.

CHAPTER 5

1. Thomas More, *The Utopia,* ed. Mildred Campbell (Princeton, N.J.: D. Van Nostrand, 1947), p. 32.

2. Ibid., p. 139.

3. Henri Baudrillart, *Bodin et son temps* (Paris, 1853). [Citations from this work are translated by S. W.]

4. Baudrillart notes both "the explosion of republican ideas" and "the naive illusion that humanity can live without laws or leaders and realize a paradise of innocence and felicity on earth." Ibid.

5. Etienne de La Boétie, *The Politics of Obedience: The Discourse of Voluntary Servitude,* trans. Harry Kurz (New York: Free Life Editions, 1975), p. 55.

6. Ibid.

7. Ibid., pp. 55–56.

8. Ibid., p. 52.

9. Ibid., p. 56.

10. Ibid.

11. Ibid., p. 50.

12. Ibid., p. 56.

13. Compare, for example, Locke's *Second Treatise of Government,* in *Two Treatises of Government,* ed. Peter Laslett (Cambridge: Cambridge University Press, 1967), chapter 5.

14. La Boétie, *Voluntary Servitude,* p. 56.

15. Ibid.
16. Ibid., p. 58.
17. Ibid., p. 60.
18. Ibid., pp. 64–65.
19. Ibid., p. 65.
20. Ibid., p. 46.
21. Ibid., p. 69.
22. Ibid., p. 50.
23. Ibid., p. 51.
24. Ibid., pp. 52–53.
25. Baudrillart, *Bodin*.
26. La Boétie, *Voluntary Servitude*, p. 55.
27. Ibid., p. 86.

CHAPTER 6

1. Jean-Jacques Rousseau, *Discourse on the Origin of Inequality*, (hereafter cited as *Origin of Inequality*), in *On the Social Contract, Discourse on the Origin of Inequality, Discourse on Political Economy*, trans. and ed. Donald A. Cress (Indianapolis: Hackett Publishing, 1983), p. 118.

2. Ibid., pp. 118–119.

3. Ibid., p. 119.

4. Ibid.

5. Ibid., p. 139.

6. Ibid.

7. I cannot recommend too highly Alexis Philonenko's *Jean-Jacques Rousseau et la pensé du malheur* (Paris: Vrin, 1984).

8. Rousseau, *Origin of Inequality*, p. 114.

9. Jean-Jacques Rousseau, *The Confessions of Jean-Jacques Rousseau: The Anonymous Translation into English of 1783 and 1790, Revised and Completed*, ed. A.S.B. Glover (New York: Heritage Press, 1955), p. 331; *Rousseau, Judge of Jean-Jacques*, in *Collected Writings of Rousseau*, trans. Judith R. Bush, Christopher Kelly, and Roger D. Masters (Hanover, N.H.: University Press of New England, 1990), p. 130; and especially the letter of 12 January 1762 in the *Lettre à Malesherbes*.

10. Jean-Jacques Rousseau, note 9 to the *Origin of Inequality*, in *A Discourse on Inequality*, trans. Maurice Cranston (New York: Penguin Books, 1984), pp. 153–154.

11. Raymond Polin called his book on Rousseau *La politique de la solitude* (Paris: Sirey, 1971).

12. Recall Rousseau's surprise and sorrow on reading the dialogue appended to a copy of *Le fils naturel* sent him by Diderot. There he discovered "this bitter and severe sentence without the least softening: *Only the wicked man is alone*." *Confessions*, p. 436.

13. John Locke, *The Second Treatise of Government*, in *Two Treatises of Government*, ed. Peter Laslett (Cambridge: Cambridge University Press, 1967), p. 368.

14. Which does not mean that natural law does not exist, in Rousseau's opinion, but that man is not conscious of it.

15. From note 9 in Rousseau, *A Discourse on Inequality*, p. 148. See also *The State of War Is Born from the Social State*, in Grace G. Roosevelt, *Reading Rousseau in the Nuclear Age* (Philadelphia: Temple University Press, 1990): "Natural man, after all, has no necessary ties to his fellow men; he can survive in good health without their assistance. Indeed, he needs the attentions of men less than he needs the fruit of the earth, and the earth produces more than enough to feed all of its inhabitants"(p. 191); and "I can imagine that in the unmediated quarrels that sometimes arise in the state of nature an irritated man might happen to kill another, either openly or by surprise. . . . War is a continual state, but the constant relationship that the state of war presupposes can rarely be found between man and man. Everything among individuals is in a continual flux which incessantly alters their interests and ties. The subject of a dispute thus appears and disappears in almost an instant, a quarrel begins and ends in a day, and while there may be conflicts and killings there is never, or at least very rarely, long-standing enmity or general war" (p. 189).

16. Rousseau, *Origin of Inequality*, p. 20.

17. Ibid., p. 139.

18. Ibid., p. 115.

19. Ibid., pp. 133–134.

20. Ibid., pp. 133–135.

21. Rousseau, *State of War*, p. 189.

22. Rousseau, *Origin of Inequality*, p. 124.

23. Ibid.

24. Ibid., p. 140.

25. Ibid., p. 133.

26. Ibid., p. 126.

27. "An animal will never know what it is to die; and knowledge of death and its terrors is one of the first acquisitions that man has made in withdrawing from the animal condition." Ibid.

28. Ibid., p. 135.

29. Ibid., p. 126.

30. Ibid., p. 139.

31. Ibid., p. 137.

32. Ibid., pp. 148, 150.

33. Rousseau, *State of War*, p. 185.

34. Alfred de Vigny, "La maison du berger," in *Poèmes philosophique*. [Citation translated by S. W.]

35. Rousseau, *Origin of Inequality*, p. 120.

36. Ibid., p. 124.

37. Ibid., p. 125.

38. Ibid., p. 127.

39. Ibid., p. 139.

40. Ibid.

41. Ibid., pp. 140–141.

42. Ibid., p. 141. Only once does Rousseau use the expression "some fortunate chance happening." The happening referred to acquaints man with fire and can only be called fortunate after other natural disasters had previously forced the human being to change his way of life.

43. Ibid., p. 143. Compare Rousseau's political text, *L'influence des climats relativement à la civilization*, written around 1750.

44. Ibid., p. 145.

45. Ibid., pp. 132, 133.

46. See chap. 6 in Polin's, *La politique de la solitude*.

47. *Origin of Inequality*, p. 144.

48. Note 15 in *Discourse on Inequality*, p. 167.

49. "Surplus awakens greed: The more one accumulates, the more one desires. Those who have much want to have all ." Rousseau, *State of War*, pp. 187–188.

50. Rousseau, *Origin of Inequality*, p. 122.

51. Rousseau, *Confessions*, p. 371.

52. Rousseau, *Origin of Inequality*, p. 145.

53. See Claude Lévi-Strauss, *La pensé sauvage* (Paris: Plon, 1962).

54. Rousseau, *Origin of Inequality*, p. 125.

55. Rousseau, *Social Contract*, p. 27.

56. See the discussion of the state of nature in the first version of the Rousseau, *Social Contract*, bk. 1, chap. 2.

57. Rousseau, *Origin of Inequality*, p. 145.

58. Rousseau, *Social Contract*, p. 23.

59. "The rich, pressed by necessity, finally conceived the most thought-out project that ever entered the human mind. It was to use in his favor the very strength of those who attacked him. . . . They all ran to chain themselves, in the belief that they secured their liberty, for although they had enough sense to realize the advantages of a political establishment, they did not have enough experience to foresee its dangers." Rousseau, *Origin of Inequality* pp. 149–150. "Subjected to the duties of the civil state without enjoying even the rights of the state of nature and without being able to use their strength to defend themselves, they would as a result be in the worst condition in which free men can find themselves." Rousseau, *On Political Economy*, p. 174. See also in the same work p. 186: "Let us summarize in a few words the social pact of the two estates. *You need me for I am rich and you are poor. Let us come to an agreement between ourselves. I will permit you to have the honor of serving me, provided you give me what little you have for the trouble I will be taking to command you.*"

60. Rousseau, *Social Contract*, p. 24.

61. Ibid., p. 72.

62. Rousseau, *Social Contract*, first version, bk. 1, chap. 2. [Citation translated by S. W.]

63. Rousseau, *Social Contract*, p. 23.

64. Ibid., p. 360.

65. Ibid., p. 361.

66. Ibid., p. 360.

67. Ibid., p. 361.

68. Ibid., bk. 2, chaps. 1, 2, 3. See Philonenko, Jean-Jacques Rousseau et la pensée du malheur, vol. 3, ch. 2 for a fascinating interpretation that shows how the eighteenth-century's interest in differential and integral calculus most nearly explains this text. There appears to be no contradiction between Philonenko's analysis and my interpretation, even though they differ. See also Rousseau's work on the government of Poland in which he writes, "The law, which is merely the expression of the general will, is certainly the product of all sectional interests, combining with and balancing one another in all their variety." *The Government of Poland*, trans. and ed. Willmoore Kendall (Indianapolis: Bobbs-Merrill, 1972), p. 42.

69. Rousseau, *Social Contract*, p. 31.

70. Ibid., p. 24.

71. Ibid.

72. Ibid., p. 26.

73. Ibid., p. 27.

74. Rousseau, *On Political Economy*, p. 167.

75. Ibid., p. 170.

76. Ibid., p. 171.

77. Jean-Jacques Rousseau, *Emile; or, On Education*, trans. Alan Bloom (New York: Basic Books, 1979), p. 235.

78. Rousseau, *Social Contract*, p. 27.

79. Ibid., p. 39.

80. Ibid., p. 26.

81. Ibid.

82. Rousseau, *Emile*, p. 290.

83. "There is in the depths of souls, then, an innate principle of justice and virtue according to which, in spite of our own maxims, we judge our own actions or those of others as good or bad. It is to this principle that I give the name *conscience*." Ibid., p. 289.

84. See Polin, *La politique de la solitude*, chap. 2.

85. Jean-Jacques Rousseau, *Constitutional Project for Corsica*, in *Political Writings*, trans. and ed. Frederick Watkins (New York: Thomas Nelson and Sons, 1953), p. 277.

86. Rousseau, *Origin of Inequality*, p. 148.

87. Rousseau, *Social Contract*, pp. 41–42.

88. Ibid., p. 46.

89. Ibid., p. 63.

90. Rousseau, *State of War*, p. 190.

91. Ibid., p. 196.

92. Ibid., p. 186.

93. Rousseau, *Origin of Inequality*, p. 150.

94. Ibid., p. 150.

95. Rousseau, *Social Contract*, p. 20.

96. Ibid., p. 44.

97. Rousseau, *The Government of Poland*, p. 67.

98. Ibid.

99. Ibid., pp 67–68.

100. Rousseau, *Social Contract*, p. 44.

101. Lycurgus "did not see that the taste for conquests was an inevitable vice in his country and more powerful than the law that repressed it." *Fragments politiques*, in *Oeuvres complètes*, (Paris: Gallimard, 1964), p. 541. [Citation translated by S. W.]

102. Rousseau, *Social Contract*, p. 68.

103. Rousseau, *The Government of Poland*, pp. 11–12 (my italics).

104. Rousseau, *Social Contract*, p. 26.

105. Ibid., pp. 34–35.

106. Ibid., p. 35.

107. Ibid., p. 48.

108. Ibid., p. 21.

109. Ibid., p. 22. See also Rousseau, *State of War*, p. 196ff.

110. Such a right draws an absolution distinction between the contract state and totalitarian states. Rousseau rightly says, "To inhabit the territory is to submit to sovereignty." He adds in a note, "This should always be understood in connection with a free state, for otherwise the family, goods, the lack of shelter, necessity, or violence can keep an inhabitant in a country in spite of himself; and then his sojourn alone no longer presupposes his consent to the contract or to the violation of the contract." *Social Contract*, pp. 81–82.

111. Rousseau, *Social Contract*, p. 79.

112. Ibid., p. 39

113. Ibid., p. 102.

114. Rousseau, *The Government of Poland*, p. 19.

115. Ibid., p. 13.

116. Ibid., chap. 3. Rousseau uses the expression "like a good mother," ibid., p. 14. In a short political text on the concept of the native land, he writes of the zeal that "will be aroused for such a tender mother." *Oeuvres complètes*, p. 536. [Citation translated by S. W.]

117. Rousseau, *On Political Economy*, p. 173.

118. Ibid., pp. 173–174.

119. Ibid., p. 177. We take this to mean the natural love of self in its fusion with what preserves it.

120. Rousseau, *Social Contract*, p. 45.

121. Rousseau, *Constitutional Project for Corsica*, p. 285.

122. Rousseau, *Social Contract*, pp. 39–40.

123. Ibid., p. 39.

124. Rousseau, *The Government of Poland*, p. 8.

125. Ibid., p. 10.

126. Ibid., p. 11.

127. "Regular armies have been the scourge and ruin of Europe. They are good for only two things: attacking and conquering neighbors, and fettering and enslaving citizens." Ibid., p. 80.

128. Ibid., chaps. 10 and 11.

129. Ibid., p. 80.

130. Rousseau, *Social Contract*, p. 19.

131. Rousseau, *The Government of Poland*, especially chaps. 2 and 4. See also the *Political Economy*: "A country cannot subsist without liberty, nor can liberty without virtue, nor can virtue without citizens. You will have everything if you train citizens" (p. 176).

132. Rousseau, *The Government of Poland*, p. 69. Compare also: "A state rich in money is always weak, and a state rich in men is always strong." *Constitutional Project for Corsica*, p. 282.

133. Rousseau, *On Political Economy*, pp. 181–182.

134. Rousseau, *Constitutional Project for Corsica*, p. 283. Love of family joins love of country and love of tilling the earth. According to Rousseau, the three are indispensable to the definition of the moral human being and the good citizen.

135. Rousseau, *State of War*, p. 188.

136. Jean-Jacques Rousseau, *Judgement on the Project for Perpetual Peace*, in Roosevelt, *Reading Rousseau in the Nuclear Age*, p. 221.

137. Ibid., p. 225.

138. "For that it would be necessary that the sum of individual interests would not outweigh the common interest, and that each one would believe that he had found in the good of all the greatest good that he could hope for for himself." Ibid., p. 224.

139. Ibid., pp. 223, 225.

140. Rousseau, *State of War*, p. 190.

141. Rousseau, *Social Contract*, p. 42.

142. Rousseau, *Constitutional Project for Corsica*, p. 278.

143. Rousseau, *The Government of Poland*, p. 2.

144. Rousseau, *Origin of Inequality*, p. 153.

145. Rousseau, *State of War*, p. 190.

146. Rousseau, *Judgement on the Project for Perpetual Peace*, p. 228.

147. Rousseau, *Rousseau, Judge of Jean-Jacques*, p. 94.

CHAPTER 7

1. See Blandine Barret-Kriegel, *L'etat et les esclaves* (Paris: Calmann-Lévy, 1979). On the topic covered in this chapter, see also Yirmiyahu Yovel, *Kant and the Philosophy of History* (Princeton, N.J.: Princeton University Press, 1989).

2. Immanuel Kant, *Idea for a Universal History with a Cosmopolitan Intent*, in *Perpetual Peace and Other Essays on Politics, History, and Morals*, trans. and intro. Ted Humphrey (Indianapolis: Hackett Publishing, 1983), p. 34.

3. Immanuel Kant, *Speculative Beginning of Human History*, in Humphrey, *Perpetual Peace and Other Essays*, pp. 57–58.

4. Immanuel Kant, *Critique of Judgment*, trans. and intro. J. H. Bernard (New York: Hafner Publishing, 1951), p. 283.

5. Immanuel Kant, *Religion Within the Limits of Reason Alone*, trans. and intro. Theodore M. Greene and Hoyt H. Hudson (New York: Harper Torchbooks, 1960), pp. 28–29.

6. Ibid., p. 30.

7. Immanuel Kant, *Critique of Practical Reason*, trans. and intro. Lewis White Beck (Indianapolis: Bobbs-Merrill, 1956), p. 31..

8. We see both to what extent Kant follows Rousseau and to what extent he departs from him.

9. Kant, *Religion*, p. 22.

10. Ibid., pp. 22–23.

11. Kant, *Critique of Practical Reason*, p. 3.

12. Ibid., p. 4.

13. Kant, *Religion*, p. 26.

14. Ibid., p. 27.

15. Ibid., p. 28.

16. Ibid., p. 29.

17. Kant, *Human History*, pp. 50–51.

18. Kant, *Universal History*, pp. 31–32.

19. Ibid.

20. Ibid., p. 32.

21. Ibid.

22. Ibid.

23. Ibid.

24. Ibid.

25. Ibid., p. 34.

26. Kant, *Religion*, p. 92.

27. Immanuel Kant, *Anthropology from a Pragmatic Point of View*, trans. and intro. Mary J. Gregor (The Hague: Martinus Nijhoff, 1974), pp. 133–134.

28. Ibid., p. 135.

29. Ibid., pp. 133–134.

30. Kant, *Universal History*, p. 30.

31. Kant, *Human History*, p. 49.

32. Ibid.

33. Ibid., p. 51.

34. Ibid., p. 52.

35. Ibid.

36. Kant, *Universal History*, pp. 29–30.

37. Ibid., p. 32.

38. Kant, *Human History*, p. 58.

39. Ibid., p. 54.

40. Kant, *Universal History*, p. 31.

41. Ibid.

42. Immanuel Kant, *The Philosophy of Law: An Exposition of the Fundamental Principles of Jurisprudence as the Science of Right*, trans. W. Hastiel (Clifton, N.J.: Augustus M. Kelley, 1974), p. 62.

43. Ibid., p. 63.

44. Ibid., p. 71.

45. Ibid., p. 90.

46. Ibid., pp. 94–95.

47. Ibid., pp. 163–164.

48. Ibid., p. 165.

49. Ibid., p. 166.

50. "[Concepts] can very probably and without criticism be *thought*, yet it may be quite impossible for them to be given; instead, they may be merely empty ideas that have either no practical use whatsoever or even one that would be disadvantageous." Immanuel Kant, *On the Proverb: That May Be True in Theory, but Is of No Practical Use* (hereafter cited as *Theory and Practice*), in *Perpetual Peace*, p. 62.

51. *Immanuel Kant's Critique of Pure Reason*, trans. Norman Kemp Smith (London: Macmillan, 1929), pp. 310–311.

52. A contradictory idea for speculative reason, because Kant has eliminated the possibility of knowing anything other than phenomena. It goes without saying that knowledge of objects that transcend phenomena and make use of *symbols* (as the dragon would have been for medieval illuminators) is of no interest from Kant's point of view.

53. Kant, *Critique of Pure Reason*, p. 642.

54. Kant, *Philosophy of Law*, pp. 45–46.

55. Ibid., p. 46.

56. Kant, *Critique of Pure Reason*, p. 300.

57. Ibid., p. 302.

58. Ibid.

59. Ibid.

60. Kant, *Universal History*, p. 33.

61. Ibid.

62. Ibid.; emphasis in the original.

63. Ibid., p. 34.

64. Ibid., pp. 34–35.

65. Ibid., p. 35.

66. Ibid., pp. 34–35.

67. Alexis Philonenko, *Etudes kantiennes* (Paris: Vrin, 1982), chap. 3.

68. Kant, *Human History*, p. 53.

69. Ibid., p. 58.

70. Kant, *Critique of Judgment*, p. 282.

71. Ibid.

72. Ibid., p. 281.

73. Ibid., p. 276.

74. Ibid., p. 279.

75. Ibid., p. 282.

76. Ibid., p. 283.

77. Ibid.

78. Ibid.

79. Kant, *Theory and Practice*, pp. 87–88.

80. Ibid., p. 62.

81. Ibid.

82. Ibid.

83. Kant continues: "For this is a matter of inner experience, and such an awareness of one's state of mind would involve an absolutely clear representation of everything pertaining to those nations and considerations that imagination, habit, and inclination conjoin to the concept of duty. This is too much to ask for. Moreover, something's nonexistence (even an unconsciously intended advantage) cannot be an object of experience." Ibid., p. 68.

84. Ibid., p. 89.

85. Ibid., p. 87.

86. Ibid., p. 72.

87. Ibid., pp. 71–72.

88. Ibid., p. 72.

89. Ibid.

90. Ibid., p. 76.

91. Ibid., p. 72.

92. Ibid., p. 77.

93. Ibid., p. 79.

94. Ibid., p. 78.

95. Ibid.

96. Ibid., p. 79.

97. Ibid., p. 89.

98. Kant, *Philosophy of Law*, pp. 176–177.

99. Alexis Philonenko, *Essais sur la philosophie de la guerre* (Paris: Vrin, 1976), p. 29.

100. Immanuel Kant, *To Perpetual Peace: A Philosophical Sketch* (hereafter cited as *To Perpetual Peace*), in *Perpetual Peace*, p. 113.

101. Ibid., p. 123.

102. Ibid., pp. 112–113.

103. Ibid., p. 113.

104. Ibid., pp. 111, 113.

105. Ibid., p. 112.

106. Rom. 13:4 (Revised Standard Version).

107. Kant, *To Perpetual Peace*, p. 113.

108. Kant, *Theory and Practice*, p. 88.

109. Kant, *To Perpetual Peace*, p. 112.

110. Ibid.

111. Kant, *Philosophy of Law*, p. 167.

112. Kant, *To Perpetual Peace*, p. 112.

113. Ibid.

114. John Locke, *The Second Treatise of Government*, in *Two Treatises of Government*, ed. Peter Laslett (Cambridge: Cambridge University Press, 1967), p. 368.

115. Jean-Jacques Rousseau, *On the Social Contract*, in *On the Social Contract, Discourse on the Origin of Inequality, Discourse on Political Economy*), trans. and ed. Donald A. Cress (Indianapolis: Hackett Publishing, 1983), p. 25. See also in bk. 3, chap. 18: "If all the citizens were to assemble in order to break the compact [the social contract] by common agreement, no one could doubt that it was legitimately broken" (p. 79).

116. Kant, *To Perpetual Peace*, p. 116.

117. Ibid.

118. Ibid., p. 117.

119. Ibid., p. 118.

120. Ibid., p. 119.

121. Ibid.

122. Ibid., p. 120.

123. Ibid.

124. Ibid., p. 123.

125. Ibid.

126. Ibid..

127. Rousseau, *On the Social Contract*, p. 24.

128. Kant, *To Perpetual Peace*, p. 124.

129. Ibid.

130. Kant, *Theory and Practice*, p. 88.

131. Kant, *To Perpetual Peace*, p. 125.

132. Ibid., p. 137.

133. Ibid., p. 138.

134. Ibid., p. 131.

135. Ibid., p. 132.

136. Ibid., p. 135.

137. Ibid.

138. Kant, *Philosophy of Law*, p. 215.

139. Ibid., p. 217.

140. Ibid., p. 214.

141. Ibid., p. 224.

142. Although Marx's ideas were shaped by his reaction against the writings of Kant and Hegel, they are nonetheless very often close to certain themes of Hegel's and even of Kant's. The *Speculative Beginning of Human History* (and other works as well) could be cited as evidence, though we should obviously not minimize the differences, indeed the contradictions. Kant and Hegel wrote as philosophers; Marx was much less concerned with philosophy.

143. Karl Marx, *Economic and Philosophic Manuscripts of 1844* (Moscow: Foreign Languages Publishing House, 1959), p. 151.

144. Karl Marx, *Capital*, trans. Ben Fowkes (New York: Vintage Books, 1976), vol. 1, p. 100.

145. Karl Marx, *Wage-Labour and Capital* (New York: International Publishers, 1933), p. 15.

146. Ibid., pp. 28–29.

147. See especially *Value, Price, and Profit* and *Capital*, bk. 1.

148. Karl Marx and Friedrich Engels, *German Ideology* (Moscow: Progress Publishers, 1964), pp. 92–93.

149. Karl Marx and Friedrich Engels, *Manifesto of the Communist Party* (hereafter cited as *Manifesto*), in *Birth of the Communist Manifesto*, ed. Dirk J. Struik (New York: International Publishers, 1971), p. 99.

150. Karl Marx, *Inaugural Address and Statutes of the International Workingmen's Association*, in Karl Marx and Friedrich Engels, *Collected Works* (New York: International Publishers, 1984), vol. 20, pp. 12–13.

151. Marx, *Manuscripts of 1844*, p. 67.

152. Ibid., p. 68.

153. Ibid., p. 69.

154. Ibid., p. 77.

155. Letter to Annenkov, 28 December 1946, in Marx and Engels, *Collected Works*, vol. 38, p. 96.

156. Ibid. See also the forward to the *Critique of Political Economy*.

157. Marx, *Manuscripts of 1844*, p. 70.

158. In the *Manifesto*, for example, the proletariat is defined as "a class of laborers who live only as long as they find work, and who find work only as long as their labor increases capital" (p. 96). We also read, "The 'dangerous class', the social scum, that passively rotting mass thrown off by the lowest layers of the old society may here and there be swept into the movement by a proletarian revolution; its conditions of life, however, prepare it far more for the part of a bribed tool of reactionary intrigue" (p. 100). The same adjective (*proletarian*) is applied to very different groups—those who are drawn into the revolution and those who start it. Again, the proletarians are "a considerable part of the population," which the bourgeoisie "rescued . . . from the idiocy of rural life" and also "more massive and more colossal productive forces" than all those of the past together, which "slumbered in the lap of social labor" (p. 94).

159. Marx and Engels, *Manifesto*, p. 120.

160. Ibid., p. 121.

161. Karl Marx, *Contribution to the Critique of Political Economy*, in Karl Marx and Friedrich Engels, *Basic Writings on Politics and Philosophy*, ed. Lewis S. Feuer (Garden City, N.Y.: Anchor Books, 1959), p. 43.

162. Marx, *German Ideology*, p. 95.

163. Marx and Engels, *Manifesto*, p. 104.

164. Marx, *Poverty of Philosophy*, in *Collected Works*, vol. 6, p. 175.

165. Marx and Engels, *Manifesto*, p. 103.

166. Ibid., p. 104.

167. It is interesting to see how V. I. Lenin interpreted the party's role, both in theory and practice. Compare *What Is to Be Done?* trans. J. Fineberg and G. Hanna (New York: International Publishers, 1969).

168. Marx and Engels, *Manifesto*, p. 91.

169. Ibid.

170. Marx, *German Ideology*, p. 93.

171. Ibid., p. 79.

172. Ibid., p. 83.

173. Ibid., p. 58.

174. Marx, *Contribution to the Critique of Political Economy*, p. 162.

175. Marx and Engels, *Manifesto*, p. 101.

176. Marx, *German Ideology*, p. 96.

177. Ibid.

178. Ibid., p. 97.

179. Ibid., p. 60.

180. Cited by M. Ruben in Karl Marx, *Oeuvres* (Paris: NRF, 1968), vol. 1, p. 1574.

181. Marx and Engels, *Manifesto*, pp. 110–111.

182. Karl Marx, *Critique of the Gotha Programme* (Moscow: Co-operative Publishing Society of Foreign Workers in the USSR, 1937), p. 28.

183. At the time of the Russian Revolution, the Bolsheviks certainly understood this "necessity," as evidenced, for example, by the massacre at Ekaterinaburg, where the members of the imperial family, especially the children, were targeted not so much as individuals but as symbols. We can say the same for all killings planned with no other reason than to eliminate the *symbols* of what is wanted destroyed.

184. Marx, *German Ideology*, p. 97.

185. Marx and Engels, *Manifesto*, p. 112.

186. Marx, *Critique of the Gotha Programme*, p. 14.

187. See Jean Bodin: "Nothing can be thought of as shared in common, except by contrast with what is privately owned. . . . It is common knowledge that no one feels any very strong affection for that which is common to all. Common possession brings in its train all sorts of quarrels and antagonisms." *The Six Books of the Commonwealth*, trans. M. J. Tooley (New York: Barnes & Noble, 1967), pp. 8, 9.

188. A book very much in vogue in 1968 treated the Marxist postulate as certainty. See Pierre Bourdieu and Jean-Claude Passeron, *Les héritiers* (Paris: Le Seuil, 1967). See also a noteworthy critique of it by philosophers of the new generation, Luc Ferry and Alain Renaut, *La pensée 68* (Paris: Gallimard, 1985).

189. The materialist interpretation leads to explanations as reductionistic as Marx's explanation of feudalism in *German Ideology*, or else laughable, like the reasons he gives in the same work for the loss of the art of stained glass.

190. Kant, *Human History*, p. 153.

191. Kant, *Critique of Practical Reason*, p. 4.

CHAPTER 8

1. Karl von Clausewitz partially explores ideas of this kind in his *On War*, ed. and trans. Peter Paret and Michael Howard (Princeton, N.J.: Princeton University Press, 1984).

2. Thucydides takes only three lines to relate this fact, without comment. *Peloponnesian War* 5.115.

3. René Descartes, *Discourse on the Method of Rightly Conducting the Reason and Seeking for Truth in the Sciences*, in *The Philosophical Works of Descartes*, edition of 1931, trans. Elizabeth Haldane and G.R.T. Ross (New York: Dover Publications, through special arrangement with Cambridge University Press, 1955), vol. 1, p. 88.

4. The words *thing* and *slave* as terms describing the child are borrowed from Marie Balmary, *Le sacrifice interdit* (Paris: Grasset, 1986).

5. René Descartes, *The Search After Truth by the Light of Nature,* in *The Philosophical Works of Descartes,* vol. 1, pp. 305, 312.

6. Ibid., p. 307.

7. Plato, *Laws* 7.808d , trans. A. E. Taylor, in Bollingen Series 71, *The Collected Dialogues of Plato,* ed. Edith Hamilton and Huntington Cairns (Princeton, N.J.: Princeton University Press, 1987).

8. Plato, *Statesman* 268d ff.

9. Plato, *Laws* 4.713a ff.

10. The French language has no word for the male human being other than *homme* [man], which is also the term designating any human being, whether male or female. Having no alternative, I will use the term *homme* every time I mean a male human being. The word *femme* [woman] is fortunately available and presents no problems. Although slang and informal speech give us options that clearly distinguish the sexes, I prefer not to use them because of their emotional, humorous, or pejorative connotations, obviously not relevant here. I am nonetheless aware that using *homme* with two meanings does not compensate adequately for the needed term. [Translator's note: English offers the translator resources for avoiding this ambiguity by replacing the generic *man* with such clear, and clearly nonsexist, terms as *humanity, humankind, person,* and so on.]

11. Plato, *Symposium* 189a ff.

12. Karl Marx, *Economic and Philosophical Manuscripts of 1844* (Moscow: Foreign Languages Publishing House, 1959), p. 101.

13. Friedrich Nietzsche, *Thus Spoke Zarathustra,* trans. Walter Kaufmann, in *The Portable Nietzsche* (New York: Viking Press, 1968), p. 178.

14. Marx, *Manuscripts of 1844,* pp. 100–101.

15. Hesiod *Works and Days* 42 ff.

16. Gen. 3:6 (Revised Standard Version).

17. Aristotle, *Nichomachean Ethics,* bks. 8 and 9.

18. Marx considers only the unilateral (and economic) relationship of a man *to* a woman. Here we are considering the general and reciprocal relationship of a man *and* a woman.

19. See Marie Balmary, *L'homme aux statues* (Paris: Grasset, 1979).

20. Once again we need a word, this time to indicate that a human being may be of either of two sexes. I am forced to invent a word. It is true that "man," in the generic sense, has flown like an angel across centuries of philosophical thought, the only difference being that philosophy, which is not theology, has never asked his or her sex—and that he or she is no angel! I shall use the word *sexation,* which someone else has probably already invented, and give it the following meaning: Sexation is an attribute of most living species, such that no member or individual of one of these species can be taken to be its perfect representative. In respect to the human species, sexation implies that man cannot be mentioned without reference to woman, and vice versa, if we would accurately grasp the concept of human being.

CHAPTER 9

1. Plato, *Statesman* 269d, trans. J. B. Skemp, in Bollingen Series 71, *The Collected Dialogues of Plato,* ed. Edith Hamilton and Huntington Cairns (Princeton, N.J.: Princeton University Press, 1987).

2. Plato, *Statesman* 271e, 273c.

3. See Plato, *Republic* 5.415d ff, trans. Paul Shorey, in *Collected Dialogues of Plato.*

4. Plato, *Republic* 6.486a

5. Plato, *Republic* 7.518c.

6. See the works of contemporary French Jewish exegetes such as André Neher and Eliane Amado-Lévy-Valensi. See also investigations such as Marie Balmary's in *Le sacrifice interdit* (Paris: Grasset, 1986).

7. Angelus Silesius, *The Cherubinic Wanderer,* trans. Maria Shrady (New York: Paulist Press, 1986), pp. 52, 110. See also the Comments in Eugène Susini's edition of the work (Paris: PUF, 1964), vol. 2, p. 145.

8. Gen. 1:31. (All biblical citations are from the Revised Standard Version.)

9. Gen. 1:27 (my italics).

10. Gen. 1:26.

11. Gen. 1:28.

12. Gen. 2:3.

13. Gen. 2:18.

14. Gen. 2:15.

15. Gen. 2:17.

16. Gen. 2:18.

17. "But for the man there was not found a helper fit for him." Gen. 2:20.

18. Gen. 2:23–24.

19. Eliane Amado-Lévy-Valensi has often noted that the first man and woman do not *speak* to each other. She has discussed implications of this fact. Some of them are repeated here. See especially *La onzième épreuve d'Abraham* (Paris: Editions Lattès, 1981), p. 29.

20. In the first chapter, man and women do not speak to each other. The narrative ends with God's satisfaction in their existence. They are there together; no separation in time prevents their speaking. Nonetheless, they have yet to speak.

21. Gen. 3:2–3.

22. Gen. 3:4–5.

23. Gen. 3:19.

24. Gen. 3:7.

25. A symbolic choice. There are both male and female fig trees. Each is sterile without the other. This is doubtless why Christ withered the fig tree that bore no fruit; it was isolated from its true being. Matt. 21:19–21; Mark 11:13, 21.

26. This has often been forgotten.

27. René Descartes, *Discourse on the Method of Rightly Conducting the Reason and Seeking for Truth in the Sciences,* in *The Philosophical Works of Descartes,* edition of 1931, trans. Elizabeth Haldane and G.R.T. Ross (New York: Dover Publications,

through special arrangement with Cambridge University Press, 1955), vol. 1, p. 119.

28. Gen. 3:22.

CHAPTER 10

1. Plato, *Statesman* 268d, 268e, trans. J. B. Skemp, in Bollingen Series 71, *The Collected Dialogues of Plato*, ed. Edith Hamilton and Huntington Cairns (Princeton, N.J.: Princeton University Press, 1987).

2. Peter Pan is a mere caricature of the *puer aeternus*, the child god of the traditional myths.

3. Gen. 4:1–16. (All biblical citations are from the Revised Standard Version.)

4. Gen. 4:9.

5. A letter also, in its way, initiates or continues a dialogue.

6. Plato, *Gorgias* 448d, trans. W. D. Woodhead, in *Collected Dialogues of Plato*.

7. Plato, *Gorgias* 472b.

8. Plato, *Timaeus* 75e, trans. Benjamin Jowett, in *Collected Dialogues of Plato*.

9. Plato, *Phaedrus* 275d, trans. R. Hackforth, in *Collected Dialogues of Plato*.

10. See Michel Villey, *Questions de saint Thomas sur le droit et la politique* (Paris: PUF, 1987).

11. Hobbes's definitive analysis of the multitude comes to mind.

12. Plato, *Republic* 6.486a, trans. Paul Shorey, in *Collected Dialogues of Plato*.

13. See Irène Pennacchioni, *De la guerre conjugale* (Paris: Mazarine, 1986).

14. Plato, *Laws* 6.782e, 783a, trans. A. E. Taylor, in *Collected Dialogues of Plato*.

15. Plato, *Timaeus* 86d.

16. Plato, *Republic* 9.572b.

17. Friedrich Nietzsche, *The Gay Science*, trans. Walter Kaufmann (New York: Random House, 1974), p. 89.

18. Sigmund Freud, *Civilization and Its Discontents*, trans. Joan Riviere (Garden City, N.Y.: Doubleday and Co., 1958) and *Beyond the Pleasure Principle*, trans. James Strachey (New York: Liveright Publishing, 1961).

19. Marquis de Sade, *The 120 Days of Sodom*, in *The Marquis de Sade: The 120 Days of Sodom and Other Writings*, trans. Austryn Wainhouse and Richard Seaver (New York: Grove Press, 1966), p. 427.

20. Unless de Sade had read the translation that appeared in France in 1796 of Kant's *To Perpetual Peace*, which could hardly have enlightened him regarding Kant's system of morality and had no influence on his own outlook.

21. De Sade, *The 120 Days of Sodom*, p. 218.

22. Marquis de Sade, *Philosophy in the Bedroom*, trans. Austryn Wainhouse and Richard Seaver, in *The Marquis de Sade: The Complete Justine, Philosophy in the Bedroom, and Other Writings* (New York: Grove Press, 1965), p. 232.

23. Marquis de Sade, *Juliette; or, The Prosperities of Vice*, trans. Austryn Wainhouse (New York: Grove Press, 1988).

24. *Philosophy in the Bedroom*, pp. 237–238.

25. Ibid., pp. 230–231.

26. Ibid., pp. 283–284.

27. Ibid., pp. 303–304.

28. Ibid., p. 310.

29. Ibid., p. 253.

30. Ibid., p. 185.

31. "Does not the most fleeting glance at natural operations reveal that destructions are just as necessary to her plan as are creations? " Ibid., p. 274.

32. Ibid., p. 221.

33. That is, the pleasure of men.

34. De Sade, *The 120 Days*, pp. 250–252.

35. De Sade, *Philosophy in the Bedroom*, p. 219.

36. Ibid., p. 332.

37. Contemporary exegesis of de Sade's works resolutely upholds this interpretation. See Albert Demazière's afterword to *Juliette*; Pierre Klossowski, *Sade mon prochain* (Paris: Editions du Seuil, 1967); Maurice Blanchot, *Lautréamont et Sade* (Paris, 1949); Gilbert Lely, *Vie du marquis de Sade* (Paris: Gallimard, 1957); and other works.

38. To take refuge in an honorable endeavor is not the same thing as engaging in it *humanly*. At the outset, the consequences are, it goes without saying, infinitely less detrimental than those of sadistic activity. But this behavior does not heal the being. The fracture merely persists in peace and quiet.

39. Plato, *Symposium* 210e, 211a, 211d, in *Collected Dialogues of Plato*.

ABOUT THE BOOK AND AUTHOR

What are the fundamental causes of war, and why does war seem so firmly rooted in human experience? After tracing the answers to these questions to biblical accounts of the genesis of the sexes and to Plato's conception of the united self, Professor Chanteur explores the failures of modern political theory to come to terms with the warlike nature of the human species.

Examining the thought of Machiavelli, Hobbes, Hegel, Nietzsche, La Boetie, Rousseau, Kant, and Marx, she finds that while there is of course a strong tradition of deploring war, many have also seen it as inevitable or even useful. Ultimately, she argues, the hope for peace lies in rediscovering a neglected aspect of human ontology: Human beings are both men and women. It is the failed dialogue between these two aspects of the complete human species that leads to the fear and suspicion of the "other" that so typifies the warlike instinct.

Combining political theory, gender analysis, and human psychology, *From War to Peace* constitutes a brilliant contribution to all these fields and is essential reading for scholars of war, peace, and human society.

Janine Chanteur is a professor at the Sorbonne, University of Paris, and secretary-general of the International Institute of Political Philosophy.

INDEX